# The Healing Dialogue
in
Psychotherapy

# The Healing Dialogue
# in
# Psychotherapy

## MAURICE FRIEDMAN

Jason Aronson, Inc.
New York and London

**Library of Congress in Publication Data**

Friedman, Maurice S.
    The healing dialogue in psychotherapy.

    1. Psychotherapist and patient.    2. Psychotherapy.
I. Title.    [DNLM:    1. Psychotherapy—methods.    2. Interview,
Psychological—methods.    3. Family Therapy—methods.
WM 420 F911h]
RC480.8.F74    1984        616.89'14        84-14504
ISBN 0-87668-730-3

To the Memory
of my Friend
LESLIE H. FARBER

# Contents

## PART II
## CONFIRMATION AND HEALING THROUGH DIALOGUE

# Preface

All therapy relies to a greater or lesser extent on the meeting between therapist and client and, in group and family therapy, the meeting among the clients. But only a few theories have singled out the meeting—the sphere of the "between"—as the central, as opposed to the ancillary, source of healing. My specific concern in this book is the way in which healing through meeting takes place in psychotherapy and family therapy. Psychotherapy in our age has often been guilty of one of the great violations of reality in that it has focused so much on the inner psychic world—the neurosis or the complex of the person—and has tended to treat parents, family, and culture as psychic symbols rather than as the concrete social context of the person's day-to-day existence. An aspect of psychology and psychiatry that has consistently been neglected, even if touched on here and there, in fact, is that of healing through meeting in the psychotherapeutic dialogue. Though it has been a minor theme in much of the literature, a strong light has never been trained on it so as to bring out its true importance and to illuminate the issues and problems that it raises.

I have balanced the presentation of dialogue in various schools of individual and family therapy with a discussion of such dimensions of healing through meeting as the unconscious and dreams, guilt, mutuality, and "inclusion" and confirmation and the "dialogue of touchstones." In this part of the book I offer many insights of my own, as well as the thought and experience of others.

Although a number of contemporary psychotherapists are included and are identified in terms of their schools, my aim is not a complete presentation of the theories of the schools, or of individual therapists. I have presented the theories of the schools only insofar as they directly impinge on healing through meeting and confirmation, and the writings from these schools have been dealt with selectively as they allow further insight into these subjects. Therapists have been discussed in roughly chronological order, without implying thereby any influence of one on the other.

What has struck me in the course of many years of reading is how many radically different and even contradictory schools of psychotherapy arrive, through one or another exponent, at some form of healing through meeting or at least of psychotherapy as a kind of confirmation that does something to repair the disconfirmation that causes "mental illness." This does not mean that all schools of psychotherapy are essentially the same. What accompanies this healing through meeting or confirmation is usually approached differently by any one school and often, though not always, it is incompatible with the theories and techniques of another school. Neither does it mean that *all* the exponents of that school may be seen as dialogical psychotherapists or even that the therapists presented here are *predominantly* dialogical therapists.

Heinz Kohut contributed so much on the subject of disconfirmation and confirmation that I originally made him an integral part of Chapters 11 and 12. I have removed him to "The Self and Its Objects" chapter only because of a more recent decision to have a separate chapter on "object relations," stemming from the main line of Freudian theory and thus a chapter in which Kohut clearly belongs. Kohut's *How Does Analysis Cure?* (1984) came to my attention too late to be incorporated into the body of this book. It extends the understanding of confirmation by adding a third category to mirroring and ideal, namely, "essential alikeness (twin-ship or alter ego transference)." Even more important for our purposes, it makes a decisive contribution to the understanding of healing through meeting, as Kohut's two earlier books do not, through its extensive discussion of empathy (Kohut 1984, Chapters 5, 6, 9, 10).

Another example is Carl Jung, who, before anyone else—with the possible exception of Ferenczi—recognized the centrality of dialogue to psychotherapy. Jung never fully reaches a Thou that is not psychologized as part of the I in his theoretical understanding. Yet he lays the ground-work for others, which, through his onetime disciple, Hans Trüb, leads to perhaps the fullest and most human presentation of healing through meeting, a phrase taken from Trüb's own posthumous book. There are important issues that arise between Martin Buber and Carl Rogers, as we shall see; yet in the body of his writing, Carl Rogers is so squarely concerned with healing through meeting as to be, without question, a dialogical psychotherapist. Fritz Perls, on the other hand, was not one. He was fond of placing Buber's I–Thou relationship at the center of his discussion of Gestalt therapy. Yet in his emphasis upon autonomy and his reliance upon techniques, he fell far short of true healing through meeting. Among a number of his followers, though, dialogue and healing through meeting have assumed a central place.

In the years I have been writing this book, my friends Dr. Richard Hycner and Dr. Richard Stanton have given me invaluable editorial and moral support. I also owe thanks to Dr. Howard Gillis, since it was as a member of his dissertation committee that I began my formulation of the distinction between empathy, identification, and inclusion, which I later expanded.

I also wish to thank Dr. Jason Aronson for urging me to write Chapter 2, "The Freudians," and for supplying me with Jules Glenn and Mark Kanzer's *Freud and His Patients* and Robert J. Langs' *The Psychotherapeutic Conspiracy*, both of which I make extensive use of in that chapter.

It is my hope that *The Healing Dialogue in Psychotherapy* will be the first of a number of books and monographs associated with the Institute for Dialogical Psychotherapy, which I co-direct with Drs. Richard Hycner and James DeLeo, both clinical psychologists in San Diego.

# Acknowledgments

The author gratefully acknowledges permission to reprint excerpts from the following sources:*

Medard Boss, *Psychoanalysis and Daseinsanalysis*, trans. L. B. Lefebre. New York: Basic Books, © 1963.

Ivan Boszormenyi-Nagy and Geraldine Spark, *Invisible Loyalties: Reciprocity in Intergenerational Family Therapy*. New York: Harper & Row, © 1973 by Ivan Boszormenyi-Nagi.

Martin Buber, *The Knowledge of Man: A Philosophy of the Interhuman*, ed. with an Introductory Essay by M. Friedman, trans. M. Friedman and R. G. Smith. New York: Harper & Row © 1966.

————, *Between Man and Man*, trans. R. G. Smith, with an introduction by M. Friedman. New York: Macmillan, © 1965.

————, *A Believing Humanism: Gleanings*, trans. with an Introduction and Commentaries by M. Friedman. New York: Simon & Schuster, © 1969 by Georges Borchardt.

Hanna Colm, The therapeutic encounter. *Review of Existential Psychology and Psychiatry*, © 1965, 5:137–159.

Joen Fagan and Irma L. Shepherd, eds., *Gestalt Therapy Now: Theory/*

---

* In order to spare the reader too many breaks in the text, I have placed the source of both quotations and paraphrases at the end of whole paragraphs and occasionally, when it is the same source throughout, at the end of two or three paragraphs. For this reason I often have more page references than there are actual quotations within the body of the paragraph. In the case of inset quotations, I have placed the source at the end of the quotation, giving the page numbers only for that quotation.

*Techniques/Applications*. New York: Science and Behavior Books, © 1970.

Leslie H. Farber, The ways of the will. *Essays Toward a Psychology and Psychopathology of the Will*. New York: Basic Books, © 1966.

————, *lying, despair, jealousy, envy, sex, suicide, drugs, and the good life*. New York: Basic Books, © 1976.

Kenneth A. Frank, ed., *The Human Dimension in Psychoanalytic Practice*. New York: Grune & Stratton, © 1983 by the American Society of Clinical Oncology.

*The Worlds of Existentialism: A Critical Reader*, ed. with Introductions and a Conclusion by M. Friedman. New York: Random House, © 1964.

Harry Guntrip, Personality structure and human interaction: the developing synthesis of psychodynamic theory. In *The International Psychoanalytical Library*, ed. J. D. Sutherland, No. 56. London: The Hogarth Press and the Institute of Psycho-Analysis, © 1961.

————, *Schizoid Phenomena, Object Relations and the Self*. New York: International Universities Press, © 1969.

Sidney M. Jourard, *Disclosing Man to Himself*. New York: D. Van Nostrand, © 1968.

C. G. Jung, The practice of psychotherapy. In *The Collected Works of C. G. Jung*, trans. R.F.C. Hull, Bollingen Series 20, vol. 16. New York: Princeton University Press, © 1954, © renewed 1982.

Mark Kanzer and Jules Glenn, eds., Freud and his patients. *Downstate Psychoanalytic Institute Twenty-fifth Anniversary Series*, vol. II. New York: Jason Aronson, © 1980.

Heinz Kohut, *The Restoration of the Self*. New York: International Universities Press, © 1977.

R. D. Laing, *The Politics of Experience*. New York: Penguin Books Ltd., © 1967.

Robert J. Langs, *The Psychotherapeutic Conspiracy*. New York: Jason Aronson © 1982.

Rollo May, *Love and Will*. New York: Norton, © 1969.

Erving and Miriam Polster, *Gestalt Therapy Integrated: Contours of Theory and Practice*. New York: Brunner/Mazel, © 1973.

Carl R. Rogers, *On Becoming a Person. A Therapist's View of Psychotherapy*. Boston: Houghton Mifflin, © 1961.

————, *A Way of Being*. Boston: Houghton Mifflin, © 1981.

Carl R. Rogers and Barry Stevens, *Person to Person: The Problem of Being Human. A New Trend in Psychology*. Lafayette, California: Real People Press, © 1967.

Harold F. Searles, The patient as therapist to his analyst, In *Tactics and*

*Techniques in Psychoanalytic Therapy*, ed. P. L. Giovacchini, pp. 95–151. Countertransference, vol. 2. New York: Jason Aronson, © 1975.

Harry Stack Sullivan, *The Interpersonal Theory of Psychiatry*, ed. H. S. Perry and M. L. Gawel, New York: Norton © 1953.

# Chapter 1

# Introduction:
# Dialogue in Psychotherapy

I have taken the phrase "healing through meeting" from the title Martin Buber gave the posthumous book by the Swiss psychoanalyst Hans Trüb (*Heilung aus der Begegnung*). As long as there has been society, something that can be recognized as healing through meeting has taken place. The parent, the teacher, the nurse, the shaman, the medicine man—anyone who lays hands on another or helps another—is involved in healing through meeting.

From the very beginning of formal psychoanalysis, healing through meeting was already built into the system as an indispensable means to the end of overcoming fixation and repression. Even if the therapeutic situation was modified by Freud's asking the patient to lie on the couch rather than to face him, it was still a meeting—in contrast to those operant conditioning and psychopharmacological forms of psychology and psychotherapy that entail little or no actual contact between psychologist and client. Freudian theory, to be sure, sees the ego as the servant of three masters—the superego, the id, and the environment—but nowhere does Freud place the meeting between self and self at its center, except in theories of transference and countertransference. "Freud fought against his humanistic personal urges through his scientism," writes Ivan Boszormenyi-Nagy, "and he abhorred Ferenczi's relational emphasis on therapeutic methods."[1]

Yet we cannot imagine Freud working year after year with people and dealing with them only as objects. When we turn to Carl Jung, who is even

---

[1]Letter from Ivan Boszormenyi-Nagy to Maurice Friedman, June 21, 1974.

more preoccupied with the intrapsychic than Freud, it is startling to realize the extent to which his *therapy* is centered on the dimension of meeting, or dialogue. In *The Undiscovered Self*, Jung says, "All over the world, it is being recognized today that what is being treated is not a symptom, but a patient" (Jung 1958, p. 12). The more the doctor schematizes, the more the patient quite rightly resists. The patient demands to be dealt with in his or her uniqueness, not just as part of a problem, and to do this the therapist must engage and risk himself or herself as a person. "The dream of half a century has run its course," says Viktor Frankl, "the dream in which what was held of value was a mechanics of the psyche and a technology of psychotherapy." In the place of this interpretation of psychic life on the basis of mechanisms and this therapy of psychic disorders with the help of techniques, Frankl puts forward healing through meeting as the true center of psychotherapy:

> Provided that one does not shudder at that so fashionable word, one can aptly speak of human meeting (*Begegnung*) as the actual agent in the modes of acting in psychoanalytic treatment. The so-called transference is also probably only a vehicle of such human meeting. . . . *Within the framework of psychotherapy, the methodology and technique applied at any given time is least effective of all: rather it is the human relationship between physician and patient which is determining* (Frankl 1973, p. 24f.).

One of the most important issues the approach of healing through meeting addresses is the extent to which healing proceeds from a specific healer—priest, sorcerer, shaman, or therapist—and the extent to which healing takes place in the "between"—in the relationship between therapist and client, among the members of a group or family, or even within a community. When it is the latter, is there a special role, nonetheless, for the therapist as facilitator, midwife, enabler, or partner in a "dialogue of touchstones?" We must also ask whether such healing takes place through an existential grace (a term I coined in *Touchstones of Reality* [Friedman 1972], which cannot be planned and counted on, however much it can be helped along. To what extent does healing through meeting imply that meeting must also be the *goal* as well as the means to that goal? And to what extent are we talking about a two-sided event that is not susceptible to techniques in the sense of willing and manipulating in order to bring about a certain result?

Another important problem that healing through meeting encounters is that of the limits of responsibility of the helper. To what extent do therapists have an ego involvement such that they feel themselves a success if the patient is healed and a failure is he or she is not? Therapists open to the new vistas of healing through meeting will feel that more is demanded of them than their professional methods and their professional role provide. The "abyss calls to abyss," or self to self, as Buber wrote in his preface, "Healing through Meeting," to Trüb's book; the technical superiority of the therapist is not required, but rather his or her actual self. In *Power and Innocence* (1972), Rollo May writes of a black woman patient who felt so powerless and so cut off from her own anger that May had to become angry for her. But he added, "I did not do this just as a technique. I really became angry." Only through his personal involvement was the woman able to gain access to her anger.

What is crucial is not the skill of the therapist, but rather what takes place *between* the therapist and the client *and* between the client and other people. The one *between* cannot totally make up for or take the place of the other. No amount of therapy can be of decisive help if a person is too enmeshed in a family, community, or culture in which the seedlings of healing are constantly choked off and the attempts to restore personal wholeness are thwarted by the destructive elements of the system. If this fact underlines the importance of supplementing one-to-one therapy with family therapy and even intergenerational (three or more generations) family therapy, such as Ivan Boszormenyi-Nagy practices and advocates, it also underlines the importance of creating that climate of trust, that confirmation of otherness, in which healing through meeting can flourish on every level. That there are tragic limitations to such healing is obvious, but it is not equally obvious that we should accept the present state of "community" as a given and restrict ourselves to the intrapsychic or to the intrafamilial.

Insanity, writes Ferdinand Ebner, is the end product of "I-solitude" and the absence of the Thou—the complete closedness of the I to the Thou. It is a spiritual condition in which neither the word nor love can reach the individual. The irrationality of insane persons lies in the fact that they talk past other persons and are unable to speak to a concrete Thou. The world has become for them the projection of their I, not just theoretically, as in idealism, but practically, and for this reason they can only speak to a fictitious Thou (Ebner 1921, pp. 47f., 81, 155). This type of psychosis is explained by Martin Buber in somewhat more poetic terms in *I and Thou*. "If a man does not represent the *a priori* of relation in his living with the world," writes Buber, "if he does not work out and realize the inborn *Thou* on what meets it, then it strikes inwards." As a result, confrontation of what is over against one takes place in oneself, and this means self-contradiction—the horror of an inner double. "Here is the verge of life, flight of an unfulfilled life to the senseless semblance of fulfillment, and its groping in a maze and losing itself ever more profoundly" (Buber 1958, p. 69f.).[2]

---

[2]Ebner's and Buber's intuition of the origins of insanity have been confirmed, as we shall see, by Viktor von Weizsäcker, a German psychiatrist who has made an important contribution to psychosomatic medicine. It was during the years that he and Buber were associated as co-editors of the periodical *Die Kreatur* that von Weizsäcker began his application of dialogical philosophy to medicine and psychiatry.

Buber's I–Thou philosophy is both descriptive *and* normative, fact *and* value. The normative comes in the difference between mere existence and authentic existence, between being human at all and being more fully human, between holding the fragments of the self together sufficiently to get by and bringing the conflicting parts of oneself into an active unity, between having partial, disparate relations with others and having fuller, more responsible ones.

The unfolding of the sphere of the between Buber calls the "dialogical." The psychological, that which happens within the soul of each, is only the secret accompaniment of the dialogical. The meaning of dialogue is not found in either one or the other of the partners, nor in both added together, but rather in their interchange. This distinction between the "dialogical" and the "psychological" constitutes a radical attack on the psychologism of our age. It makes manifest the fundamental ambiguity of those modern psychologists who affirm the dialogue between person and person, but who are unclear as to whether this dialogue is of value in itself or is merely a function of the individual's self-acceptance and self-realization.

Only as a partner can a person be perceived as an existing wholeness. To become aware of a person means to perceive his or her wholeness as person defined by spirit: to perceive the dynamic center that stamps on all utterances, actions, and attitudes the recognizable sign of uniqueness. Such an awareness is impossible if, and as long as, the other is for me the detached object of my observation; for that person will not thus yield his or her wholeness and its center. It is possible only when he or she becomes present for me.

Mutual confirmation is essential to becoming a self—a person who realizes his uniqueness precisely through relations to other selves whose distance from him is completed by his distance from them. True confirmation means that I confirm my partner as this existing being even while I oppose him. I legitimize him over against me as the one with whom I have to do in real dialogue. This mutual confirmation of persons is most fully realized in "making present," an event that happens partially wherever persons come together, but, in its essential structure, happens only rarely. "Imagining the real," as Buber also calls this event, is no empathy or intuitive perception, but rather a bold swinging into the other that demands the most intense action of one's being in order to make the other present in his wholeness, unity, and uniqueness. One can only do this as a partner, standing in a common situation with the other, and even then one's address to the other may remain unanswered and the dialogue may die in becoming.

In friendship and love, imagining the real, or "inclusion," is mutual. In the helping relationships, however, it is necessarily one-sided. The patient cannot equally well experience the relationship from the side of the therapist or the pupil from the side of the teacher without destroying or fundamentally altering the relationship. This does not mean that the therapist is reduced to treating the patient as an object, an It. The one-sided inclusion of therapy is still an I–Thou relationship founded on mutuality, trust, and partnership in a common situation, and it is only in this relationship that real healing can take place.

If "all real living is meeting," all true healing also takes place through meeting. If the psychotherapist is content to "analyze" the patient,

> i.e. to bring to light unknown factors from his microcosm, and to set to some conscious work in life the energies which have been transformed by such an emergence, then he may be successful in some repair work. At best he may help a soul which is diffused and poor in structure to collect and order itself to some extent. But the real matter, the regeneration of an atrophied personal center, will not be achieved. This can only be done by one who grasps the buried latent unity of the suffering soul with the great glance of the doctor: and this can only be attained in the person-to-person attitude of a partner, not by the consideration and examination of an object (Buber 1958, p. 132f.).

A common situation, however, does not mean one which each enters from the same or even a similar position. In psychotherapy, the difference in position is not only that of personal stance, but also of role and function, a difference determined by the very difference of purpose that led each to enter the relationship. If the goal is a common one—the healing of the patient—the relationship to that goal differs radically as between therapist and patient, and the healing that takes place depends as much upon the recognition of that difference as upon the mutuality of meeting and trust.

Martin Buber gives us a further insight into the implications of dialogue for psychotherapy in his discussion of the way in which the great *zaddikim* (the leaders of the Jewish mystical communities of Hasidim in eighteenth- and nineteenth-century Eastern Europe) healed those who came to them for help. To obtain a right perspective, we must bear in mind, writes Buber, that the relation of a soul to its organic life depends on the degree of its wholeness and unity.

> The more dissociated the soul, the more it is at the mercy of its sicknesses and attacks, the more concentrated it is, the more it is able to master them. It is not as if it conquered the body; rather through its unity it ever again saves and protects the unity of the body (Buber 1960, p. 142f.).[3]

---

[3]Since this essay was written in 1921, it is most unlikely that it was influenced by Robert Assagioli's use of the term psychosynthesis. Indeed, the influence may have been the other way around, since Buber and Assagioli later became friends.

This process can best be effected, according to Buber, "through the psychosynthetic appearance of a whole, united soul laying hold of the dispersed soul, agitating it on all sides, and demanding the event of crystallization." Here the term "psychosynthetic" is clearly used in conscious contrast with "psychoanalytic" to suggest the procedure from wholeness as contrasted with the procedure from isolated parts and complexes. The unified soul shapes a center in the soul that is calling to him and at the same time takes care that this soul does not remain dependent upon him. The helper does not place his own image in the soul that he helps. Instead he lets him "look through him, as through a glass, into being and now discover being in itself and let it be empowered as the core of living unity" (Buber 1960, p. 132f.).

This type of help stands in sharp contrast to the doctor and the psychotherapist who give others technical aid without entering into relationships with them. Help without mutuality is presumptuousness, writes Buber; it is an attempt to practice magic.

> As soon as the helper is touched by the desire, in however subtle a form, to dominate or enjoy his patient, or to treat the latter's wish to be dominated or enjoyed by him as other than a wrong condition needing to be cured, the danger of falsification arises, beside which all quackery appears peripheral (Buber 1965a, p. 95).

For the therapist, the distinction between arbitrary and true will rests on a quite real and concrete experiencing of the client's side of the relationship. Only if the therapist discovers the "otherness" of the client will he or she discover his or her own real limits and what is needed to help the client. He or she must see the position of the other in that person's concrete actuality, yet not lose sight of his or her own. Only this will remove the danger that the will to heal will degenerate into arbitrariness.

In therapy, will and decision within dialogue are decisive. Therapy should not proceed from the investigation of individual psychological complications, but rather from the whole person; for it is only the understanding of wholeness as wholeness that can lead to the real transformation and healing of the person and of that person's relationships with others. None of the phenomena of the soul is to be placed in the center of observation as if all the rest were derived from it. The person ought not to be treated as an object of investigation and encouraged to see himself as an "it." He should be summoned "to set himself to rights," says Buber, to bring his inner being to unity so that he may respond to the address of being that faces him. Such response means the transformation of the urges, of the "alien thoughts," or fantasy. We must not reject the abundance of this fantasy, but rather transform it in our imaginative faculty and turn it into actuality. "We must convert the element that seeks to take possession of us into the substance of real life."

# Part I

# DIALOGUE IN THE SCHOOLS OF PSYCHOTHERAPY

# Chapter 2

# The Freudians

## Sigmund Freud

Sigmund Freud used dialogue as a central tool in his psychoanalysis; yet he was not, for all that, a "dialogical psychotherapist." His concern was primarily with the intrapsychic, and only secondarily with the interpersonal, and as far as his theory went, as opposed to his actual practice, he was not at all concerned with the "interhuman" or the "between." On the other hand, he did recognize, as we shall see, that at times there is direct communication between one unconscious and another; he made bold use of a one-on-one method that could not be replicated under laboratory conditions; he himself coined the terms "transference" and "countertransference" out of his own experience as an analyst; and, as the founder of psychoanalysis, he is the single most important antecedent of those individuals and schools of contemporary therapy that we shall consider in Part I, "Dialogue in the Schools of Psychotherapy." If we do not succeed in finding many dialogical perspectives *in* Freud's psychotherapy, we shall at least gain some dialogical perspectives *on* his psychotherapy.

Freud distinguishes between two kinds of unconscious, one capable of becoming conscious, such as something we are not thinking of but can think of if we wish to, and another that cannot become conscious, because it is repressed by the censor as too dangerous to the ego. The former Freud calls the "preconscious," the latter the "unconscious" proper. Although repressed, the unconscious is still the basic, determining force. We are "lived" by unknown and uncontrollable forces. "The ego constantly carries into action the wishes of the id as if they were its own." It rationalizes the desire of the id. "The ego represents what we call reason and sanity, in contrast to the id which contains the passions." The ego only comes into existence as a splitting off from the id, as a result of identifying with the parents in the first years of life. The character of the ego, to Freud, is nothing other than a precipitate of abandoned "object-choices." The word "object" here is particularly appropriate, for Freud does not see "cathexis" as an essential relation with another person, but rather as an instinctual relation with oneself through the other person. It is like a closed circuit in which the other person is the intermediate transmitter, but never really the initiator or receiver.

By a similar process, the ego-ideal, or "superego," is developed, according to Freud's book *The Ego and the Id*, published in 1923. The ego-ideal originates in a direct and immediate identification with the father. The father becomes the image of man, both in the sense of what it means to be a man, a male, and also in the superego that governs the character ideals. The superego not only says, "You *ought* to *be* like your father in these and these ways," but also "You *must not be* like him in these other ways, which are his prerogatives." Social feelings rest on the basis of a common ego-ideal, with the result that "the tension between the demands of conscience and the actual attainments of the ego is experienced as a sense of guilt."

Culture serves the double purpose "of protecting humanity against nature and of regulating the relations of human beings among themselves" as Freud writes in *Civilization and Its Discontents* (1958). The decisive step toward civilization comes when the power of a united number of persons is substituted for the power of a single person. This united strength never involves more than a social contract. It cannot convert man into a unit in an organic whole, like the ant or the bee. Man will always defend his claim to individual freedom against the will of the multitude, Freud says, and this makes central the task of finding a satisfying solution to the problem of individual claims and the claims of the civilized community. "It is one of the problems of man's fate whether this solution can be arrived at in some particular form of culture or whether the conflict will prove irreconcilable" (Freud 1958, p. 41).

Freud's view of civilization and its discontents leads him to the curious position of making moral judgments against the superego, which he has defined as the sole source of moral judgments. "In commanding and prohibiting with such severity," he complains, "it troubles too little about the happiness of the ego, and it fails to take into account sufficiently the difficulties in the way of obeying it—the strength of instinctual cravings in the id and the hardships of external environment" (Freud 1958, p. 102). As a result, Freud sees the therapist as "obliged to do battle with the superego and work to moderate its demands." From his moral judgment of the ethical standards of the individual superego, Freud turns to a moral judgment of the ethical standards of the cultural superego, the norms of society. It, too, enjoins a moral "ought," which cannot possibly be fulfilled. It presumes unlimited power of the ego over the id such as does not exist even in normal people. This exorbitant demand leads to revolt or neurosis, or makes the individual unhappy.

In Freud's image of the human, then, there is no place for freedom and spontaneity—with one curious, yet all-important exception. However Freud may explain it theoretically, the goal of psychoanalysis is the liberation of the individual from past fixations and traumas so that there is the freedom to respond to and live with the reality of the present. The ego, to Freud, is the reality-tester. Its function of helping the individual to adjust to reality and to modify or to strike compromises between the demands of superego and id leads to real freedom. A corollary of this fact is Freud's tendency to regard consciousness itself as freedom, especially when it succeeds in recognizing repressed material and integrating it into the ego. The goal of Freudian psychoanalysis—"Where id was ego shall be"—itself describes a movement from psychological determinism to personal freedom.

To Freud, more than to any other person, goes the credit and the blame for ushering in the age of the Psychological Man. On the credit side are deeper insights into human passions and conflicts, into the complex inner divisions and internecine strife of man, in general, and of modern, civilized man, in particular. Also on the credit side is that moral concern that makes Freud desire to limit the harsh reign of the superego in favor of the more moderate combinations of repressions and instinctual satisfactions a liberated and mature ego can afford. Freud's juxtaposition of the reality and pleasure principles and, later, of the love instinct and the death instinct affords him a delicately balanced realism that accepts the tragic limitations of life, yet believes in the melioristic possibilities afforded by reason when it operates in psychoanalysis as a neutral scientific instrument of inquiry.

On the debit side is the overwhelming and overweening individualism that makes Freud reduce the social relationships between persons to secondary products of individual, instinctual gratification. Even more serious for the image of the human is the psychologism that translates the meaning of human and interhuman existence into the intrapsychic—internal, psychic categories and dimensions.[1]

David Bakan has suggested an important modification of our criticism of Freud's emphasis upon the intrapsychic at the expense of the interpersonal. In Freud's stress upon the need for transference in order to overcome the repression of the patient, Bakan sees

---

[1] The preceding paragraphs are based upon Maurice Friedman, *To Deny Our Nothingness: Contemporary Images of Man*, 3rd rev. ed. (1978), with a new Preface and Appendices (Chicago: The University of Chicago Press Phoenix Books, 1978). Ch. 11. "Sigmund Freud," pp. 191 205.

a profound intuition about the relationship between the intrapsychic and the social. If the isolation of the individual from the larger *social telos* could be overcome, if contact and communication between the individual and at least one other person in the larger social body could be established, the person might be healed. In other words, if the social telos could again be brought into play so as to integrate the individual organism into the larger society, the latter equally conceived as an organism, the telic decentralization within the organism might be overcome (Bakan 1969, p. 47).

We can gain a more concrete dialogical perspective on Freud if we turn to his relationship to his early patients insofar as we have access to them from Freud's literary case studies and the commentaries on them. Jules Glenn writes that Freud recognized that a therapeutic alliance had to be established with his patients, and he took steps to facilitate this development: "If one exhibits a serious interest in him, [the analyzand] carefully clears away the resistances that crop up at the beginning and avoids making certain mistakes" then transference from persons "by whom he was accustomed to be treated with affection" will occur. The analyst should not analyze the transference until it has become a resistance (Glenn 1980b, p. 15).

In the case of the Rat Man (so called because of his preoccupation with a torture in which rats are released on the buttocks of a criminal and bore their way through the anus), "Freud went beyond these suggestions and attempted to further the patient's confidence in and commitment to treatment by assuring him that he, the patient, was an intelligent and stable man who would benefit from analysis," writes Glenn. Glenn contrasts Freud's retreat from analyzing Dora and the "homosexual woman" with his patience with the Rat Man and the Wolf Man. Freud fed the Rat Man, sent him a postcard, supplied the words that completed the Rat Man's description of his torture, and urged him to bring his girlfriend's picture to him and to tell him her name. Glenn suggests that part of the reason Freud terminated the analyses of Dora and the "homosexual woman" was Freud's failure to recognize that their defense mechanisms were typical of adolescents, plus his own erotic attraction to them, which made him less tolerant of their hostile apathy than that of his male patients. He underestimated their affection and desire for help, while overestimating their aggressive desires for revenge. Freud ignored the main issue for Dora and overlooked her adolescent love of truth that made her seek a man of integrity, her hope of finding a neutral, non-incestuous, non-corrupt mentor.

Melvin Scharfman suggests that Freud's treatment of Dora was of secondary importance to him, his primary concern being the advancement of his own psychoanalytic theory. Freud focused on penis envy and oedipal fantasies, but ignored the real disappointments that Dora experienced with her father and Herr K., who sought to seduce her. The result was nonhealing through mismeeting, to coin a phrase opposite to Buber's:

> There are several points in the analysis where Freud defended both Herr K. and the patient's father, telling Dora that she really knew how much they loved her. All of this was said to a young woman who had experienced rather intensive disappointment in both of these men. Her analysis might have been a chance at having a different kind of relationship with a man. She needed to go through the intermediate phase of development of the younger girl in which she has a relationship with a man that is not immediately sexualized, but rather one in which she feels accepted as a person, while still looking for some derivatives of oedipal wishes in terms of the wish to feel loved, admired, paid attention to (Scharfman 1980, p. 55).[2]

Robert Langs similarly points to a misalliance dimension in Dora's case—interactions between Freud and Dora that undermined the goals of the therapy. Freud was slow to recognize the transference elements in Dora's communications, and he tended to link them to genetic material from her early childhood without fully appreciating the implications of his relationship with her. Through his continued contact with Dora's father and Herr K., Freud violated the one-to-one quality of the analytic relationship, threatened the confidentiality of the analysis, and distorted his own image as someone linked to the two men who had disappointed her. Mark Kanzer, too, sees Freud as avoiding Dora's transference and the insight her dreams might have given him into her relationship with him. Dora was constantly pressured to confirm Freud's interpretations and had little opportunity to freely bring forward her own associations, fantasies, and ideas. Instead of analyzing Dora's ambivalence toward him and its relation to her realistically grounded distrust of all adults and authority figures, summarizes Isidor Bernstein, Freud emphasized Dora's libidinal or sexual conflicts, ignored her aggression toward him, associated with her important adults, and conducted her analysis in an authoritarian and didactic manner! Freud seemed, in fact, to be telling Dora that he hardly needed her for the analysis, thus repeating earlier depreciations of her importance. Carried away by the excitement of his discovery of the new world of dreams and the unconscious, Freud fell prey to premature interpretations that strengthened Dora's defenses. Later Freud was to criticize himself for not dealing with transference problems soon enough.

Even with the Rat Man, Freud had only a minimal awareness of transferences, as Stanley Weiss has pointed out:

---

[2]Compare Scharfman 1980, pp. 52, 56f.

During the Rat Man's psychoanalysis, interpretations were limited to the unconscious. Transference interpretations were tentatively made and limited primarily to the positive transference. Current transferences, especially negative transferences, were frequently dismissed or displaced into the past and not permitted to win attention in the present (Weiss 1980, p. 207).

Similarly, Robert Langs depicts Freud as escaping the current situation between himself and the Rat Man by reconstructing the Rat Man's childhood hostility toward his father. "This was characteristic of Freud's technique at the time, in that Freud consistently avoided the day residues and current precipitants of his patient's transference reactions, nor did he take cognizance of any realistic perceptions and reality-based reactions to himself." Mark Kanzer suggests that Freud's warm impulses that led him to feed the Rat Man and send him a postcard seriously disrupted the therapeutic alliance at a critical time. He also suggests that negative therapeutic reactions may have arisen from Freud injecting images and metaphors that influenced the Rat Man and ignored the patient's use of language and images of considerable import.

On the positive side, Kanzer cites Elizabeth Zetzel's reconstruction from Freud's notes on his treatment of the Rat Man (published long after the official case itself) that Freud "could be seen to a greater extent as a real person, warmly interested in the patient, aware at times of counter-transference difficulties, and utilizing encouragement and educational measures." Kanzer also summarizes Judith Kestenberg's portrayal of Freud as a good parent who was patient, understanding, and compassionate. Freud countered the Rat Man's fuzzy thinking with precise formulations, taught him to form new object- and self-images, and served as a dependable model in the place of his confused and disturbed parents. Analyzing himself as he went along (his own laughter, incredulity, and conflicts), he was able to effect such self-scrutiny in the Rat Man as well (Langs 1980a, p. 218; Kanzer 1980a, p. 239; Kanzer 1980b, p. 242f.).

Another famous early case of Freud was that of the Wolf Man, who had repeated dreams of ferocious white wolves. "The reader of the Wolf Man case gets the impression that it was more enriching for Freud than for his famous patient," remarks Harold Blum, commenting on Freud's scientific and literary genius and the likelihood that the analysis was primarily elucidated and organized in Freud's mind. Robert J. Langs suggests that Freud contributed to a therapeutic misalliance in the case of the Wolf Man through giving him direct advice, seeing his fiancée, discussing personal matters from his own life, demanding gifts, and giving him free analytic sessions. All these "deviations" from what would today be standard psychoanalytic technique "fostered and enhanced a series of pathogenic unconscious fantasies and identifications that interfered with a lasting inner resolution of the Wolf Man's pathology." Freud's extensions of the boundaries of the patient–analyst relationship promoted a seductive atmosphere, a submissive, passive-feminine stance in the Wolf Man, as well as an unconscious image of Freud as seductive, masculine, and powerful (Blum 1980, p. 342; Langs 1980c, pp. 380–82). The conclusion that Langs reaches is of importance for a dialogical approach to psychoanalysis:

> The manner in which the analyst creates and maintains the analytic setting and relationship is continuously and unconsciously monitored by the patient. These ground rules and boundaries reflect crucial aspects of the analyst's identity and functioning, and deeply influence the patient's sense of security and trust, the important ongoing identificatory aspects of his relationship with the analyst, and the nature of the patient's intrapsychic fantasies, unconscious perceptions and projections (Langs 1980b, p. 383).

The summary–conclusion of Mark Kanzer and Jules Glenn also contributes to a dialogical perspective on psychoanalysis:

> The current disposition to see the analytic process as involving a two-person relationship has led us to focus upon Freud as well as the patient in the interchanges between them. His intuitive and pioneering interventions are part of the fascination that the cases hold and his choice of language and metaphors often indicates, on the basis of extensive self-analytic and biographical commentaries, the inner depths from which his conceptions arise and the suggestive influences that pass reciprocally between the patient and himself. In this sense, we regard ourselves as carrying forward an essential task of psychoanalysis that could rarely appear in Freud's published works: the alternations between the analysis of the patient and the self-analysis of the therapist (Kanzer and Glenn, 1980, p. 430f.).

## Robert Langs

In his book *The Psychotherapeutic Conspiracy* (1982), Robert J. Langs also attempts to carry forward an essential task of psychoanalysis of the same two-sided nature, namely, rejecting the overuse of transference and emphasizing the intrapsychic that went with it in favor of recognizing the unconscious interaction between analyst and patient and the bipolar reality that that entails. Langs holds that Freud invented transference as a way of reassuring Josef Breuer that he did not contribute to the seductive behavior of his patient, Anna O., thus persuading Breuer to permit the publication of their joint book *Studies on Hysteria* in 1895. This concept enabled Breuer, Freud, and subsequent therapists to see the patient's actions and expressions toward them as pure distortion, uninfluenced by any unconscious interactions on their part. "The therapist is viewed as a foil or kind of blank screen onto which the patient projects or enacts his or her sexual and other entirely unfounded and distorted feelings."

Based on his reading of Freud's writings and early case histories, Langs also points out that "therapists tended in those early years to reveal a great deal of themselves and their personal lives to their patients." What is most important for Langs is not just the denial of the strong mutual attraction between Breuer and Anna O., but also the strong motivation for therapist and patient alike to conspire to avoid the terrifying truths aroused by the psychotherapeutic experience. The therapist who exposes the patient's most private and intimate secrets must be prepared to confront his or her own past life and current inner mental world (Langs 1982, pp. 84f., 90f.).

Langs claims that Freud created the field of psychoanalysis on the foundation of just this psychotherapeutic conspiracy, itself based on the concept of transference:

> For Freud it was impossible to conceive that a physician could lose control sexually on any level when it came to his or her relationship with a patient. While perturbed, he was clearly not terrified by his patient's amorous behavior to the point of taking flight, at least not physical flight. Instead, he immediately decided that her behavior could have nothing to do with his own personal attractiveness or, for that matter, with anything whatsoever that he had done. To account for it, he proposed an entirely different source: the patient's earlier love for her father or some other comparable figure, mistakenly transferred onto Freud as the therapist. In all, the therapist was seen merely as a player being used for the enactment of the patient's drama (Langs 1982, p. 98f.).

Langs is not denying that transference exists. What he is saying, rather, is that "quite often a patient's reactions to a therapist, direct and encoded, are in keeping with sound unconscious perceptions of the implications of the therapist's interventions" and that when the therapist applies the term transference to such occurrences, it is a defensive error. "The experiences that Freud studied, and that formed the basis for his invocation of the concept of transference, were mainly those in which his own inputs were highly charged." Langs concluded that what enabled Freud to continue as a therapist, whereas Breuer fled, and to found psychoanalysis with its talking cure, was essentially a self-protective lie: "On balance, Freud's invention of transference contained a small measure of truth and a large measure of falsification" (Langs 1982, pp. 126, 129–131).

In those days, Langs points out, countertransference was totally ignored: "The emotional problems of the analyst, and the broader subject of the conscious and unconscious nature of his or her contributions to the patient's therapeutic experience, was afforded virtually no consideration at all." In 1910, to be sure, Freud coined the term countertransference and identified it as a limiting factor in analytic work. But he never wrote a major paper on the subject, says Langs, and paid only minimal attention to it in his later writing. Freud, thus, set the stage for a tendency to place virtually all the blame for any disturbance in the therapeutic interaction on the patient. This emphasis on the sickness of the patient and the implied health of the analyst is actually curative, since it provides some relief from emotional suffering for guilt-ridden patients! (Langs 1982, p. 140f.).

According to Langs, the most important consequence of all this is that the emphasis in Freud's psychoanalysis was placed squarely on the intrapsychic at the expense of the interpersonal: "There was a strong correlation between the theory that transference is entirely a product of the imagination of the patient and the belief that emotional disturbance develops in comparable fashion—from within" (Langs 1982, p. 151). Freud saw unconscious inner mental struggles and conflicts as the central factor in emotional sickness.

> External reality and relationships with others were acknowledged only peripherally, mainly as sources of gratification or trauma. While Freud eventually did provide a basis for a study of the role of what are called object relationships in emotional disturbances, it remained for modern-day psychoanalysts to begin to take this sphere—the interpersonal sphere—into account. To this very day, this factor is afforded only limited consideration (Langs 1982, p. 148).

A corrective to this one-sided emphasis on the intrapsychic at the expense of the interpersonal is beginning to take shape from within psychoanalysis itself. Langs writes

> While some analysts are now engaged in attempts to correct these basic errors and to face the unconscious basis of a patient's neurosis full force, regardless of its sources (including their own inputs), there is as yet no major and acknowledged mode of treatment in use that consistently takes this key factor into account. There is, however, a new descendant of psychoanalysis that is beginning to stake a claim in this respect. It is called the *bipersonal* or *communicative* (interactional) *approach* to psychotherapy (Langs 1982, p. 160).

For Langs, the key to this new bipersonal or communicative approach is what he calls "trigger decoding," decoding the encoded messages of the patient's dreams and free associations first of all in terms of the day residues and other present, reality-based material. Trigger decoding is based on the recognition of the presence of a continuous and spiraling communicative interaction between the patient and those of importance to him or her, in particular, the therapist. "The therapeutic relationship and interaction is quickly established as the major arena within which the battle against the patient's neurosis is carried out." The therapist's errors in intervention will evoke *nontransference* to earlier authority figures whose behavior was seductive or threatening to the patient.

Instead of seeing dreams as entirely figments of the patient's imagination and the product of unconscious wishes and fantasies, trigger decoding recognizes an important source of dreams in threatening unconscious perceptions of others, including the therapist. Trigger decoding recognizes that no message exists in isolation. A message always has a context. It is a response to another message and involves both conscious and unconscious communication. "Trigger decoding requires of the therapist a capacity for self-knowledge and self-awareness that is difficult to achieve and even harder to maintain." The result is that there exists only a little *truth therapy*—arriving "at the truth of the patient's neurosis in light of the ongoing therapeutic and communicative interaction between the patient and therapist"—and a great deal of *lie* or *lie-barrier therapy*—"avoiding, falsifying, covering over, or otherwise defending against these fundamental truths" (Langs 1982, pp. 206–232).

Our concern here cannot be the 300 lie therapies that Langs identifies (all of those listed in Richie Herink's *The Psychotherapy Handbook* [1980], including two of my own—"Dialogue Therapy" and "Meeting Therapy") or the fact that Langs sees every form of present-day psychotherapy as "designed unconsciously as a way of enabling therapists to dump many aspects of their own inner problems into their patients." Rather, it is with the fact that Langs sees Freud and classical psychoanalysis as falling squarely into lie therapy:

> Freud had the wisdom to create psychoanalysis out of the ashes of the cathartic method. He had the courage to probe deeper into the origins and underlying truths of his patients' emotional disorders. Nonetheless, he too required a series of tenets that would assure a maintenance of lie-barrier qualities to psychoanalytic work. These involved the belief that the patient's associations reflected conscious and unconscious fantasies and were entirely devoid of valid unconscious perceptions. They entailed the use of the concept of transference as a means of denying the therapist's contribution to the therapeutic interaction and to the patient's communications. They therefore involved the denial of important aspects of reality as they pertained to the therapeutic experience, and often to the early life experiences of his patients as well (Langs 1982, p. 281).[3]

The consequences of this for classical psychoanalysis are grave in the extreme:

---

[3]Compare pp. 9, 242, 244f., 248 in Langs (1982).

Because of its lie-barrier foundation, clinical psychoanalysis has not been able to integrate truly new clinical findings and ideas into the mainstream of its thinking and clinical practices. The entire conceptualization of an active, two-person therapeutic interaction is repudiated out of hand, since it cannot be integrated into present psychoanalytic thinking, which is devoted entirely to the postulated intrapsychic happenings within the patient (Langs 1982, p. 249).

A sound form of psychotherapy, in contrast, would give up seeing the analyst as a detached, healthy observer and interpreter and would acknowledge the analyst's vulnerabilities, countertransferences, and active unconscious participation in the therapeutic interaction. "There would be the painful realization that a large portion of the patient's communications involve an unconscious working over of the therapist's sickness." Langs sees psychoanalysis alone as giving us a basis for a discovery of the actual truth, and he sees the *unconscious* needs of patients and, to some extent, therapists as providing the greatest impetus for the shift within psychoanalysis from lie to truth therapy (Langs 1982, pp. 263f., 282f., 305, 314f.). Langs, like all the others who offer us dialogical perspectives in psychotherapy, rests squarely on the foundation that Freud provided—the relation between therapist and client.

Steven Kepnes' discussion of the use of narrative in psychoanalysis offers us a radically different dialogical perspective in Freud. Following French linguistic psychoanalyst Jacques Lacan, many therapists are now approaching Freudian psychoanalysis as a hermeneutical discipline that is primarily concerned not with pure science, but rather with a personal story or "root narrative." "Psychotherapy," says Kepnes, "is the art of bringing this root narrative first to articulation and then retelling or interpreting it in such a way that new possible ways of being in the world are opened." Seen from this standpoint, the neurotic is caught in a part of a whole story, the endless repetition of an infantile conflict. The psychoanalytic task of helping neurotics bring their acted-out stories to the level of verbal articulation was aptly called the "talking cure" by Anna O., the patient of Josef Breuer and Freud. "The entire process of psychoanalysis," writes Kepnes, "may be seen as a process of opening blockages of memory, correcting distortions, setting life events in a proper sequence, and creating a coherent life narrative."

Through giving the patient a sense of personal history and continuity, this life narrative also gives him or her a sense of self-identity. This is done, in part, through the interpretation that introduces elements of change and reconstruction into the patient's personal tale, thus enabling the patient to find possibilities for altering his or her image and understanding of himself or herself. A sense of self order and meaning is maintained by successively reinterpreting and revising the life story. Neurosis, by the same token, results from a failure to reinterpret one's life story at times of personal crisis, such as the passage into adulthood or old age. Present events call for a revision of past history, and this reordering of our personal story helps us to reorganize our lives and see new possibilities. Both Buber and Freud view narrative as a way of retrieving significant life events, writes Kepnes (1982, pp. 27–30).[4]

---

[4]In footnote 2, p. 32, Kepnes (1982) writes: "American interpreters differ from Lacan in their humanism, in their assertion of the existence of a 'substantial self.'"

# Chapter 3

# The Jungians

## Carl Jung

Carl G. Jung has played an important part in the history of dialogical psychotherapy. In his later statements on psychotherapy, Jung goes far beyond Freud in the direction of recognizing the otherness and uniqueness of the patient and the therapist. If he falls headlong into psychologism in his philosophy of religion, in his statements on psychotherapy he transcends it—and implicitly modifies his image of Psychological Man in so doing.

From his discovery that delusions and hallucinations have a human meaning—Jung tells us in *Memories, Dreams, Reflections*—he came to hold "that psychiatry, in the broadest sense, is a dialogue between the sick psyche and the psyche of the doctor . . . a coming to terms between the sick personality and that of the therapist, both in principle equally subjective." This means that doctor, and patient, must become a problem to the other if psychotherapy is to be effective. The rapport between the two must be a close one in which there is "a constant comparison and mutual comprehension," a "dialectical confrontation of two opposing psychic realities" in which the doctor must expose himself to the heights and depths of human suffering. Jung still uses the language of Psychological Man in referring to doctor and patient as "two opposing psychic realities." Yet he sees this psychic confrontation as one that occurs face to face and eye to eye, one in which the patient, as well as the doctor, has something to say. "The crucial point is that I confront the patient as one human being to another. Analysis is a dialogue demanding two partners" (Jung 1961,

p. 132f.). Jung demands that the therapist enter into the crisis not as competent practitioner, but rather as a person who is risking himself:

> In any thoroughgoing analysis the whole personality of both patient and doctor is called into play. There are many cases which the doctor cannot cure without committing himself. When important matters are at stake, it makes all the difference whether the doctor sees himself as a part of the drama, or cloaks himself in his authority. In the great crises of life, in the supreme moments when to be or not to be is the question, little tricks of suggestion do not help. Then the doctor's whole being is challenged (Jung 1961, p. 241).

In his essays, *The Practice of Psychotherapy*, Jung repeatedly stresses that he sees therapy as a "dialectic process," and he equates this dialectic process with "a dialogue or discussion between two persons." There is still a touch of psychologism here, to be sure, since Jung defines a person as a "psychic system which, when it affects another person, enters into reciprocal reaction with another psychic system." Jung quite rightly points out the difference between this "most modern formulation of the psychotherapeutic relation between physician and patient" and the orthodox Freudian "view that psychotherapy was a method which anybody could apply in stereotyped fashion in order to reach the desired result."

In particular, the dialectical procedure means giving up authority and desire to influence in favor of a comparison of mutual findings in which the patient is free to take his part unhampered by the therapist's assumptions. "My reaction is the only thing with which I as an individual can legitimately confront my patient." This individual treatment is the only one that is scientifically responsible, Jung said. Any other attitude "amounts to therapy by suggestion." The therapist is involved as deeply as the patient, for which reason Jung demanded, even before Freud, that the analyst himself be analyzed. In the dialectical procedure, the doctor must emerge from his anonymity and give an account of himself. "What happened to the patient must now happen to the doctor, so that his personality shall not react unfavorably on the patient." Only if the doctor has as much insight into his own psychic processes as he expects from his patient, will there be that "relationship of mutual confidence, on which the therapeutic success ultimately depends."

For all Jung's emphasis on rapport and mutual confidence, his ultimate vision of the therapist–patient relationship is one of two individual psychic processes, each of which is aided through interaction with the other, but each of which necessarily regards the other as a function of his own becoming. The therapist is no longer the agent of treatment. He is "a fellow participant in *a process of individual development*" (italics added). This means giving up any set presuppositions, methods, and techniques in favor of a dialectical procedure that will be suitable to individuality, which "is absolutely unique, unpredictable, and uninterpretable." It also means recognizing "the multiple significance of symbolic content." Jung distinguishes here between "the analytic–reductive and the synthetic–hermeneutic interpretation." The latter we are already familiar with from his teaching on archetypes and individuation. Yet he also says that he frequently will use a Freudian or an Adlerian approach to a particular patient. This seeming flexibility is really a relativism similar to Jung's interpretation of religion. All approaches may be accepted precisely because their meaning is transformed in terms of the unconscious process of individuation. If an individual resists any serious attempt to change him, Jung says, then the doctor must either quit the treatment or risk the dialectical procedure.

> In all such cases the doctor must leave the individual way to healing open, and then the cure will bring about no alteration of personality but will be the process we call individuation in which the patient becomes what he really is (Jung 1954, p. 10).[1]

What is surprising is not that Jung's emphasis upon dialogue between therapist and patient retains a psychic bent, but rather that he goes so far in his insistence upon mutuality within that bent. When the therapist enters the dialectical procedure as questioner and answerer, "no longer is he the superior wise man, judge, and counsellor; he is a fellow participant who finds himself involved in the dialectical process just as deeply as the so-called patient." The therapist must, in fact, "give serious consideration to the possibility that in intelligence, sensibility, range, and depth the patient's personality is superior to his own." The prime rule for Jung is that the individuality of the sufferer has the same value, the same right to exist, as that of the doctor.

Jung emphasizes the mutual, *unconscious* influence of therapist and patient. The therapist is in danger of "psychic infection," of getting entangled in the neurosis of his patient; yet if he tries too hard to guard against this influence, he robs himself of his therapeutic efficacy. "Between this Scylla and this Charybdis lies the peril, but also the healing power" (Jung 1954, pp. 8, 10, 19).

> For, twist and turn the matter as we may, the relation between doctor and patient remains a personal one within the impersonal framework of professional treatment. By no device can the treatment be anything but the product of mutual influence, in which the whole being of the doctor as well as that of his patient plays its part. In the treatment there is an encounter between two irrational factors, that is to say, between two persons who are not fixed and determinable quantites but who bring

---

[1]See also pp. 3, 5, 8, 18, 116 in Jung 1954.

with them, besides their more or less clearly defined fields of consciousness, an indefinitely extended sphere of nonconsciousness. Hence the
personalities of doctor and patient are often infinitely more important
for the outcome of the treatment than what the doctor says and thinks
. . . if there is any combination at all, both are transformed . . . . [The
doctor's] influence can only take place if the patient has a reciprocal
influence on the doctor (Jung 1954, p. 71).

This reciprocal influence means, for Jung, that the doctor is as much
"in the analysis" as the patient. "He is equally a part of the psychic process
of treatment and therefore equally exposed to the transforming influences." To be effective, the therapist must strive to meet his own therapeutic
demand. He must *become* the person through whom he wishes to influence
his patient. "The touchstone of every analysis . . . is always this person-to-
person relationship, a psychological situation where the patient confronts
the doctor upon equal terms, and with the same ruthless criticism that he
must inevitably learn from the doctor in the course of his treatment." Jung
contrasts this freely negotiated personal relationship with "the slavish and
humanly degrading bondage of the transference." To Freud, as once to
Jung, the transference of early childhood attachments to the therapist was
the heart of therapy. As Jung developed his own stance, he came to see the
person-to-person relationship as the channel through which the patient
discovers "that his own unique personality has value, that he has been
accepted for what he is, and that he has it in him to adapt himself to the
demands of life" (Jung 1954, pp. 72f., 137).

None of this will take place if the therapist continues to hide behind a
method and shuts himself off from being influenced as a person. What is
more, "even the most experienced psychotherapist will discover again and
again that he is caught up in a bond, a combination resting on mutual
unconsciousness." Even the individual neurotic Jung sees, at one point at
least, in interpersonal terms that would not be inconsonant with Sullivan
and Fromm. "A neurosis is more a psychosocial phenomenon than an
illness in the strict sense," writes Jung. "It forces us to extend the term
illness beyond the idea of an individual body whose functions are disturbed, and to look upon the neurotic person as a sick system of social
relationships" (Jung 1954, pp. 24, 178).

Therapy is as varied as human individuals. "I treat every patient as
individually as possible, because the solution of the problem is always an
individual one," says Jung in *Memories, Dreams, Reflections.* A different
language is needed for every patient, for only individual understanding,
only that understanding that arises in the direct dialogue between patient
and therapist, will do. This is a position Jung elaborates still further in one
of his last books, *The Undiscovered Self* (1958). There he points out that
self-knowledge cannot be based on theoretical assumption, for "it is not

the universal and the regular that characterize the individual, but rather the unique." Although man has to be known as a comparative unity for general purposes, his uniqueness cannot be compared with anything else, and it is this uniqueness that is "of paramount importance for understanding man." The doctor can have knowledge of man on the basis of scientific principles, but he can have understanding of his patient as a human being only through the dialogue that reveals his or her uniqueness. The therapist

> is faced with the task of treating a sick person, who, especially in the case of psychic suffering, requires individual understanding. The more schematic the treatment is, the more resistances it—quite rightly—calls up in the patient, and the more the cure is jeopardized. . . . Today, over the whole field of medicine, it is recognized that the task of the doctor consists in treating the sick person, not an abstract illness (Jung 1958, p. 12).

That this approach to medicine is based upon his image of the human, Jung makes clear through contrasting scientific education based on statistical truths in which the individual is a marginal phenomenon with what he holds to be the real human image: "The individual . . . as an irrational datum is the true and authentic carrier of reality, the concrete man as opposed to the unreal ideal or normal man to whom the scientific statements refer." Similarly, Jung's stress on the dialogue between therapist and patient has as a corollary a hitherto missing emphasis on the direct relationship between person and person. "Real and fundamental change in individuals," he writes in *The Undiscovered Self*, "can come only from the personal encounter between man and man, but not from communistic or Christian baptisms en masse, which do not touch the inner man." Jung recognizes that the mass state, for all its emphasis on the group, is an enemy of "mutual understanding and relationship of man to man." Yet such human relationship is urgently needed for the real cohesion of our society, "in view of the atomization of the pent-up mass man, whose personal relationships are undermined by general mistrust." Love can only exist where mutual projections of the shadow are withdrawn, and in love—mutual, trusting human relationship—the real cohesion and strength of society belongs. "Nothing promotes understanding and rapprochement more than the mutual withdrawal of projections." A conscious recognition and consideration of our imperfections, of the shadow, is necessary if human relationship is to be established. Thus Jung integrates his basic, more individualistic image of the human with his new emphasis on relationship by picturing the process of self-knowledge and individuation as a mutual one. The "between," however, is still subsidiary to the process of personal development within each individual (Jung 1958, pp. 10–13).

Jung's earlier work, *The Psychology of Transference* (1946; see Jung 1954), gives us still further insight into this change. Jung speaks there of the "recent past" in which the State "proved to be the most efficient machine for turning out mass men" and warned that if the inner consolidation of the individual is not conscious it will occur spontaneously and take the "form of that incredible hardheartedness which collective man displays towards his fellow men."

> He becomes a soulless herd animal governed only by panic and lust: his soul, which can live only in and from human relationships, is irretrievably lost. But the conscious achievement of inner unity clings desperately to human relationships as to an indispensable condition, for without the conscious acknowledgment and acceptance of our kinship with those around us there can be no synthesis of personality (Jung 1954, p. 232f.).

It is striking that Jung's reaction against the collective and the mass men that it produces leads him not to still greater individualism but rather to an affirmation of the relationship between persons. In *The Psychology of Transference*, in fact, Jung makes a statement that comes as close as anything he wrote to recognizing the importance of meeting and the I–Thou relationship:

> The underlying idea of the psyche proves it to be . . . an hermaphroditic being capable of uniting the opposites, but who is never complete in the individual unless related to another individual. The unrelated human being lacks wholeness, for he can achieve wholeness only through the soul, and the soul cannot exist without its other side, which is always found in a "You." Wholeness is a combination of I and You, and these show themselves to be parts of a transcendent unity whose nature can only be grasped symbolically (Jung 1954, p. 243f.).

In a footnote to the phrase "transcendent unity" Jung makes it clear that he does not mean some synthesis that would abolish the difference of the two individuals. But he also makes it clear that he does not mean meeting with a Thou in Buber's sense. Rather, what he has in mind is the integration of what one has projected onto the Thou:

> I do not, of course, mean the synthesis or identification of two individuals, but the conscious union of the ego with everything that has been projected into the "You." Hence wholeness is the result of an intrapsychic process which depends essentially on the relation of one individual to another. Such a relationship paves the way for individuation and makes it possible, but is itself no proof of wholeness. The projection upon the feminine partner contains the anima and sometimes the self (Jung 1954, p. 244, *n.* 15).

## James Hillman

In his book *The Myth of Analysis* (1972), the contemporary Jungian thinker James Hillman develops these thoughts of Jung's further in connection with the Greek myth of Eros and Psyche, which he interprets as the myth of I and Thou rather than of the lone hero journey. If we can go with another only as far as we have gone with ourselves, this also means "that we can go with ourselves *only as far as we have gone with another.*" Human relationship is the indispensable condition, but the world and its humanity still remain "the vale of soul-making," in Keats' words. If we focus on relationships, Hillman warns, we make the mistake of making the instruments and means more important than the end (Hillman 1972, p. 25). At the same time Hillman, even more explicitly than Jung, adopts Buber's terminology of the I–Thou relationship and dialogue, only to locate it, as Jung himself does, within the realm of the psyche and its projections:

> Dialogue is not a bridge constructed between isolated skin-encased subjects and objects, I's and Thou's, but is intrinsic, an internal relationship, a condition of the soul's immanence. The I–Thou is a necessity, a given a priori with the gift of soul. So soul becomes the operative factor in converting the it into a Thou, making soul of objects, personifying, anthropomorphizing through psychizing, turning into a partner the object with which it is engaged and in which it has implanted soul. Through our souls, as our dreams, projections, and emotions show, we are immanent in one another. That souls are ontologically entailed means that we are existentially involved. . . . Thus involvement becomes the first condition for admission to the psychic realm, to the field of psychology (Hillman 1972, p. 27).

If anything, Hillman has gone farther than Jung in the direction of recognizing the centrality of the I–Thou relationship to the self. Yet as his own earlier warning shows, it remains the means to the end of the "making," or individuation, of the soul. We do not really meet the soul of the other as "other," but only as it is immanent in our own souls in "our dreams, projections, and emotions." "The opus which challenges the creative, limits its potential, and tests it ultimately is always the other human soul," and these limitations "are felt in any relationship as the fulfillment and the tragedy of the human connection." Nonetheless, the methods must not be "confused with the aim, which is not sensory awareness, visual imagination, or group feeling and involvements but rather psychic consciousness: the experience of life as a mythical enactment and of the soul as the focus of individual destiny."

> Even where the opus is another soul, psychological creativity operates through one's own sense of soul as its instrument, like the tuning fork or the lyre which strikes a chord, setting in vibration tones in others, back and forth, reciprocally, mutually in harmony and discord (Hillman 1972, p. 28).

Training in participation with others is a necessary first-level attempt to awaken psyche by making us aware of the soul as it is extended through others.

## Edward Whitmont

Edward Whitmont has gone beyond both Jung and Hillman in the direction of a genuine meeting that is not just the means to the end of an intrapsychic process of individuation. In *The Symbolic Quest* Whitmont points out that, as used by Jung, the Eros principle is a function of relationship, an urge to get involved with concrete people rather than with ideas or things "but to get involved for the sake of the personal, subjective, emotional union rather than for the sake of any meaning or awareness of oneself or of one's partner."

> Hence this urge toward involvement, unity and relationship must not be confused with what we have come to call relatedness in the sense in which Buber, for instance, uses the term when he postulates a consciously empathic I–Thou *Begegnung*, that is a meeting, confrontation or encounter. Such a *Begegnung* is a "recognition," a relationship of mutual creative involvement and understanding, of distance as well as of nearness.

Eros, in contrast, does not mean basic "knowing" in its biblical sense of loving understanding, but rather only human contact, involvement, and merging that is still indifferent to understanding.

Whitmont does not stop at this differentiation, but goes on to call for a full and true human relatedness:

> True human relatedness requires more than erotic involvement, it requires confronting distance as much as connecting nearness, creative understanding as well as emotional involvement, aggressive challenge as much as patient inaction, waiting, caring and bearing. . . . Full human I–Thou relatedness cannot simply be an Eros function, as it has usually been presented in the writings of analytical psychology; it arises out of the interaction of Yang and Yin in their double polarity of love and challenging aggressiveness, of creative understanding and emotional gestation. It requires distance and separateness no less than involvement, the conscious integration of anger and hostility no less than that of love and friendliness. Hence it constellates and invokes the wholeness or

totality of our human potential. Relatedness is the external interpersonal aspect of individuation. One cannot fully and truly relate to a "Thou" without encountering the deepest Self; in turn one cannot encounter the Self through introversion only. Our human fullness requires the actual meeting with a "Thou" (Whitmont 1969, p. 174f.).

"Individuation occurs through realization," Whitmont emphasizes elsewhere, "genuine experiencing in actual encounters or situations; it is not sufficient to depend on theoretical understanding (Whitmont 1969, p. 296).

## Arie Sborowitz

The European Jungian analyst Arie Sborowitz has written a long monograph in which he attempts to combine the essential elements of Jung's and Buber's teaching through viewing such Jungian categories as "introjection," "projection," and "identification" as the negative obstacles to positive relationship. To Sborowitz, Jung's emphasis on "destiny" and Buber's emphasis on "relationship" are complementary concepts that together make up an adequate conception of psychology (Sborowitz 1948, pp. 9–56).

The emphases of Buber and Jung are not so compatible as Sborowitz thinks. The integration of the personality is not an end in itself to Buber as it is to Jung: one becomes whole in order to be able to respond to what meets one. Jung ignores the fact that the essential life of the individual soul "consists of real meetings with other realities," writes Buber. Although Jung speaks of the self as including both the I and the "others," the "others" are clearly included not in their actual "otherness," but only as contents of the individual soul that shall, just as an individual soul, attain its perfection through individuation.

> The actual other who meets me meets me in such a way that my soul comes in contact with his as with something that it is not and that it cannot become. My soul does not and cannot include the other, and yet can nonetheless approach the other in this most real contact. This other, what is more, is and remains over against the self as the other, no matter what completeness the self may attain. So the self, even if it has integrated all of its unconscious elements, remains this single self, confined within itself. All beings existing over against me who become "included" in my self are possessed by it in this inclusion as an It. Only then when, having become aware of the unincludable otherness of a being, I renounce all claim to incorporating it in any way within me or making it a part of my soul, does it truly become Thou for me (Buber 1957a, p. 88f.).

## Hans Trüb

What Sborowitz failed to accomplish through an intellectual synthesis the Swiss psychiatrist Hans Trüb made a reality in his own life in his dialogical anthropology—the fusion of Jung's analytical psychology with Buber's philosophy of dialogue. Trüb belonged to Jung's Psychology Club in Zurich and was so close to Jung personally that Jung's wife Emma went to Trüb for therapy on Jung's recommendation. Trüb did not synthesize Jung and Buber. He included Jung's psychological–dialectical approach to therapy within his own anthropological–dialogical approach, but he came down decisively in favor of the dialogical rather than the dialectical. Psychology looks only at *psychic occurrences* and is adequate only to them. But the whole person can be grasped only by the anthropological point of view that looks only at man's situation in the world.

In the *psychological–dialectical* procedure, the psychiatrist employs the contact with the patient on the level of consciousness in order to gain insight and admission to the irrational processes in his or her "unconscious." The aim is to harmonize "in themselves" the antitheses expressing themselves in the polarity of the conscious "I-complex," on the one hand, and the autonomous contents of the unconscious, on the other. In the *anthropological–dialogical* procedure, in contrast, the therapist posits that the Thou capable of being addressed in the patient is identical with the self capable of answering, thus directing the patient to the total dialogue.

For Trüb, the *dialectical* attitude of the psychologist, with its methodological and systematic focus on the contradictory multiplicity of the psyche, had to be coordinated with and subordinated to the *dialogical* attitude of the partnership relationship that rejects both method and system in favor of "the person-to-person meeting, each and every time unique, each and every time demanding a decision." No matter how significant and reliable the self-illuminating insights achieved by the analysis of depth psychology may be in any given case, they demonstrate their curative force decisively only when the patient abandons the stand he took during the analysis and throws himself *as himself* into the world of real objects and meetings.

By making conscious the images by which the patient is passively assaulted in his unconscious, the analysis enables the patient to meet the reality of the world steadily. Introspective analysis, for Trüb, in marked contrast to Jung, does not open up for us an inner world in which one can live, a world that has to compete with reality. "Rather it puts us in possession of the *world of images* with which alone we are truly enabled to meet the one and only real world." The neurotic person reacts to reality, but he no longer opens himself to it. The result of this flight from reality is a profound, uncanny, and inexplicable dread out of which the patient constructs within himself a system of barely penetrable protections and defenses. Conversely, the uncovering of these inner psychic defense mechanisms by means of depth psychology can only truly succeed if it recognizes that they are based in the self's *personally* executed flight from meeting (Trüb 1973, pp. 500–503).

Only mutual personal trust assures the positive treatment of such a neurosis. The therapist's recognition of the presence of another provides him with a yardstick for psychoanalytic work. "How far I must and may follow up psychological work with this person confronting me is always to be decided on the basis of personal relationship." When the patient does execute an authentic about-face toward the world, this is experienced by both partners in the relationship "as an autonomous act, bursting forth out of freedom, startling." The therapist may even fear it since it ends, often abruptly, the rational procedure in the process of psychological realization. The therapist both hopes for and dreads this result:

> For when it appears, the patient is lost to us at a blow as an object of treatment, and that which remains to be done proceeds from a fundamentally new point of departure. For now the problem lies *between* us. The situation from now on is an obviously dialogical one (Trüb 1973, p. 504).

In his essay, "Individuation, Guilt, and Decision," Hans Trüb describes how he went through a decade-long crisis in which he broke with his personal and doctrinal dependence on Jung in favor of the new insights that arose through his friendship with Martin Buber. What had the greatest influence on Trüb was not Buber's doctrine but rather meeting with him person to person, and it is from this meeting that the revolutionary change in Trüb's method of psychotherapy proceeded (Trüb 1935, pp. 529–542, 553). Put in terms of the image of the human, we could say that it was not the human image Buber consciously presented in his writings and speaking that influenced Trüb, but rather the human image that Buber communicated in his dialogue with Trüb—an image, therefore, that included the basic attitudes of both men and the dialogue between them rather than an image of any visual form or conceptual content.

Trüb writes that, in time, he found himself fully disarmed by the fact that in conversation Buber was not concerned about the ideas of his partner, but rather about the partner himself. It became ever clearer to Trüb that in such unreserved interchange it is simply not possible to bring any hidden intention with one and to pursue it. In this dialogue, one individuality did not triumph over the other, for each remained the same. Yet Trüb emerged from this meeting "renewed for all time, with my knowledge of the reality of things brought one step nearer to the truth." Particularly important for Trüb seems to have been Buber's practice of "inclusion," or experiencing the other side, which Trüb describes as letting a soft tone sound and swell in himself and listening for the echo from the other side (Trüb 1935, p. 554).

Trüb describes how in his work with his patients he became aware of the invariable tendency of the primary consciousness to become monological and self-defeating. He also tells how this closed circle of the self was again and again forced outward toward relationship through those times when, despite his will, he found himself confronting his patient not as an analyst, but rather as a human being. From these experiences he came to understand the full meaning of the analyst's responsibility. The analyst takes responsibility for lost and forgotten things, and with the aid of his psychology he helps to bring them to light. But he knows in the depths of his self that the secret meaning of these things that have been brought to consciousness first reveals itself *in the outgoing to the other* (Trüb 1935, pp. 543–550).

> *Psychology* as science and *psychology* as function know about the soul of man as about something in the third person. . . . They look down from above into the world of inner things, into the inner world of the individual. And they deal with its contents as with their "objects." They give names and they create classifications while carefully investigating the manifold connections and presenting them vividly in meaningful systems.
>
> But the psychotherapist in his work with the ill is *essentially a human being*. . . . Therefore he seeks and loves the human being in his patients and allows it . . . to come to him ever again (Trüb 1973, p. 497).

The personal experience that moved Trüb from the dialectical psychology of Jung to the dialogical anthropology of Buber was, he tells us, an overwhelming sense of guilt. This guilt was no longer such as could be explained away or removed, for it was subjectively experienced as the guilt of a person who had stepped out of a real relationship to the world and tried to live in a spiritual world above reality. Trüb, like Buber, holds that guilt is an essential factor in the person's relations to others and that it performs the necessary function of leading him to desire to set these relations right.

True guilt, in contrast to neurotic guilt, takes place *between* person and person. It is an ontological reality of which the feeling of guilt is only the subjective and psychological counterpart. For this reason, Buber says that guilt does not reside in the person but that he stands, in the most realistic sense, in the guilt that envelops him. Similarly, the repression of guilt and the neuroses that result from this repression are not merely psychological phenomena, but rather real events between persons. Therefore, Buber holds, the person who is sick from existential guilt must follow a path made up of three stages in order to be healed. First, he must illuminate his guilt by recognizing that, however different he may now be, he is the person who took this burden of guilt on himself; second, he must persevere in this illumination; and third, he must repair the injured order of the world, either with the person he wronged or by establishing a new dialogical relation at some other point. In T. S. Eliot's *The Cocktail Party*, Sir Henry Harcourt-Reilly tells Edward that he must learn to live with his guilt, but there is nothing that he can do about it in relation to the person to whom he is guilty. Buber, in contrast, holds that guilt means a rupture of the dialogical relationship, an injury of the existential order of "the common," and as such must be repaired by again entering into dialogue with that person or with the world (Buber 1965b, pp. 531–539).

Real guilt is the beginning of *ethos*, or responsibility, writes Trüb in his essay, "From Self to World" (1947), but before the patient can become aware of it, he must be helped by the analyst to become aware of himself in general. This the analyst does through playing the part both of confidante and big brother. The neurotic is given the understanding the world has denied him, which makes it more and more possible for him to step out of his self-imprisonment and into a genuine relation with the analyst. In doing this, Trüb says, the analyst must avoid the intimacy of a private I–Thou relationship with the patient *and* the temptation of dealing with the patient as an object. This means, in effect, that he must have just that dialogical relationship of concrete, but one-sided inclusion on which Buber insists in his Postscript to *I and Thou*. It cannot become the mutual inclusion of friendship without destroying the therapeutic possibilities of the relationship. But neither can it make the patient an It. The analyst must be able to risk himself and to participate in the process of individuation.

The analyst must see the illness of the patient as an illness of relations with the world, Trüb writes. The roots of the neurosis lie both in the patient's closing himself off from the world and in the pattern of society itself and its rejection and nonconfirmation of the patient. Consequently, the analyst must change at some point from the consoler who takes the part of the patient against the world to the person who puts before the patient the claim of the world. This change is necessary to complete the second part of the cure—the establishment of real relationship with the world that can only take place in the world itself. On the analyst falls the task of preparing the way for the resumption in direct meeting of the interrupted dialogical relationship between the individual and the community. The psychotherapist must test the patient's finding of himself by the criterion of whether his self-realization can be the starting point for a new personal meeting with the world. The patient must go forth whole in himself, but he must also recognize that it is not his own self, but rather the world with which he must be concerned. This does not mean, however, that the patient is simply integrated with or adjusted to the world. He does not cease to be a real person, responsible for himself; but at the same time he enters into responsible relationship with his community (Trüb 1973, pp. 497–499).

In *Healing through Meeting*, Trüb states his approach to psychotherapy through a systematic confrontation with the psychology of Jung. One's self, the center of one's personality, becomes actualized only as one discloses oneself as a partner to the world, and so, too, the living sense of psychic processes, both healthy and pathological, is revealed only through this self-disclosure. Therefore, to know his patient the psychotherapist must recognize him in his partnership with the world—an objective knowledge is not enough. The therapist must experience the patient as a partner in his own meeting with him. It is through this eye-to-eye confrontation that the patient's capacity for meeting begins to be restored.

> By viewing the isolated patient from the beginning as one who has sacrificed his capacity for dialogue in withdrawing his self from meeting with the world, and by addressing him immediately, anthropological psychotherapy sets him up as a fellow human being, a Thou, the original partner in a fully human meeting. It seeks out this stubborn self, this introvert captive of the psyche, and will not release it. It summons this self by name as the one called upon to answer, the one personally responsible. And by addressing it in this manner, it challenges the self to disclose itself in its self and to individuate itself in the new dialogue with the physician-partner and beyond him in intercourse—and not merely the introverted kind—with the world (Trüb 1973, p. 500f.).

For Trüb, the dialogical meeting is both the starting point and the goal of therapy. The success or failure of the cure focuses on the risk of this meeting. The tension of psychic conflict that derives from the contradiction of the conscious and unconscious arrives at a psychotherapeutic resolution in the framework of this basic partnership. "The healing process takes place between *this* physician and *this* patient, in the totality of their personal confrontation" (Trüb 1973, p. 502). The therapist embodies for the patient a loving inclination of the world that seeks to restore the patient's dispirited and mistrustful self to a new dialogical meeting with the forces of nature and history. Thus, the therapist quiets and harmonizes the psychic tension of the patient not only according to the latter's wish, but also as a partner penetrating the personal basis of his being, the actual origin of that elemental introversion that nourishes all neuroses. The unconscious is precisely the personal element that is lost in the course of development, the element that escapes consciousness. In dealing with this lost element, the psychotherapist cannot point to a truth he *has*, but only to a truth to be sought *between* him and the patient. Only thus can he equalize again the enormous advantage given him by the fact that the other one seeks him out and asks him for help. Thus the equality of respect for which the humanistic psychologist seeks is attained, according to Trüb, not by the insistence on a complete mutuality of situation, but rather by the recognition of the *betweenness* itself as the place where real meeting, real healing, and real finding occurs.

It is very important, of course, that the therapist not demand responsibility in dialogue before the patient is ready for it. That is why the reconstruction of the capacity for dialogue must go hand in hand with the methodical attempt to loosen and dismantle the complex defense mechanisms in the psychic realm of expression as fast as the recuperating self permits. "Without this supplemental assistance of depth psychology, what is dialogically expected of the patient's self in the meeting situation with the world would place too great a demand on it and expose it to the danger of regression" (Trüb 1973, p. 502).

But Trüb does *not* hold, like Jung and his followers, that one must first become individuated and only then enter into a dialogue with others. The therapist, Trüb says, must keep in view "the one true goal of healing, the unlocking of the locked up person for the meeting with the world" (Trüb 1973, p. 503). Only this enables the therapist to answer *both* for the patient *and* for the world. Only by so doing can the therapist risk personal commitment, even to the neurotic self-entanglement of the patient. Only starting from the meeting as partner can physician and patient hold their ground with a positive attitude in the face of the cure's completion, which generally occurs unexpectedly and which may be compared, Trüb suggests, to a leap over the abyss. All this implies no choice between the inner personal wholeness and the social self, such as Jung makes in his repeated valuing of the inner personal wholeness over the social self. On the contrary, "the willingness of the self to meet the world, the situation of a living dialogue, that is between within and without, should be striven for and furthered *simultaneously* with the effort to attain a psychic integration of the self" (Trüb 1973, p. 503). When the psychological cooperation and dialectical interaction of patient and therapist is conducted dialogically, with mutual personal trust between therapist and patient, then there gradually awakens and grows in the patient at one and the same time, and as corollaries of the same happening, a new confidence in himself *and* in the other (Trüb 1973, p. 504f.)[2]

It is to Hans Trüb that Buber points, in "Healing through Meeting," as the man who broke the trail as a practicing psychotherapist in the recogni-

---

[2]These selections were translated for Friedman 1973 by William Hallo and are the only published translations in English of Trüb 1952.

tion and realization of the therapeutic possibilities of dialogue. Speaking of the crisis through which the psychotherapist passes when he discovers the paradox of his vocation, Buber writes:

> In a decisive hour, together with the patient entrusted to and trusting in him, he has left the closed room of psychological treatment in which the analyst rules by means of his systematic and methodological superiority and has stepped forth with him into the air of the world where self is exposed to self. There, in the closed room where one probed and treated the isolated psyche according to the inclination of the self-encapsulated patient, the patient was referred to ever-deeper levels of his inwardness as to his proper world; here outside, in the immediacy of one human standing over against another, the encapsulation must and can be broken through, and a transformed, healed relationship must and can be opened to the person who is sick in his relationship to otherness—to the world of the other which he cannot remove into his soul. A soul is never sick alone, but there is always a betweenness also, a situation between it and another existing being. The psychotherapist who has passed through the crisis may now dare to touch on this.
>
> This way of frightened pause, of unfrightened reflection, of personal involvement, of rejection of security, of unreserved stepping into relationship, of the bursting of psychologism, this way of vision and of risk is that which Hans Trüb trod. . . . Surely there will not be wanting men like him—awake and daring, hazarding the economics of the vocation, not sparing and not withholding themselves—men who will find his path and extend it further (Buber 1969, p. 142f.).

This book offers evidence that the persons Buber called for do exist.

# Chapter 4

# The Interpersonal Approach

## George Herbert Mead

One of the pioneers in the discovery of the "social self" was the American social psychologist and philosopher George Herbert Mead. The fundamental emphasis of Mead in his central book, *Mind, Self, and Society*, is that the self is a product of the social process, rather than something that exists independently of and prior to that process. "Selves can only exist in definite relationship to other selves."

> The self is not something that exists first and then enters into relationship with others, but it is, so to speak, an eddy in the social current and so still a part of the current. It is a process in which the individual is continually adjusting himself in advance to the situation to which he belongs, and reacting back on it (Mead 1934, p. 182).

For Mead, the earliest stage of the development of the self is "the internationalization and inner dramatization, by the individual, of the external conversation of significant gestures which constitutes the chief mode of interaction with other individuals belonging to the same society." Mead shows the self arising in a child through play and the game in which the child takes the attitude of the other and carries on a conversation with the other. This taking on the role of the other is perhaps the most basic point in Mead's social behaviorism.

One of Mead's most fruitful ideas is his distinction between the two different selves that appear together and constitute the personality—the "I" and the "Me." The Me is the organized response of the other that we have taken into ourselves, and the I is our reaction to this organized response. Only through both of these—the internalization and the response—do we acquire conscious selves. There remains, nonetheless, an element of the unexpected and unpremeditated in the response of the I that is not present in the Me. "The Me represents a definite organization of the community there in our own attitudes, and calling for a response, but the response that takes place is something that just happens." This means that for all Mead's characterization of the self as "an eddy in the social current," he leaves room for an element of freedom and spontaneity through which the becoming of the individual can be understood as a *dialogue* between the person and his image of the human rather than as an entirely conditioned reaction. The corollary of this recognition of the freedom and spontaneity of the I is Mead's insistence that, for all its individuality, the I is a social self that can be realized only in relation with others.

One realizes oneself as a self, according to Mead, only as one takes the attitude of the other. One takes this attitude over against one's self, in fact; for the self only has meaning in its existence over against the other self. Through language, for example, one "gets a new soul." "He puts himself into the attitude of those that make use of that language. He cannot read its literature, cannot converse with those that belong to that community without taking on its peculiar attitudes." Communication, for Mead, is the organizing process in the community that makes possible "putting one's self in the place of the other person's attitude, communicating through significant symbols." This taking of the attitude of the other is the basis of human sympathy; it means a sympathetic identification with the other and a tendency to respond to his or her social situation in the way he or she does. "What is essential is the development of the whole mechanism of social relationship which brings us together, so that we can take the attitude of the other in our various life-processes."[1]

## Alfred Adler

The American psychiatrist Harry Stack Sullivan developed his image of the human far more under the influence of George Herbert Mead and American pragmatism than of Freud. But we must also recognize, in the case of Sullivan, as of Rollo May and Erich Fromm, the direct and

---

[1]For an excellent presentation of the thought of George Herbert Mead, see Paul Pfuetze's comparative study of Mead and Buber, originally published as *The Social Self*, then later reprinted by Harper Torchbooks and later still by Greenwood Books under the title *Self, Society, and Existence*.

indirect influences of Alfred Adler and his school of "Individual Psychology." "Adler's psychology is essentially a dynamics of interpersonal relationships," writes Henri Ellenberger. "It never considers the individual in an isolated and static situation, but sees him in the light of his actions and of the reactions of his environment." In fact, Adler saw neurosis, depression, perversion, criminality, and even psychosis as varieties of disturbances in the relationship of the individual with the community. The Oedipus complex, which Freud accepted as normative, Adler saw as the result of faulty education, and both parents and siblings were for Adler partners against whom the child could measure his strength. For Adler, lack of understanding in interpersonal relationships produced mental illness, from which he held that a more general knowledge of man could facilitate social relationships. In contrast to Freud, Adler saw an individual's basic drive as lying not in any death or fighting instinct, but rather in community feeling.

Adler's approach to therapy was also closer to "healing through meeting" than Freud's. Instead of lying on a couch with the therapist sitting behind it, the Adlerian patient sits face to face with the therapist; both chairs are equal in size. The therapist brings in other members of the family if it seems helpful. Nor is there the Freudian emphasis upon the great value of paying for one's therapy.

Ellenberger sees the shift of psychoanalysis to ego psychology under the so-called "Neo-Freudians" as, to a great extent, an adaptation of Adlerian concepts by prominent members of the William Alanson White Institute and the Association for the Advancement of Psychoanalysis. Psychoanalytic terminology, however, is preseved. Particularly important here were the American psychotherapists Harry Stack Sullivan, Karen Horney, Erich Fromm, and Clara Thompson (Ellenberger 1970, pp. 613f., 620, 638).

## Harry Stack Sullivan

Harry Stack Sullivan takes interpersonal relations as the true nexus of the self and, by the same token, of mental health and mental illness. Sullivan distinguishes between the pursuit of satisfactions, which pertains to bodily needs, and the pursuit of security, which pertains to cultural needs. It is the latter, not the former, which he holds to be crucial in mental illness. The child is formed and educated through the anxiety experienced from the disapproval of significant others or the relief and pleasure felt from their approval. The personality is a larger whole than the self. Many of the impulses and performances of the personality are not noted because they are outside the awareness of the self. A curious reversal takes place.

Instead of anxiety's serving to prevent one's feeling, thinking, or doing what significant others disapprove, it serves to protect the self from the awareness that it is engaging in such disapproved activities.

Relationships with other people are an indispensable part of one's development as a person and a self. "The human being requires the world of culture, cannot live *and be human* except in communal existence with it." This is absolutely true in the earlier phases of personality development, but it is true in a different sense when the child moves from the juvenile to the preadolescent stage. Only then does there arise a capacity to love in which "the satisfactions and the security which are being experienced by someone else, some particular other person, begin to be as significant to the person as are his own satisfactions and security" (Sullivan 1940, pp. 18, 20).

> If another person matters as much to you as do you yourself, it is quite possible to talk to this person as you have never talked to anyone before. The freedom which comes from this expanding of one's world of satisfaction and the security to include two people, linked together by love, permits exchanges of nuances of meaning, permits investigations without fear of rebuff or humiliation, which greatly augments the consensual validation of all sorts of things (Sullivan 1940, p. 20).

"Consensual validation" means a truth, a world, that is discovered with others, not by being objectively established, but rather by being interpersonally shared and tested out. This is the period in which a real world community is illuminated. Instead of being imprisoned within one's self in autistic, self-referring isolation, one is open to some comparing of notes, checking, and counterchecking. This consensual validation leads one to feel human in a new sense—through the appreciation of the common humanity of people, through sympathy for the other, whether known directly or only by report.

When a person does not experience this consensual validation, he or she not only fails to develop his or her feeling of humanity, but he or she also fails to develop as a person, becoming less and less aware of interpersonal performances, and as a result, more and more dissociated. Only by skillful use of responsive speech, "our most specialized tool of communication," can we overcome the privacy of our personal worlds. Those who do not succeed in bridging this gap lead existences that are unstable and less than human, inauthentic, not in terms of some moral judgment, but in terms of their existence itself. On the other hand, Sullivan holds that "one achieves mental health to the extent that one becomes aware of one's interpersonal relations."

Sullivan explicitly rejects Freud's notion of the formation of the conscience as an introjection of the values of the father and/or the mother.

What Sullivan is concerned with is the actual anxiety-diminishing and anxiety-increasing experiences of the child in interpersonal relations with significant others. In other words, Sullivan is substituting dynamic relationship—verbs—for the more static, noun-based thinking of Freud: "This dynamism is an explanatory conception; it is not a thing, a region, or what not, such as superegos, egos, ids, and so on."

Instead of holding with Freud that man "has an actual need for being cruel and hurtful to his fellows," Sullivan sees malevolence and hatred developing from the child's experience of being denied tenderness. If a child expresses a need for tenderness, and that child's parents reject and even hurt the child, then as a juvenile the child "makes it practically impossible for anyone to feel tenderly toward him or to treat him kindly," beating them to it by a display of hatred. Malevolence, as Sullivan sees it, is "just an elaboration of this warp," the vicious circle that comes when parents fail "to discharge their social responsibility to produce a well-behaved, well-socialized person" (Sullivan 1953).

If Jung errs on the side of valuing the inner man as against the social, and Freud straddles the fence on this issue, Sullivan goes to the other extreme in making the sole criterion of authentic personal existence being "well behaved" and "well socialized." The impossible only became possible in Nazi Germany because so many Germans were so well behaved and well socialized in relation to that particular society that they did not dare to stand against it! Sullivan seems to have no room in his thinking for Socrates' drinking a cup of hemlock because the Athenians considered him a threat to good behavior and good socialization.

Although Sullivan seems to have founded his whole system on anxiety, he later attests that loneliness can brush aside the activity of the self-system. "Under loneliness, people seek companionship even though intensely anxious in the performance. . . . The fact that loneliness will lead to integrations in the face of severe anxiety automatically means that loneliness in itself is more terrible than anxiety." This means that our relations to others are not just a system of being approved or disapproved, but rather that we need them for themselves and not just for their bolstering of our own selves.

Sullivan distinguishes three "needs": "the need for personal security—that is, for freedom from anxiety; the need for intimacy—that is, for collaboration with at least one other person; and the need for lustful satisfaction, which is connected with genital activity in pursuit of the orgasm." The fact that Sullivan speaks of "the need for intimacy" shows the psychologism that still dominates his thinking. He has already defined intimacy as caring about the other person's needs as much as one's own. If this is so, such persons cannot be a "need" of mine without making my concern for their needs a function of my own needs and therefore, by definition, less of a concern for them than for myself. But this is as much of a language vestige as it is a reduction of the relationship to the other to a function of the self. Sullivan not only recognizes that the need for intimacy and that for lust cannot be identified, he also points out that they are often quite at variance with each other as well as with the need for security.

Sullivan includes in his interpersonal psychiatry an open relationship to another person that would have been quite impossible for Freud, for whom love at its best could never be anything but a mutual exploitation for the fulfillment of individual, instinctual needs. This open relationship is not attained in our culture. "The cultural influences which are borne in upon each person include very little which prepares members of different sexes for a fully human, simple, personal relationship together." The result is often a split between lust and intimacy in which the former is directed to "the prostitute" and the latter to "the good girl." The satisfaction of lust, then, takes place at the cost of one's self-esteem, while the relationship that allays loneliness and anxiety is not a full relationship. Nor is this split only present in adolescence. Some of Sullivan's most biting comments are reserved for the false part that sex plays in our culture—not as the satisfaction of a genuine need, but rather as a means of enhancing prestige: "In this culture the ultimate test of whether you can get on or not is whether you can do something satisfactory with your genitals or somebody else's genitals without undue anxiety and loss of self esteem."

In his discussion of "late adolescence," Sullivan presents his most complete image of what it means to be fully human. Late adolescence begins with discovering what one likes in the way of genital behavior and how to fit it into the rest of one's life, and it proceeds *through unnumbered educative and eductive steps to the establishment of a fully human or mature repertory of interpersonal relations, as permitted by available opportunity, personal and cultural.*" The goal of being fully human means, to Sullivan, freedom of living. But since living takes place in interpersonal relations, these relations must be real ones. Sullivan sees a restriction to freedom of living not in the fact that the individual is prevented by others from full "self-expression," but rather in the fact that many people settle for "pseudo-social ritual": "Each person is busily engaged with people, but nothing particularly personal transpires. . . . There are a remarkable number of people who have ways of being social as the devil without having anything to do with the other people concerned." Thus, Sullivan's use of the term "interpersonal" is not merely descriptive, but normative as well. Not every type of relationship between people leads to the "fully human," but only that into which people really enter as persons and in which they really have to do with others.

For Sullivan, maturity, self-respect, and genuine interpersonal relations are necessary corollaries. Only immature people derogate others for the sake of their own security, and in so doing, demonstrate their own lack of self-respect. Mature people will be recognized by their sympathetic understanding of the limitations, interests, possibilities, and anxieties of those with whom they live. Thus, the *need* for intimacy that leads to collaboration with others also leads to a transcending of the language of individual needs in favor of "a very lively sensitivity to the needs of the other and to the interpersonal security or absence of anxiety in the other" (Sullivan 1953).

## Erich Fromm

In contrast to Freud's psychology, with its biological individualism and its innate competitiveness and aggression, Erich Fromm sees the key problem of psychology as "that of the specific kind of relatedness of the individual towards the world and not that of the satisfaction or frustration of this or that instinctual need *per se.*" Following Karl Marx and Harry Stack Sullivan, Fromm sees people as *primarily* social beings, i.e., social in their very selves and not just in their needs. Psychology, as a result, is "psychology of interpersonal relationships." Fromm disagrees emphatically with Freud's view that history is the result of psychological forces that in themselves are not socially conditioned. But he also disagrees with those theories, "more or less tinged with behaviorist psychology," that assume "that human nature has no dynamism of its own and that psychological changes are to be understood in terms of the development of new habits as an adaptation to new cultural patterns" (*Escape from Freedom*). Human nature is not infinitely malleable, and the human factor is one of the dynamic elements in the social process.

In *Escape from Freedom*, Fromm goes beyond Freud and Sullivan in his emphasis on freedom, which he sees as characterizing human existence as such.

> Human existence begins when the lack of fixation of action by instincts exceeds a certain point; when the adaptation to nature loses its coercive character; when the way to act is no longer fixed by hereditarily given mechanisms. In other words, *human existence and freedom are from the beginning inseparable* (Fromm 1941, p. 32).

Human freedom, however, depends on the successful emergence of the individual from his primary ties to an individualized state. He finds fulfillment not through organic or symbiotic union with others, but rather through "his active solidarity with all men and his spontaneous activity, love and work, which unites him again with the world . . . as a free and independent individual." But the loss of the ties that gave people security, plus coercive economic, social, and political conditions, often make freedom an unbearable burden. The result is "sadomasochism"—an unhealthy, nonproductive, dominance–submission relation to others—and with it the loss of the true self. Sado-masochism, as Fromm uses the term, is not a sexual phenomenon, or even an expression of hostility, as Freud later saw sadism, but rather an attempt to overcome the anxiety produced by being a separate person through a symbiotic union with another in which that separateness is forgotten. For this reason, a sadist is as dependent on the person he dominates as a masochist is on the person who dominates him. In fact, says Fromm, the two always go together.

Fromm sees freedom as a corollary of the wholeness of the personality. "Positive freedom consists in the spontaneous activity of the total, integrated personality." Such spontaneity comes through the acceptance of the total personality and the elimination of the split between reason and nature. The foremost component of spontaneity is love—not the dissolution of the self in another person or the possession of another, but rather the spontaneous affirmation of others while preserving the individual self. Love, for Fromm, means the overcoming of separation without the elimination of otherness. Work, too, is a part of spontaneity—not compulsion or domination of nature, but rather an act of creation that unites one with nature without dissolving one in it. "The basic dichotomy that is inherent in freedom—the birth of individuality and the pain of aloneness—is dissolved on a higher plane by man's spontaneous action."

Freedom and the organic growth of the self are possible, says Fromm, only if one respects the uniqueness of the self of other persons as well as one's own self. Fromm characterizes love, in *Man for Himself* and in *The Art of Loving*, as "care, responsibility, respect, and knowledge." These terms all imply a mutual relation with others that sees the other as of value in himself. Fromm recognizes this explicitly in taking responsibility back to its root meaning of "respond" and in further defining love as "the wish for the other person to grow and develop" and as "the expression of intimacy between two human beings under the condition of the preservation of each other's integrity." Love, to Fromm, is "a paradoxical two-in-oneness" in which both separateness and togetherness prevail. It means the response to another in his uniqueness, accepting him *as he is*:

> Responsibility could easily deteriorate into domination and possessiveness, were it not for a third component of love, *respect*. Respect is . . . the ability to see a person as he is, to be aware of his unique individuality. Respect means the concern that the other person should grow and unfold as he is. Respect, thus, implies the absence of exploitation. I want the loved person to grow and unfold for his own sake, and in his own ways, and not for the purpose of serving me (Fromm 1956, p. 28).

In opposition to Freud, Fromm holds, in *Beyond the Chains of Illusion*, that the most powerful motive for repression is not fear of castration, but of isolation and ostracism. "Man has to be related, he has to find union with others, in order to be sane." Like Sullivan, therefore, Fromm sees man's strongest fear as the loneliness that threatens his sanity. This often leads the individual to blind himself to the reality behind the illusions his group puts forward, rather than risk ostracism. Yet man is also afraid of isolation from the humanity inside him, from his conscience and reason. When a society is not human, the individual is forced into a conflict between social and human aims. He can only resolve this conflict in favor of the human if he "has transcended the limits of one's society and has become a citizen of the world." One source of such transcending, Fromm suggests, is his unconscious, which to Fromm is neither good nor evil, rational nor irrational, but all of these—all that is human. The unconscious is the whole man, the universal man, minus the social part, whereas consciousness is the social man, "the accidental limitations set by the historical situation into which an individual is thrown." "To become aware of one's unconscious," therefore, "means to get in touch with one's full humanity and to do away with barriers which society erects within each man and, consequently, between each man and his fellowman."

In *Beyond the Chains of Illusion* (1962), Fromm tells how he began with the "strictly orthodox Freudian procedure of analyzing a patient while sitting behind him and listening to his associations." This procedure turned the patient into the object of a laboratory experiment for Fromm. He was able to fit the patient's dreams into his theoretical expectations, but he was still talking *about* the patient rather than *to* him. Eventually, he found a new way: "Instead of being an observer, I had to become a participant; to be engaged with the patient; from center to center, rather than from periphery to periphery." That this means an even more radical departure from the traditional method than Harry Stack Sullivan's "participant observer" is suggested by Fromm's remark to me that he not only sees therapy as "healing through meeting" but that he also believes that the therapist himself is healed in the process.

This stress on participation does not mean that Fromm is under any illusion about therapy being fully mutual. Even while he felt himself fully engaged, as he had never been before, and learned that he could understand his patient rather than interpret what he said, he discovered that he could at the same time remain fully objective—seeing the patient as he is, and not as Fromm might want him to be. "To be objective is only possible if one does not want anything for oneself, neither the patient's admiration, nor his submission, nor even his cure." The therapy takes place for the sake of the cure, but a genuine wish to help will protect the therapist from being hurt in his self-esteem when the patient does not improve or from being elated about "his" achievement when the patient gets well (Fromm 1962, pp. 149f., 154f.).[2]

## Frieda Fromm-Reichmann

Although Frieda Fromm-Reichmann made no important *theoretical* contribution to dialogical psychotherapy, she was a pioneer in applying Freud's and Sullivan's approaches to interpersonal psychiatry to direct, long-term work with schizophrenics. Sullivan, too, worked with schizophrenics with impressive results. But Fromm-Reichmann became legendary in this respect to all who knew her. Through the immense popularity of *I Never Promised You A Rose Garden*, she has become known, anonymously, to millions as the understanding, warm, and human therapist who worked directly with the author of the book in St. Elizabeth's Hospital in Washington, D.C. Even more important was her work in Chestnut Lodge, the psychiatric facility of The Washington School of Psychiatry, the faculty of which she chaired after Harry Stack Sullivan and before Leslie H. Farber.

In her one book, *Principles of Intensive Psychotherapy*, Fromm-Reichmann gives us a rich harvest of examples of her understanding of healing through meeting from her own practice and that of others with whom she worked closely. To Fromm-Reichmann, Sullivan's concept of the therapist as "participant observer" included spontaneous and genuine responses on the part of the therapist and even, in some cases, reassuring touch and gestures of affection. This does *not* include transforming the professional relation into a social one or seeking personal gratification from the dialogue with the patient. But it does include confirmation of patients as worthy of respect and "meeting them on the basis of mutual human equality."

Fromm-Reichmann rejects Freud's death instinct in favor of a recognition of hostility as rising from unhappy interpersonal experience. What is more, actions on the patient's part, such as silence, are not invariably manifestations of hostility. They may be expressions of trust. The therapist may be the first person in the patient's life who has presented him with the gift of a degree of interpersonal security that makes it unnecessary for him to speak or, as one patient described this friendly silence: "The happiness to dare to breathe and vegetate and just to be in the presence of another person who does not interfere." Again, although Fromm-Reichmann acknowledges Freud as one of her teachers and repeatedly

---

[2]For a full-scale discussion of Fromm, see Friedman 1978, Chapter 13.

stresses the importance of the therapist's analysis, she reverses the popular "Freudian" notion that genital maturity is the criterion of recovery in favor of the recognition that good sex is an expression of good human relationship, that healing in the one realm of meeting produces healing in the other: "A person who is reasonably free from anxiety, greed, envy, and jealousy and who is able to experience interpersonal intimacy will be capable of expressing this in terms of satisfactory sexual activities" (Fromm-Reichmann 1950, pp. 25, 138).

# Chapter 5

# Carl Rogers and Humanistic Client-Centered Therapy

In a discussion of Ludwig Binswanger's "Case of Ellen West" (Binswanger 1958), which he entitles "The Loneliness of Contemporary Man," Carl Rogers (1980, pp. 164–180) points to Buber's "healing through meeting" as the center of therapy. The greatest weakness of Ellen West's treatment, in Rogers' opinion, is that no one involved in it seems to have related to her as a *person*, a person "whose inner experiencing is a precious resource to be drawn upon and trusted." She was dealt with as an object, and helped to *see* her feelings, but not to *experience* them. She herself recognizes that the doctor can give her discernment, but not healing. She utters a desperate cry for a relationship between two persons, but no one hears her. "She never experienced what Buber has called healing through meeting. There was no one who could meet her, accept her, as she was." Rogers draws from the case of Ellen West the lesson that whenever or however the therapist makes an object of the person—"whether by diagnosing him, analyzing him, or perceiving him impersonally in a case history"—he stands in the way of his therapeutic goal. The therapist is deeply helpful only when he relates as a person, risks himself as a person in the relationship, experiences the other as a person in his own right. "Only then is there a meeting of a depth which dissolves the pain of aloneness in both client and therapist" (Friedman 1973, p. 484f.).

In *Client-Centered Therapy*, Rogers (1951) states that the role of the counselor in "nondirective" therapy is not, as is often thought, a merely passive *laissez-faire* policy, but rather an active acceptance of the client as a person of worth for whom the counselor has real respect. Client-centered therapy stresses above all the counselor's assuming the internal frame of reference of the client and perceiving both the world and the client through the client's own eyes. It is important in the process of the person's becoming that he know himself to be understood and accepted by the therapist. This means "an active experiencing with the client of the feelings to which he gives expression," a trying "to get *within* and to live the attitudes expressed instead of observing them." This implies, at the same time, a certain distance and absence of emotional involvement—an experiencing of the feelings from the side of the client without an emotional identification that would cause the counselor to experience these feelings himself, as counselor. Finally, it implies a laying aside of the preoccupation with professional analysis, diagnosis, and evaluation in favor of an acceptance and understanding of the client based on true attitudes of respect that are deeply and genuinely felt by the therapist (Rogers 1951, pp. 20–45, 55). Rogers is willing to extend this respect and trust even to a patient in danger of committing suicide or one who has been institutionalized.

> To enter deeply with this man into his confused struggle for selfhood is perhaps the best implementation we now know for indicating the meaning of our basic hypothesis that the individual represents a process which is deeply worthy of respect, both as he is and with regard to his potentialities (Rogers 1951, p. 45).

A corollary of client-centered therapy is the recognition that good interpersonal relationships depend upon the understanding and acceptance of the other as a separate person, "operating in terms of his own meanings, based on his own perceptual field." Rogers sees the recognition of the separateness of others as made possible through a relationship in which the person is himself confirmed in his own being. A person comes to accept others through his acceptance of himself, and this, in turn, takes place through the acceptance of the child by the parent or of the client by the therapist (Rogers 1951, pp. 520–522). The real essence of therapy, correspondingly, is not so much the client's memory of the past, his explorations of problems, or his admissions of experiences into awareness as his direct experiencing in the therapy relationship.

> The process of therapy is, by these hypotheses, seen as being synonymous with the experiential relationship between client and therapist. Therapy consists in experiencing the self in a wide range of ways in an emotionally meaningful relationship with the therapist (Rogers 1951, p. 172).

As early as 1952, Rogers defined the person as a fluid process and potential "in rather sharp contrast to the relatively fixed, measurable, diagnosable, predictable concept of the person which is accepted by psychologists and other social scientists to judge by their writings and working operations." The person as process is most deeply revealed, Rogers wrote, in a relationship of the most ultimate and complete acceptance, a relationship Rogers described, in Buber's terms, as "a real I–Thou relationship, not an I–It relationship." The person moves in a positive direction toward unique goals that the person himself can but dimly define (Rogers 1952).

In his book, *On Becoming a Person*, Rogers (1961) tells how he changed his approach to therapy from the intellectual question of how he could treat the patient to the recognition that changes come about through *experience* in a *relationship*. He found that the more genuine he was in a relationship, the more aware he was of his own feelings, the more willing he was to express his own feelings and attitudes, the more he gave the relationship a *reality* the patient could use for his own personal growth. He also found that the more he could respect and like the patient, showing a warm regard for him as a person of unconditional self-worth and accepting each fluctuating aspect of the other, the more he was creating a relationship the patient could use. This acceptance necessarily includes a continuing desire to understand the other's feelings and thoughts, which leaves him really free to explore all the hidden nooks and frightening crannies of his inner and often buried experience. This includes, as well, complete freedom from any type of moral or diagnostic evaluation.

Rogers' "deep empathic understanding," which enables him to see his client's private world through his eyes, is close to Buber's "experiencing the other side," or "inclusion." Rogers states that "when I hold in myself the kind of attitudes I have described, and when the other person can to some degree experience these attitudes, then I believe that change and constructive personal development will *invariably* occur" (Rogers 1961, p. 35). This faith in the latent potentialities that will become actual "in a suitable psychological climate," seems to expect of "healing through meeting" an effectiveness that goes beyond the concrete situation with its often tragic limitations. If the parent creates such a psychological climate, "the child will become more self-directing, socialized, and mature" says Rogers (1961, p. 37). Through relationship, the other individual will experience and understand the repressed aspects of himself, will become better integrated and more effective in functioning, closer to the person he would like to be, "more of a person, more unique and more self-expressive," and he "will be able to cope with the problems of life more adequately and more comfortably" (Rogers 1961, p. 38).

In this connection Rogers uses Buber's phrase, "confirming the other," accepting the person not as something fixed and finished, but as a process of becoming. Through this acceptance, Rogers says, "I am doing what I can to confirm or make real his potentialities." If, on the contrary, writes

Rogers, one sees the relationship as only an opportunity to reinforce certain types of words or opinion in the other, as Verplanck, Lindsley, and B. F. Skinner do in their therapy of operant conditioning, then one confirms him as a basically mechanical, manipulatable object and he tends to act in ways that support this hypothesis. Only a relationship that "reinforces" *all* that he is, "the person that he is with all his existent potentialities," Rogers concludes, is one that, to use Buber's terms, *confirms* him "as a living person, capable of creative inner development" (Rogers 1961, p. 55f.).

As a therapist, Rogers writes,

> I enter the relationship not as a scientist, not as a physician who can accurately diagnose and cure, but as a person entering into a personal relationship. Insofar as I see him only as an object, the client will tend to become only an object.
>
> I risk myself, because if, as the relationship deepens, what develops is a failure, a regression, a repudiation of me and the relationship by the client, then I . . . will lose . . . a part of myself.

The therapist conducts the therapy without conscious plan and responds to the other person with his whole being, "his total organismic sensitivity."

> When there is this complete unity, singleness, fullness of experiencing in the relationship, then it acquires the "out-of-this-world" quality which therapists have remarked upon, a sort of trance-like feeling in the relationship from which both the client and I emerge at the end of the hour, as if from a deep well or tunnel. In these moments there is, to borrow Buber's phrase, a real "I-Thou" relationship, a timeless living in the experience which is *between* the client and me. It is at the opposite pole from seeing the client, or myself, as an object. It is the height of personal subjectivity (Rogers 1961, pp. 201–203).

Through his willingness to risk himself, and his confidence in the client, the therapist makes it easier for the client to take the plunge into the stream of experiencing. This process of becoming opens up a new way of living in which the client "feels more unique and hence more alone," but at the same time is able to enter into relations with others that are deeper and more satisfying and that "draw more of the realness of the other person into the relationship."

The three chapters that Rogers contributed to *Person to Person*, chapters he wrote in 1962 and 1963, have in common the assertion that the traits in the therapist that most facilitate effective therapy are congruence, unconditional positive regard, and empathic understanding. Of these three the most indispensable, says Rogers, with an emphasis that arrived relatively late in his thought, is *congruence*:

> Personal growth is facilitated when the counselor is what he *is*, when in the relationship with his client he is genuine and without "front" or facade, openly being the feelings and attitudes which at that moment are flowing in him. . . . It means that he comes into a direct personal encounter with his client, meeting him on a person-to-person basis. It means that he is *being* himself, not denying himself (Rogers 1967a, p. 90).

Even when the counselor is annoyed with or bored by or dislikes his client, it is preferable for him to be real than to assume a façade of interest and concern and liking he does not feel. What he can do is recognize that it is *his* feeling of being bored which he is expressing and not the supposed fact that his client is a boring person. When the therapist expresses this feeling, which has been a barrier between him and the client, the client will express himself more genuinely in turn because the therapist has dared to be a real, imperfect person in the relationship. Although the qualities of unconditional positive regard and empathic understanding may be easier to achieve, it is better for the counselor to be what he is than to pretend to possess these qualities (Rogers 1967a, pp. 90–92).

One of the questions that is often raised concerning Rogers' approach to psychotherapy is how his emphasis on congruence in the therapist is to be reconciled with his call for "unconditional positive regard." This emphasis is an older one in Rogers' thought and means a warm, positive, and accepting attitude toward what *is* in the client that facilitates change. The therapist's prizing the client in a total, nonpossessive way rather than placing conditions upon his acceptance makes constructive change more likely to occur. One answer that might be given to this question is that the therapist cares for what the client *is* as a person and not just what he does. Another is that if the two principles are in conflict, then the therapist must be genuine, i.e., congruent, but need not turn his feelings toward the client into a judgment of the client.

In his essay "Learning to Be Free," Rogers makes unconditional positive regard the second essential condition of good therapy. In "The Interpersonal Relationship," he places it third after empathy, or empathic understanding, as he calls it in the earlier essay. Rogers' stress on accurately seeing into the client's private world *as if* it were his own, without ever losing that *as if* quality, is very close to Buber's definition of "inclusion" as the bipolar experiencing of the other side of the relationship without leaving one's own ground: "When the counselor can grasp the moment-to-moment experiencing occurring in the inner world of the client, as the client sees and feels it, *without losing the separateness of his own identity* in this empathic process, then change is likely to occur" writes Rogers (italics added). At the same time, Rogers warns that when the therapist is truly open to the way that life is experienced by his client—

taking the client's world into his own and seeing life in his way—he runs the risk of being changed himself. But he must also succeed in communicating the fact that he has or is trying to have empathic understanding of the client if meaningful change is to occur (Rogers 1967a, p. 92f.).

In his discussion of empathy, Rogers adds a caution that was largely absent from his earlier work and that serves as a corrective to his assertions that change is *bound* to occur:

> I have learned, especially in working with more disturbed persons, that empathy can be perceived as lack of involvement; that an unconditional regard on my part can be perceived as indifference; that warmth can be perceived as a threatening closenesss, that real feelings of mine can be perceived as false (Rogers 1967a, p. 96).

Rogers would *like* to behave in such a way that what he is experiencing in relationship to the client would be perceived unambiguously by the client. But he recognizes that this is complex, and hard to achieve. In the case of a really disturbed person, even this would seem to be an understatement! Yet at the end of "The Interpersonal Relationship" Rogers asserts that congruence, empathy, and unconditional positive regard "will have a high probability of being an effective, growth-promoting relationship" not only for maladjusted individuals who come on their own initiative seeking for help, but also for "chronically schizophrenic persons with no conscious desire for help."

This extension to schizophrenia of his approach to therapy is the other important change in Rogers' teachings since his dialogue with Buber in 1957. Commenting on a study of psychotherapy with schizophrenics in his third and final contribution to *Person to Person*, Rogers begins by recognizing that the clinic client's inevitable focus on exploring and experiencing of self once he has tasted its "bitter-sweet satisfactions" does not hold for the hospitalized schizophrenic. Nonetheless, he reported that "the more successful schizophrenic cases showed the greatest increase in depth of self-exploration from early to late, greater even than the successful neurotic cases." The schizophrenic who improves does so because he has really entered into therapy, spontaneously and feelingly expressing personally relevant material in an active, struggling, fearful exploration of self (Rogers 1967b, p. 184f.).

In this same essay, Rogers emphasizes the centrality of healing through meeting if possible even more strongly than in any of his earlier writings: "It is the existential encounter which is important. . . . In the immediate moment of the therapeutic relationship consciousness of theory has no helpful place." Thinking of theory during the relationship itself, as opposed to afterward, is detrimental to the therapy because it leads the therapist to be more of a spectator than a player. "If theory is to be held at all, it seems to me that it should be held tentatively, lightly, flexibly, in a way which is freely open to change, and should be laid aside in the moment of encounter itself."

If the therapeutic relationship has little to do with theory or ideology, it also has little to do with techniques.

> In this respect I believe my views have become more, rather than less, extreme. I believe it is the *realness* of the therapist in the relationship which is the most important element. . . . Probably this is a "trained humanness" . . . but in the moment it is the natural reaction of *this* person. For one, an impatient, no-nonsense, let's put-the-cards-on-the-table approach is most effective, because in such an approach he is most openly being himself. For another it may be a much more gentle, and more obviously warm approach, because this is the way *this* therapist is. Our experience has deeply reinforced and extended my own view that the person who is able *openly* to be himself at that moment, as he is at the deepest levels he is able to be, is the effective therapist. Perhaps nothing else is of any importance (Rogers 1967b, p. 186f.).

If Rogers does not arrive at an explicit recognition of the *difference* between acceptance and confirmation that Martin Buber stressed in the 1957 dialogue with him, he *seems* to imply it in his comment on one of the therapists in this study:

> One in particular is moving more and more toward allying himself with the hidden and unrevealed person in the schizophrenic, and openly "clobbering" the defensive shell. In his work there is a real similarity to Rosen or Whitaker. He is sensitively and obviously committed to the person who is hiding, but he is quite violently and sometimes sarcastically critical of the psychotic symptoms, the fear of relating, the defenses and avoidances. Perhaps partly because this approach is congenial to him as a person, he is finding it effective (Rogers 1967b, p. 187f.).

The last sentence, of course, is meant to illustrate "congruence" and shies away from any general recognition that the therapist may have to struggle with the client against himself, as Buber says in his distinction between confirming and accepting the patient.

Rogers concludes by expressing his great personal satisfaction "that we have been able to help withdrawn, bizarre, hopeless individuals become human beings," and to Rogers this means persons, whether they are labeled schizophrenic or not:

> Behind the curtains of silence, and hallucination, and strange talk and hostility, and indifference, there is in each case a person . . . if we are skillful and fortunate we can *reach* that person, and can live, often for brief moments only, in a direct person-to-person relationship with him. To me that fact seems to say something about the nature of schizophre-

nia. It says something too about the nature of man and his craving for and fear of a deep human relationship (Rogers 1967b, p. 191f.).

There is no suggestion here of full mutuality between therapist and client and there is a realism about the fact that the person-to-person meeting is often a matter of moments only that is very close to Buber's position in his dialogue with Rogers five years earlier.

In 1967, Rogers published a brief statement that can well serve as a summation of his own view on healing through meeting:

> I find that when I am able to let myself be congruent and genuine, it often helps the other person. When the other person is transparently real and congruent, it often helps me. In those rare moments when a deep realness in one meets a deep realness in the other, it is a memorable I–Thou relationship, as Buber would call it. Such a deep and mutual personal encounter is experienced by me as very growth enhancing. A person who is loved appreciatively, not possessively, blooms and develops his own unique self. The person who loves non-possessively is himself enriched (Rogers 1967c, p. 18f.).

For Rogers, as for Fromm, healing through meeting works both ways. For both Rogers and Fromm, meeting is sometimes seen as an end in itself and sometimes only as a means to the end of personal becoming and self-actualization. This ambiguity comes through particularly clearly in Rogers' most recent book, *A Way of Being*, in which he puts forward two different and, in some ways incompatible, touchstones of reality—self-actualization and the I–Thou relationship. In one place he writes of the "actualizing tendency as the fundamental answer to the question of what makes an organism tick," (Rogers 1980, p. 119). In another he writes:

> In those rare moments when a deep realness in one meets a deep realness in the other, a memorable "I–Thou relationship," as Martin Buber would call it, occurs. Such a deep and mutual encounter does not happen often, but I am convinced that unless it happens occasionally, we are not living as human beings (Rogers 1980, p. 19).

Although they reside comfortably together in Rogers' thought, these two touchstones of reality are not really compatible. *Either* the I–Thou relationship is seen as a function of self-actualization, and the real otherness of the Thou is lost sight of in the emphasis on the development of the organism, or the I–Thou relationship is seen as a reality and value in itself, in which case self-realization becomes a by-product and not a goal and, what is more, a by-product that is produced not through a pseudo-biological development, but rather through the meeting with what is really other than the self.

# Chapter 6

# Object-Relations and Self-Psychology

Originally, like R. D. Laing, I was inclined to see the so-called "object-relations" theorists who have sprung up among the British Freudians and have spread to America as an extension of Freud's own tendency to speak of the "love object," and nothing could be a clearer way of reducing the partner in dialogue to an "It." I have come to realize more recently that within the mainstream of Freudian theory there has developed an impressive approximation of confirmation through therapy and even healing through meeting. If, as Harry Guntrip points out, no adequate theory of the relations *between* persons has as yet been put forward to take account of Buber's I–Thou relationship, nonetheless a respectable start has been made, one that may conceivably in the near future burst the bounds of psychologism and blossom into such a theory.

This "object-relations" school of Freudian therapy is of particular importance in providing a sophisticated groundwork for our understanding of the origins of psychopathology in disconfirmation and the limited, but nonetheless real hope of confirmation through therapy. The psychodynamic theory of Melanie Klein, D. W. Winnicott, and W. R. D. Fairbairn of the British school of psychoanalysis offers a synthesis of the biological approach, on the one hand, and the sociological and social–psychological, on the other. According to these writers, Freud's original distinction between the conscious and the unconscious is less important than the distinction between the two worlds of outer reality and inner reality in which everyone of us lives at the same time. Fairbairn defines psychology as the study of the relationship of the individual to its "objects," and psychopathology as the study of the relationships of the ego to its internal objects.

## Melanie Klein

Melanie Klein made a much needed correction to Freud when she was compelled to recognize through her clinical work that conflicts typical of the Oedipal phase occur at a far earlier age than three to five years and, accordingly, that the infant psyche is not initially as objectless and auto-erotic as was hitherto believed, but rather is object-related to the mother's breast from the beginning. But in contrast to those who followed her, Melanie Klein's account of the inner world owes more to the projection and reintrojection of innate sadism than to external bad handling of the infant. The superego becomes for her a blanket term covering the whole world of internalized objects in which the ego seeks the aid of good objects in its struggle with its persecuting bad figures. The bad objects that arouse our rage in outer reality become necessary to us to enforce control of our impulses, and we forestall their punishment by taking over their repressive functions ourselves. Whereas Freud discovered the libidinally needy self in the unconscious and mistook it for an impersonal id, Melanie Klein recognized that the ego is originally unified and only splits in the course of internal-object formation. Thus the Freudian ego is a later development, which arises out of the splitting of the original ego. Winnicott, Fairbairn, and Guntrip accord to Melanie Klein the honor of carrying forward Freudian psychoanalysis to the place where it could become a true psycho-dynamic theory of the human being as a person.

## W. R. D. Fairbairn

Fairbairn reversed Freud's absorption of the human being into the scientist and the impersonal type of psychology that went with it by insisting that "the investigations of psycho-analysis should be conducted at the level of personality and personal relations." Instead of starting, as Freud did, from stimulation of the nervous system, Fairbairn holds that "the libido is not primarily pleasure-seeking but object-seeking." Starting with a unitary dynamic ego, the child adopts as its first defense to deal with an unsatisfying personal relationship the mental internalization, or introjection, of the (un)satisfying object. This leads, as in Klein, to an ego-splitting in which its conflicts take on a relatively permanent, internal, structural form, but Fairbairn departs from Klein in regarding every part of the complex as a developed aspect of the original unitary dynamic ego. As a result, structure and energy do not represent the ego *versus* psychobiological instinct, but rather both are aspects of the active and organized psychic self. Neither "impulses" nor "instincts" can be understood apart from the self and its relations to its objects.

This "object-relations" theory becomes particularly important for Fairbairn in the understanding of the "schizoid person." He holds that at the bottom of all psychopathological processes is the disturbed development that results when the mother does not succeed in making the child feel she loves him for his own sake and as a person in his own right. Thus, we have a fully explicit statement of the origin of psychopathology in disconfirmation.

> The tone of voice, the kind of touch, the quality of attention and interest, the amount of notice, and the total emotional as well as physical adequacy of breast feeding, are all expressions of the genuineness or otherwise of the mother's personal relationship to the infant. . . . The breakdown of genuinely personal relations between the mother and the infant . . . dominates all other and more detailed particular issues such as oral deprivation, anal frustration, genital disapproval, negative and over-critical discipline (Guntrip 1961, p. 284).[1]

When there is an inadequate genuine relationship between the mother and the infant, a schizoid person is produced, one who suffers the tragedy of being torn by an intense need of a good love-object and an equally intense fear of an object-relationship. Usually such a person's love-hunger is hidden from the outer world beneath a mask of detachment or emotional apathy, and his libidinal object-relationships are confined to his inner world. The schizoid is terrified of exploiting good objects to the point of destruction, which would also mean the loss of the helplessly dependent ego that emotionally identifies with the object. As a result, conflicts over love object-relationships "are an intense and devastating drama of need, fear, anger and hopelessness." At about the time Buber was propounding his anthropology of distancing and relation, Fairbairn stated that the more mature a relationship, the less it is characterized by primary identification. Primary identification means the lack of real otherness, the failure to differentiate the object. When identification persists at the expense of differentiation, a markedly compulsive element enters into the individual's attitude toward his objects, and this is precisely what typifies schizoid individuals who do not primarily repress intolerably guilty impulses or intolerably unpleasant memories, as Freud thought, but rather intolerably bad internalized objects. Following this schema, Fairbairn regards schizoid problems as belonging wholly to the pre-moral level of psychic life, depressive problems as belonging to a pathologically moral level, and true morality (and with it we would add true guilt) as belonging

---

[1] I base my discussion of Fairbairn in these pages on the extensive treatment of his work by Guntrip 1961. Guntrip devotes Chapters 13 to 16 and much of what follows, from pages 361 to 404, to Fairbairn.

to maturity. Neurotic guilt necessarily acts as a resistance in psychotherapy and blocks the way to maturity and existential guilt.

For Fairbairn, infantile dependence takes the place of the Oedipus complex as the hard core of psychoneurosis. The Oedipus complex is the end product of processes in which the infant psyche loses both its own unity and its capacity to deal with its objects as "wholes" in a satisfactory way. Thus, the overcoming of the Oedipus complex and the formation of the superego is better understood as "the struggle to repress an elaborate unresolved infantile dependence on parents and ultimately on the mother, under the pressure of the need to adjust to the demands of outer life on an increasingly grown-up level."

By the same token, the unconscious in its true nature is a personal, even though hidden, inner world in which the infantile parts of the ego continuously have intense emotional relationships with its equally infantile internalized objects. As a result, "the inner world is one in which only immature relationship-patterns exist," and these, in turn, determine the kinds of immature object-relations people sustain in their outer world. If the central ego is, in principle, free to develop mature personal relations characterized by equality, mutuality, spontaneity, and stability, the infantile parts of the ego are tied down to patterns of childish relations to bad objects. Mature behavior in the outer world is constantly interfered with by immature reactions in and from the inner world, and this is the origin of psychic compulsions.

## Heinz Kohut

The significance for us of Heinz Kohut of the American school of object-relations theorists is not any contribution to the understanding of healing through meeting, but rather his understanding of confirmation. Kohut insists that confirmation and disconfirmation do not turn only on the mother, but rather on both parents. Extrapolating from the language of Freud and Ronald Fairbairn, Kohut coined the term "selfobject" for persons the infant experiences as part of itself. "The expected control over them is, therefore, closer to the concept of the control which a grown-up expects to have over his own body and mind than to the concept of the control which he expects to have over others." Kohut distinguishes between two kinds of self-objects—the mirroring one and the idealized parental imago. The mirroring self-object responds to and confirms the child's innate sense of vigor, greatness, and perfection, which Kohut also refers to as the "grandiose, exhibitionist self." The idealized parent imago is one to whom the child can look up and with whom he can merge as an image of calmness, infallibility and omnipotence. What Kohut has done, essentially, is to divide the self analytically into one part that stresses the self that does the relating and another part that stresses what the self is relating to, both parts, of course, understood originally as needing to be in relation to significant others. Having done this, he then puts them back together synthetically.

> A firm self, resulting from the optimal interactions between the child and his selfobjects, is made up of three major constituents: (1) one pole from which emanate the basic strivings for power and success; (2) another pole that harbours the basic idealized goals; and (3) an intermediate area of basic talents and skills that are activated by the tension-arc that establishes itself between ambitions and ideals (Kohut and Wolf 1978, p. 414).

When the child's mirroring and idealizing needs have been sufficiently responded to, then *minor*, non-traumatic failures in the responses of the mirroring and idealizing self-objects gradually teach the child that it cannot control them and leads to a replacement of them by a self, which is not a replica of the self-objects. "The child that is to survive psychologically is born into an empathetic-responsive human milieu."

Parents empathically sense and respond to the disturbances in the child's psychological balance. The sensing is of far greater importance psychologically than the actions the parents take to set things right, for it helps the child consolidate his nuclear self via transmuting internalization. The child has two chances as it moves toward the consolidation of the self, the one provided by its empathically responding merging-mirroring-approving self-object, the other by the parent who permits and enjoys the child's idealization of and merger with him or her. Loosely identifying these with the father and mother, respectively, Kohut suggests that if the mother fails to establish a firmly cohesive self in the child, the father may yet succeed in doing so (Kohut 1977, pp. 85f., 185f.).

Kohut sees the child's self as developing through an interaction between its innate equipment and the parent's selective encouragement and discouragement, not through the parents' philosophy of child-rearing but rather through their own nuclear selves. "It is not so much what the parents *do* that will influence the character of the child's self, but what the parents *are*." In this he is close to Buber's understanding of confirmation as growing out of the interhuman relation between being and being. But Kohut tends to express himself in intrapsychic language, and insofar as he possibly can, he stays close to the psychoanalytic tradition in which he is rooted.

Kohut sees the child as able to cope with serious traumata if embedded in a healthily supportive matrix, and that matrix, for Kohut, is "a mature, cohesive parental self that is in tune with the changing needs of the child." Behind Kohut's psychoanalytic jargon, we can glimpse actual human confirmation at work:

> However grave the blows may be to which the child's grandiosity is exposed by the realities of life, the proud smile of the parents will keep alive a bit of the original omnipotence, to be retained as the nucleus of the self-confidence and inner security about one's worth that sustain the healthy person throughout his life. . . . However great our disappointment as we discover the weaknesses and limitations of the idealized selfobjects of our early life, their self-confidence as they carried us when we were babies, their security when they allowed us to merge our anxious selves with their tranquility—via their calm voices or via our closeness with their relaxed bodies as they held us—will be retained by us as the nucleus of the strength of our leading ideals and of the calmness we experience as we live our lives under the guidance of our inner goals (Kohut and Wolf 1978, p. 417).

It follows from this view of the origin of the self that faulty interactions between the child and his self-objects produce a diffuse or seriously damaged self, depending on the source of the damage. On this basis, Kohut constructs a typology of "narcissistic behavior and personality disorders": Among these are the understimulated self, the fragmenting self, the overstimulated self, and the overburdened self. Kohut also singles out "mirror-hungry personalities" who "thirst for self-objects whose confirming and admiring responses will nourish their famished self"; "ideal-hungry personalities" who "are forever in search of others whom they can admire for their prestige, power, beauty, intelligence, or moral stature," since only through looking up to them can they experience themselves as worthwhile; and "alter-ego personalities" who "need a relationship with a self-object that by conforming to the self's appearance, opinions, and values confirms the existence, the reality of the self." All three of these personalities are prone to look restlessly for one replacement after another. In contrast to them are the "contact-shunning personalities" who avoid social contact and become isolated just because their need for others is so intense: "The intensity of their need not only leads to great sensitivity to rejection," but also "to the apprehension that the remnants of their nuclear self will be swallowed up and destroyed by the yearned-for all-encompassing union" (Kohut and Wolf 1978, pp. 418–422).

In the cases of those whose selves are thus damaged, Kohut finds the genesis of their problems not in classical Freudian drive conflict, but rather in inadequate confirmation or disconfirmation. It is not the child's wish for food, for example, which is the primary psychological configuration, but rather its need for "a food-giving self-object." If this need remains unfulfilled to a traumatic degree, then the joyful experience of being a whole, appropriately responded-to self disintegrates, and the child retreats to a fragment of the larger experiential unit, i.e., to depressive eating. In general, if the unresponded-to child "has not been able to transform its archaic grandiosity and its archaic wish to merge with an omnipotent self-object into reliable self-esteem, realistic ambitions, attainable ideals," then drive fixations and abnormalities of the ego result. Defects of the self do not arise even from serious realistic deprivations, but rather from narcissistic disturbances of the parents, often due to their own latent psychosis, which make them unable to respond empathically. When the empathic resonance is good, the child's spreading anxiety will be transmuted into calmness. When it is not, the child will either be drawn into the panic of the parents or will wall itself off from the parents (Kohut 1977, pp. 81f., 87, 89).

In similar fashion, Kohut denies Freud's assertion that destructive aggression is an innate instinct of man. Aggression, rather, is a constituent of the child's assertiveness and under normal circumstances remains alloyed to the assertiveness of the adult's mature self. "Destructive rage, in particular, is always motivated by an injury to the self." Hence the psychological "bedrock" to which the analysis can penetrate is not some destructive biological drive, but rather a serious narcissistic injury inflicted by the self-object of childhood—one that threatens the cohesion of the self. Sadism and masochism, for example, are a product of the breakup of the primary psychological unit, "an attempt to bring about the lost merger (and thus the repair of the self) by pathological means, i.e., as enacted in the fantasies and actions of the pervert." A child's sexual overstimulation and conflicts arising from observing his parents in sexual intercourse, similarly, are crystallization points for intermediate memory systems that can be traced back to the much more important absence of the parents' empathic responses to the child's need to be mirrored and to find an object for his idealization (Kohut 1977, pp. 116f., 128, 187–189).

> The deepest level to be reached is not the drive, but the threat to the organization of the self (in behavioral terms, the depressed child, the hypochondriacal child, the child who feels that he is dead), the experience of the absence of the life-sustaining matrix of the empathic responsiveness of the self-object (Kohut 1977, p. 123).

Kohut ascribes the conflicts of id and superego of which Freud spoke to "Guilty Man" typical of the nineteenth century. These are adequate in explaining psychoneuroses. But the more typical illnesses of the twentieth century, according to Kohut, are the disorders of the self that he links with "Tragic Man":

> The psychology of the self is needed to explain the pathology of the fragmented self (from schizophrenia to narcissistic personality disorder) and of the depleted self (empty depression, i.e., the world of unmirrored

ambitions, the world devoid of ideals)—in short, the psychic disturbances and struggles of Tragic Man (Kohut 1977, p. 243).

Kohut distinguishes between narcissistic behavior and personality
disorders, which he sees as temporary breakups of the nuclear self and
hence, in principle, treatable, and psychoses and borderline states, which
he sees as permanent or protracted disorders of the self and hence, in
principle, untreatable. In the treatment of narcissistic behavior and personality disorders, both *mirroring* and the *idealizing transference* are re-
vived, the former to make up for an insufficiently or faultily responded-to
childhood need for accepting and confirming, the latter to make up for an
insufficiently responded-to need for merger with a source of "idealized"
strength and calmness. The aim of the treatment is the firming of the
formerly enfeebled self so that it can again pursue the action-poised
program that holds the tension between ambitions and ideals and thus
lead a fulfilling, creative–productive life.

To facilitate this, the therapist must not come on with the typical
Freudian maturity- and reality-morality that censures the patient's manifest narcissism. This will repress the already repressed narcissistic needs.
Or the therapist "will increase the depth of the split in the personality that
separates the sector of the psyche that contains the unresponded-to autonomous self from the noisily assertive one that lacks autonomy—and he
will block the unfolding of the narcissistic transference." The unfulfilled
narcissistic needs of the patient's childhood, which he must get in touch
with, accept, and express lie deeply buried beneath a clamorous assertiveness, guarded by a wall of shame and vulnerability (Kohut and Wolf 1978,
pp. 413, 423f.).

Seen from this standpoint, the patient's resistances are not, as in
traditional Freudianism, resistances to bringing the unconscious into the
conscious in order to protect the personality from experiencing the fears
of childhood concerning its drive-wishes. Rather, they are the corollary of
the need to confirm the reality of the self: "The resistances are the activities
of the archaic nuclear self, which does not want to re-expose itself to the
devastating narcissistic injury of finding its basic mirroring and idealizing
needs unresponded to, i.e., the resistances are motivated by disintegration
anxiety" (Kohut 1977, p. 136).

Kohut considers "an analysis completed when by achieving success in
the area of compensatory structures it has established a functioning self—
[a] psychological sector in which ambitions, skills, and ideals form an
unbroken continuum that permits joyful creative activity." Particularly
significant in this continuum is the psychological equilibrium that is
reached between the *product*—the extension of the patient's self in which
the patient is absorbed and which he takes joy in perfecting—and the

*self*—the center of productive initiating that yields the exhilarating experience of producing the work. "Although I am thus joyfully aware of myself," Kohut has a patient say in an imaginary communication, "I no longer become hypomanically overstimulated while creating, nor do I fear, as I used to, that my self will be drained away into the product of my creativeness" (Kohut 1977, pp. 63, 17).

The success of the analysis is measured thus by the cohesion and firmness of the patient's self that make it the reliable initiator and performer of joyfully undertaken activities: "The strengthened self becomes the organizing center of the skills and talents of the personality and thus improves the exercise of these functions; the successful exercise of skills and talents, moreover, in turn increases the cohesion, and thus the vigor, of the self." Put negatively, the analysand's self has ceased to react to the loss of self-objects with fragmentation, serious enfeeblement, or uncontrollable rage. Put positively, it has become "able to function as a more or less self-propelling, self-directed, and self-sustaining unit which provides a central purpose to his personality and gives meaning to his life" (Kohut 1977, pp. 134f., 138f.).

Since these goals are accomplished through the revival of the mirroring and idealizing transference, we might conclude that in order to heal the narcissistic wounds, the therapist must in some way meet the patient in the process of treatment to make up for his parents' failure to meet him. Yet on this issue of the actual therapeutic relationship, Kohut has little to say in *The Restoration of the Self* (1977). In this respect he remains something of a traditional analyst, relying on "scientific empathy," on knowing as an instrument of healing. In summarizing his views on the analyst's attitude in the analytic situation, Kohut writes:

> It must never become the goal of the analyst to provide an *extra* measure of love and kindness to his patients—he will provide substantial help to his patients only through the employment of his special skills and through the application of his specialized knowledge (Kohut 1977, p. 261).

## Harry Guntrip

In contrast to Kohut, Fairbairn and Harry Guntrip draw conclusions from their object–relations theory that lead in the direction of a therapy of healing through meeting. "I am convinced," wrote Fairbairn in 1955, "that it is the patient's relationship to the analyst that mediates the 'curing' or 'saving' effect of psychotherapy" in transforming "earlier pathogenic relationships . . . under the influence of the transference into a new kind of relationship which is at once satisfying and adapted to the circumstances of outer reality." This leads Fairbairn and Guntrip to reject the traditional restriction of the functions of the therapist to the dual one of a screen upon which the patient projects his fantasies and a colorless instrument of interpretative technique. Instead, they see the real personal relationship between patient and analyst as the truly therapeutic factor on which all others depend.

This process of personal liberation and regrowth is compelled to be a more active one on the part of both patient and analyst than the original classic technique allowed for. Thus, there is greater, though not total, mutuality between therapist and client. Insight, recall of infantile memories, and catharsis depend on the relationship with the analyst not only for their effectiveness, but also for their very existence, and what is important here is not just "transference, but the total relationship existing between the patient and the analyst as persons." From this standpoint, the ultimate aim of psychoanalysis becomes helping "the patient to tolerate the conscious re-experiencing of his profoundly repressed and fundamentally weak infantile ego, which he has spent his life trying to disown in his struggle to feel adult." What makes this conscious re-experiencing possible is "a relationship with his analyst which is more reliable and mature than that which he originally had with his parents, one in which he comes to feel accepted as himself a real person."

The importance of psychoanalysis in this process is that "there is little hope of releasing a patient from this concentration camp in his unconscious unless we can discover and expose to him his motives for staying there and help him to recognize that he is really aiming, in spite of appearances, at self-preservation, but by the wrong methods." What makes this so very difficult is the fear of a collapse into nothingness in which object-relations are broken off and the ego emptied, leading, if it continues, to increasing apathy and psychic death. "The entire world of internal bad objects is a colossal defense against loss of the ego by depersonalization." The choice between good and bad objects is not so disastrous as that between any sort of objects and no objects at all.

"The emotional heart of the personality has drawn back inside out of reach of being hurt." This repressed self retains the primary capacity for spontaneous and vigorous growth once it is freed from fears, and there, asserts Guntrip, lies the ultimate hope of psychotherapy. The "true self" is not frozen in cold storage awaiting a second chance to be reborn, as Winnicott holds. "Though itself hidden, it exercises a powerful backward pull on all the rest of the personality in proportion as pressure, fear and anxiety are experienced in real life." It is the true source of all regressive phenomena and phobias, for the neurotic has been driven without option in infancy to make this drastic regression to maintain his very existence and spends the rest of his life struggling against it. The major obstacle to psychoanalysis is the fact that patients feel that illnesses founded on internal bad-object relations are the only means of safeguarding the integrity of their ego. Therefore, the only hope in psychotherapy "lies in seeing through and overcoming the fears of loss of independence in good-object relations and the chance of this is what the psychotherapist offers."

This hope is only present if the patient is very sure of the quality and motives of the therapist, and therapists must halt with humility before the final question of whether we are expecting more of this particular patient than he is capable of, even with our support. "Radical analytical psychotherapy" may offer support for the ego of everyday life that tries to cope with the outer world with depleted resources while resisting the strain of the inner one; it analyzes the intermediate internal bad-objects world; and it provides "a safe symbolic womb for the Regressed Ego" in which the patient can feel understood and accepted so that the regressed ego emerges with renewed vigor to revitalize the rest of the personality. But all of this depends upon the patient's relationship of trust to his therapist, for only this makes possible a genuine development toward inner strength and maturity (Guntrip 1961).

In the Preface to his book, *Personality Structure and Human Interaction*, Guntrip tells that in his earlier studies of religion he had been thoroughly trained in the "personal relations" school of thought of John Macmurray and Martin Buber. Guntrip's emphasis throughout his major theoretical writings on psychoanalysis remains not only on the person in his uniqueness, but also on that person's relations to other persons and to the internalized "objects" that arise from these relations. Guntrip claims that psychological science today is developing into the science of personality and of object-relationships, "which means basically *Human Relationships*." This includes the fact that each person is a subject who internalizes the other so that each enters into the content of the other's personality. If this falls short of genuine meeting, it offers us insight into the obstacles to such meeting. Guntrip defines the basic psychopathological process, in fact, as an introverted development, leading to internalized objects, splitting of the ego, and loss of realistic contact with the outer world.

Following this line of thought, Guntrip revises classical Freudian psychobiology by seeing sexual difficulties

> as due not to the constitutional strength of the sex instinct, but to the developmental immaturity of the whole personality, and more specifically to the internal and unconscious perpetuation in the psyche of the frustrating object-relations of early life. Neurotic suffering is not due to the repression of strong and healthy constitutional sexuality, but to the struggle to master infantile and immature sexual needs which are kept alive by the situation in the unconscious inner world (Guntrip 1961, p. 77).

Where Freud sees human nature as innately self- and pleasure-seeking, socialized only under very heavy pressure, Guntrip holds that good personal relationship is in itself the basic need and aim of man and that aggression and pleasure-seeking only result from the frustration of this primary aim.

In *Schizoid Phenomena, Object Relations and the Self* (1969), Guntrip pursues the implications of the ideas of *Personality Structure and Human Interaction* (1961) for psychotherapy with the clinical material he gathered in the years since. "The rebirth and regrowth of the lost living heart of the personality is the ultimate problem psychotherapy now seeks to solve," states Guntrip, in close parallel to Buber's statement that the real heart of psychotherapy is "the regeneration of an atrophied personal centre." Asserting that the love relationship is the essential goal of human life, Guntrip and Fairbairn see the schizoid as the person who dreads the very love relationships that he longs for for fear of being robbed of freedom and independence. The schizoid sets up a permanent, unsatisfactory compromise, a half-way house in which however much he tries to make contacts he is also always withdrawing. The part of the self that struggles to keep in touch with life is continually threatened by the withdrawn self that has the power to draw the rest of the personality into itself. "A regressed illness is usually a conflict between a struggle to keep going at all costs, and a longing to give up, in which the latter drive is of dire necessity winning over the former."

Following Buber in the first part of *I and Thou*, Guntrip holds that birth is mere separation. But this separation "will speedily result in isolation, in the snuffing out of the nascent personal ego, unless good mothering at once restores 'connexion' of such a kind that it can lead to the evolution or realization of the potential ego of the infant, and therewith of personal relationships."

> In every human being there is probably, to some extent, a lonely person at heart, but in the very ill, it is an utterly isolated being, too denuded of experience to be able to feel like a person, unable to communicate with others and never reached by others (Guntrip 1969, p. 220).

Only a therapeutic relationship capable of filling the gap left by inadequate mothering can rescue the patient from succumbing to the terrors of ultimate isolation. No ego can develop a significant individuality of its own without relationship, but the weakened ego always fears it will be swamped by the other person in a relationship.

Every personality has, to some degree, a schizoid core of the self. "Mental health must consist in having enough basic ego-relatedness and therefore ego-strength, to be . . . able either to withdraw into a privacy that is not empty or venture forth into relationships without fear." Underlying this language, one can discern the two central statements of Buber's *I and Thou*: "All real living is meeting" and "by the graciousness of its comings and the solemn sadness of its goings, it [the I–Thou relationship] teaches us to meet others and to hold our ground when we meet them."

Guntrip, following Winnicott, spells out the implications of this position for confirmation by distinguishing between a "female" element of "being" and a "male" element of "doing."

> The female element is best exemplified in the maternal feeling that evokes and fosters an experience of "being" in the infant as a starting-point of all personality growth; the capacity to feel with, and then to feel for, the capacity to feel oneself as "in relationship," the basic permanent experience of ego-relatedness, of which the sense of "being" is the core, and without which the psyche loses all sense of its own reality as an ego. . . . The experience of "being" is the beginning and basis for the realization of the potentialities in our raw human nature for developing a "person" in personal relationships (Guntrip 1969, p. 254).

Conversely, the disconfirmed person's capacity for experiencing a state of "being" is primarily dissociated, left unrealized at the start of development, as a result of which the individual does not become a person. The conscious ego, the ego of separation, of acting and being acted on, derives its strength from the deepest unconscious core of the self that has never lost the feeling of "being-at-one-with" the maternal source of its life. Here is a new variant of Lao-tzu's "the way to do is to be," one fully in accord with Buber's own use of the Taoist *wu-wei*, "non-doing," as the central quality of the I–Thou relationship.

In contrast to Freud's notion of projecting a father-image onto the universe, Guntrip puts forward Buber's "yearning for the cosmic connexion," or in Guntrip's own words, "the need of the human being to retain a fundamental sense of organic unity which is at the same time a latent sense of relationship." Like Winnicott, Fairbairn, and Balint, and unlike Kohut, Guntrip holds that it is primarily the *mother*'s relation to the infant that enables it to develop a capacity for an I–Thou relationship. "It is hard for individuals in our culture to realize that true independence is rooted in and only grows out of primary dependence." The core of the self can hardly be an isolate, since the factual basis of the possibility of identity and being is the experience of being-at-one-with and of incipient relationship.

> Two things must remain inviolate if a human personality is to remain strong: (i) an inner core of the sense of separate individuality, of "me-ness," of ego-identity, strong enough both to relate and accept communication from, or at need to withdraw from the outer world without anxiety over possible ego-loss; (ii) a still deeper ultimate core of the

feeling of "at-oneness" which is the soil out of which the sense of separateness can grow (Guntrip 1969, p. 266).

In applying this essentially dialogical approach to psychotherapy, Guntrip sees the difficulties in treating the schizoid person as lying in his compromise in which he can neither fully accept nor fully reject the therapist. Therefore, such a person can be helped only by a "radical psychotherapy which goes beyond the resolution of specific conflicts to the fundamental regrowing of the whole personal self," Buber's "atrophied personal center." Again, the relationship with the therapist creates the situation in which theory and technique can be applied to the solution of the patient's problems. Psychotherapy is a process in which transference relationships, both positive and negative, are worked through until they lead on and give way to a good realistic relationship between therapist and patient. There is no evading transference analysis, since, however good the therapist is, it still takes the patient a very long time to accept him as a liberating person with whom the patient can find a true self of his own. After Oedipal transference phenomena are analyzed, however, the confirming meeting between therapist and client again becomes central:

> Now the therapist must be the kind of person with whom the patient can find some sense of reality in his own experience of him, and who can at times see something in the patient that he cannot see for himself, because he has never adequately experienced it. The therapist must now sense, not the patient's repressed conflicts but his unevoked potentialities for personal relationship and creative activity, and enable him to begin to feel "real". . . . The only thing about the therapist that does really concern him [the patient] . . . is whether the therapist as a real human being has a genuine capacity to value, care about, understand, see, and treat the patient as a person in his own right. . . . [He must have] *the capacity to respect and to be concerned about the other person's reality in himself and apart from oneself, and to find true satisfaction in helping the other person to find and be his own properly fulfilled nature* (Guntrip 1969, p. 337).

Now we are squarely on the ground of healing through meeting. Guntrip quotes R. D. Laing at the Sixth International Congress of Psychotherapy: "We live on the hope that authentic meeting between human beings can occur." True psychotherapy only happens when the therapist and patient find the person behind each other's defenses. Deep insight, as Fairbairn points out, only develops inside a good therapeutic relationship. What is therapeutic, when it is achieved, is "the moment of real meeting." This experience is transforming for both therapist and patient because it is not what happened before, i.e., transference, but what has never happened before, a genuine experience of relationship. For this to take place, there must be what Buber has called a one-sided inclusion:

> The psychotherapist must be primarily a human being who has faced
> and sufficiently understood himself to be worthy to be admitted into the
> patient's private pain and sorrow. He will understand the patient's inner
> life . . . because he can feel with and for the patient; and he knows, not
> just theoretically but in his own experience, what the patient is passing
> through. . . . Only that enables the patient no longer to feel alone
> (Guntrip 1969, p. 353).

The psychotherapist must give the patient the mature parental love he did
not receive from his own parents, the love that enables him to enter into a
mature relationship of adult mutual respect, equality, and affection in
friendship and to enter, without anxiety or guilt, into an erotic relationship with an extrafamiliar partner. Only thus can the patient "lose his
schizoid fear of human contact and involvement, and find relationships
enriching and fulfilling."

Guntrip sees the object-relations theory, emerging from the work of
Melanie Klein and Fairbairn, as a process of exploring and formulating
the I–Thou relationship. At the same time, Guntrip recognizes that the
term "object-relations," "begins to date," precisely because, to go back to
my original position, "it reminds one of Freud's 'sexual object' which was
there to gratify an instinct, not to provide a two-way relationship." Object-
relations theory has as yet no adequate way of conceptualizing the mutual
relationship in which there can be no "turning the tables" because it is not
"one-up-and-the-other-down." This reality, which object-relations theory
cannot yet conceptualize, raises the fundamental question: How far can we
know and be known by one another?

> Object-relations theory . . . does have a truly psychodynamic theory of
> the development of the individual ego in personal relations; but not of
> the complex fact of the personal relationship itself between two egos.
> From Freud's ego and superego, through Melanie Klein's internal ob-
> jects, projection and introjection, to Fairbairn's splitting of both ego and
> objects in relationships, and finally Winnicott's tracing of the absolute
> origin of the ego in the maternal relationship, we have a highly impor-
> tant view of what happens to the individual psyche under the impact of
> personal relations in real life. But the theory has not yet properly
> conceptualized Buber's I–Thou relation, two persons being both ego and
> object to each other at the same time, and in such a way that their reality
> as persons becomes, as it develops in the relationship, what neither of
> them would have become apart from the relationship. This is what
> happens in good marriages and friendships (Guntrip 1969, p. 389).[2]

---

[2]See also Guntrip 1969, pp. 12, 22f., 45, 57, 61, 74, 93, 164, 221f., 231, 238, 240f., 253,
255, 258, 267–279, 292, 294, 317, 330, 344, 350–359, 363f., 385, 388f., 420, 423f.

# Chapter 7

# Existential Therapists

## Viktor von Weizsäcker

The German psychiatrist Viktor von Weizsäcker places healing through meeting at the center of his "medical anthropology," which begins with the recognition of the difference between the objective understanding of some-*thing* and the "transjective" understanding of some*one*. The therapist can only understand the patient if he begins with questions addressed to a person rather than objective knowledge about an object. Only through the real contact of the therapist and the patient does objective science have a part in the history of the latter's illness. If this contact is lacking, all information about functions, drives, properties, and capacities is falsified. This comradeship of therapist and patient takes place not in spite of technique and rational thought, but rather through and with them. The smooth functioning of the objective practitioner lasts just as long as there is a self-understood relation between therapist and patient, unnoticed because unthreatened. But if this *de facto* assent to the relationship falls away, then the objectivity is doubtful and no longer of use (Weizsäcker 1973, pp. 405–407).

Von Weizsäcker expands this relationship of therapist and patient into an all embracing distinction between objective therapy and "inclusive," or "comprehensive" therapy, using the latter word in Buber's sense of *Umfassung*, or experiencing the other side of the relationship. The most important characteristic of an inclusive therapy, in von Weizsäcker's opinion, is that the therapist allows himself to be changed by the patient, that he allows all the impulses that proceed from the person of the patient to affect him, that he is receptive not only with the objective sense of sight, but also with hearing, which brings the I and Thou together. Only through this ever-new involvement of his personality can the therapist bring his capacities to full realization in his relation with his patient.

> Only through this conscious dominion of a *relationship* over the psychic process, in this long and from-case-to-case-ever-newly-offered chain of sacrifices and new involvements of the personality, can the doctor be educated in that which enables him to encompass the resistances and to set the projected goal beyond the circumscribed area of objective therapy (Weizsäcker 1973, p. 408).

It helps in this process if the therapist recognizes that even the needs, physical or psychic, that cut the patient off are facts of the relationship between person and person, variants that lift that relationship to another level. That objective approach to therapy that leads the judging mind to disengage itself from the moment of the experiencing contact rests on a false image of the human. "He is then thought of as a being of size, surface, area, weight, function, desire, consciousness, characteristics and capabilities of all sorts," all of which are false judgments, false images. Von Weizsäcker applies this dialogical approach even to psychotics. What makes us mistrustful of many psychotics, he writes, is that their self-deification and self-degradation lack all moderation. The cause of this overvaluation of the self is the isolation of the psychotic, the fact that he has no Thou for his I. The result of the absence of a Thou is an inner double. This illusion of the double is unavoidable after a man has lost his connection with a Thou, von Weizsäcker writes, for the state of aloneness that he has reached then is unbearable. "The cleavage of the I represents— for a moment—the relationship of the I to the Thou which has become unattainable" (Weizsäcker 1973, pp. 407, 409).

The reciprocity of relationships is, without doubt, the least explored part of medical anthropology until now, according to von Weizsäcker. When one arrives at the very ground of events, explanations cease and things are as they are. But "the relationship of man to man plays a powerful role, and in this relationship first arises much of that which one calls ability, character, disposition and heredity." Pathology, after Freud, must be not only individual, but also social, von Weizsäcker concludes (Weizsäcker 1973, p. 410).

# J. L. Moreno

J. L. Moreno centers his "Philosophy of the Third Psychiatric Revolution" in *Begegnung*, a term he himself used as early as 1914 and one he prefers to translate into English as "encounter" because this emphasizes the *gegen* ("against") part of the concept. Encounter "encompasses not only loving, but also hostile and threatening relationships." Encounter "means meeting, contact of bodies, confronting each other, facing each other, countering and battling, seeing and perceiving, touching and entering into each other, sharing and loving, communicating with each other in a primary, intuitive manner by speech or gesture, by kiss and embrace, becoming one." Applied to his psychodrama, people play each other's roles: two people live and experience one another—as actors, each in his own right. Moreno distinguishes this from any type of emotional, intellectual, or scientific rapport, as from *Einfühlung* (empathy). *Begegnung* is *Zweifühlung*—"an intuitive reversal of roles, a realization of the self through the other," an experience of total reciprocity in which each sees through the eyes of the other. It is, as for Gestalt therapy, "here and now," but it is not "I and Thou." Rather Moreno claims that it is an I–I relationship in which the thou *becomes* and exists in the *I*. All this, for him, adds up to psychodrama, in which people play various roles and thus dramatically get at the deep problems that they could not reach if there were only therapist and patient present.

The common characteristic of all encounter experience is "telic" sensitivity or reciprocity, putting ourselves into the situations of others and being aware of the clues they give us as to how they want us to act. Such telic sensitivity is essential to the success of both individual and group psychotherapy. Transference leads the therapist and the patient to talk past each other. Empathy and counterempathy run parallel but do not add up to a telic relationship. Empathic sensitivity to another is possible without mutual love and can be used to dominate and injure the other. Telic sensitivity of a truly mutual nature is "trainable." It is particularly important in psychodramatic productions in which the director and auxiliary egos are confronted not only with which clues to use, but also with far more clues that they must let "pass." This is not only a question of selection, but also of timing: "Once the protagonist and auxiliary ego decide which clue is right and appropriate, they must rapidly use it before it is too late; otherwise, they may lose contact with each other" (Moreno 1973, pp. 468–471).

The impact of Moreno's psychodrama on "encounter groups," Perlsian Gestalt techniques, and group psychotherapy is probably far greater than has been recognized. But because of the nature of the role reversals in psychodramas, it has also had at least an indirect effect upon the development of family therapy.

## Rollo May

Along with his insightful introductory essays to *Existence*, Rollo May's greatest contribution to our understanding of healing through meeting is his 1969 book, *Love and Will*. To the influence on Rollo May of Freud,

Kierkegaard, Heidegger, Tillich, and Binswanger, we must also add that of Harry Stock Sullivan and the William Alanson White Institute of Psychiatry, Psychoanalysis, and Psychology in New York City, with which May for many years identified himself, plus that of the Viennese psychoanalyst Alfred Adler, with whom May worked for two summers as a younger man.

Unless the therapist is oriented toward *helping* the patient, writes May, the patient will not, and in some ways *cannot* reveal the profound roots of his problems. When such a suffering person receives no help, then the need for relationship expresses itself perversely in the daimonic—the desire to inflict pain and torture to prove one can affect somebody:

> When inward life dries up, when feeling decreases and apathy increases, when one cannot affect or even genuinely *touch* another person, violence flares up as a daimonic necessity for contact. . . . This is one aspect of the well-known relationship between sexual feelings and crimes of violence (May 1969, p. 30f.).

May suggests that the way out of this dilemma of isolation and loneliness is directing and channeling that daimonic energy, which, undirected, acts as an *impersonal* force driving us toward blind assertion in rage or sex. Consciousness can integrate the daimonic, make it personal, and this is the purpose of psychotherapy. But psychotherapy cannot accomplish this without the support of community. "The community gives a humanly trustworthy, interpersonal world in which one can struggle against the negative forces." Only within such a community of support can we identify with the negative that haunts us, not in order to fight it off, but rather to take this previously rejected element in us into ourselves (May 1969, pp. 126, 133).

When the daimonic is admitted in the course of therapy through the expression of anger, animosity, and even hatred for a spouse, the result is often a totally surprising feeling of love toward this partner. Correspondingly, when aggression toward a partner is suppressed, love is also suppressed. "To be able to experience and live out capacities for tender love requires the confronting of the daimonic."

We constructively channel the daimon through exercizing our "capacities to love in an active, outgoing concern for the other's welfare, for the sharing of pleasure and delight as an I with a Thou, for a communion of consciousness with his fellows" (May 1969, pp. 148f., 153).

Although the sources of May's teaching of the daimonic are originally Greek, and more immediately, the theology of his friend Paul Tillich, it has a striking resemblance to the Talmudic and Hasidic teaching of serving God with the "evil urge" that lies at the heart of Martin Buber's philosophy of dialogue. May devotes a chapter of *Love and Will* to the daimonic in dialogue, with explicit reference to Buber and Harry Stack Sullivan.

"The most important criterion which saves the daimonic from anarchy is *dialogue*," writes May.

> For dialogue implies that man exists in relationship. The fact that dialogue is possible at all—that it is possible, in favorable circumstances, for us to understand each other, stand where the other is standing—is, in itself, a remarkable point. Communication presupposes community, which, in turn, means a communion between the consciousness of the persons in the community. This is a meaningful interchange which is . . . a built-in aspect of the structure of human intercourse (May 1969, p. 155f.).

"The word *logos* (meaningful structure of reality), is the anchor of this term, *dia-logos*," writes May. "If we can talk about the daimonic meaningfully, we already are in the process of integrating it into the structure of our lives" (May 1969, p. 156). Here May is quite close to Buber's own interpretation of the Heracleitian *logos* as the speech-with-meaning through which we raise our thoughts and experiences as "I" into the realm of the "We" and build up a common cosmos, or world (Buber 1966, Ch. 4).

Dialogue also governs the relationship of wish and will, as May treats these in his chapter, "Wish and Will." "*The wish in interpersonal relationship requires mutuality*," May quotes Father William Lynch. Along with wish and will, May also stresses "intentionality." Intentionality involves "the *totality* of the person's orientation to the world at that time, including that person's unconscious as well as conscious being. May also points out that there is a willing *with* the body and from *within*, "a willing of *participation* rather than *opposition*." This personal wholeness of wishing, willing, and intentionality is inseparable from our dialogue with the world. The patient in therapy does not develop a sense of identity and *then* act. Rather he experiences his identity *in* the action itself (May 1969, pp. 216, 234, 240, 244).

In his chapter, "Intentionality in Therapy," May points out that "detachment and psychopathic acting out are the two opposite ways to escape confronting the impact of one's intentionality." Intentionality is central to May's approach to healing through meeting; for "intentionality is based upon a meaning-matrix which patient and therapist share" (May 1969, p. 266f.). For this sharing to be therapeutically helpful, the therapist must practice that imagining of the real side of the other without losing his own that Buber calls inclusion:

> I must be able to participate in my patient's meanings but preserve my own meaning-matrix at the same time, and thus unavoidably, and rightfully, interpret for him what he is doing—and often doing to me. The same thing holds true in all other human relationships as well:

friendship and love require that we participate in the meaning-matrix of the other but without surrendering our own. This is the way human consciousness understands, grows, changes, becomes clarified and meaningful (May 1969, p. 262).

Still another dimension of healing through meeting that May sets forth is that of *decision* and *responsibility*, two terms that he uses together to distinguish them from will. Responsibility involves *responding*, and decision also is a pattern of response:

*Decision*, in our sense, creates out of the two previous dimensions a pattern of acting and living which is empowered and enriched by wishes, asserted by will, and is responsive to and responsible for the significant other-persons who are important to one's self in the realizing of the long-term goals. If the point were not self-evident, it could be demonstrated along the lines of Sullivan's interpersonal theory of psychiatry, Buber's philosophy, and other viewpoints. They all point out that wish, will, and decision occur within a nexus of relationships upon which the individual depends not only for his fulfillment but for his very existence (May 1969, p. 268).

Given this emphasis upon will, wish, responsibility, and decision taking place in dialogue, it is not surprising that May sees love and will as united as a task and an achievement. "For human beings the more powerful need is not for sex per se but for relationship, intimacy, acceptance, and affirmation." Love pushes us toward a new dimension of consciousness precisely because it is based on the original "we" experience. "Contrary to the usual assumption, we all begin life not as individuals, but as we" (May 1969, pp. 311, 316).

In a conversation with Richard Stanton, May said that he obtained his understanding of dialogue through Buber, Marcel, and Tillich, "and got it formulated through my exposure to Sullivan . . . because of his locating the problem in interpersonal relations rather than *in* one person or another." Without dialogue, May added, "we are not human . . . community and communication are essential." A baby will first focus his or her eyes at a distance of 19 centimeters, the distance between the baby at the breast and the mother's face to which it looks up. May also acknowledged, in this conversation, that verbal behavior is not the substance of depth communication between persons and is often indeed an intellectual defense against the possibility of dialogue. The transparency which the American psychologist Sidney Jourard called for is a state of successful dialogue, said May, whereas the degree of psychological illness is gauged by the degree of lack of dialogue:

In schizophrenics you find it [dialogue] completely lacking. . . . This is the context in which one ought to see catatonia. . . . All these kinds of things are withdrawals . . . where there's no dialogue at all. . . . In the long run, one is "cured" in psychotherapy only as he becomes part of the fellowship of man. . . . *The way I use therapy* is—in principle at least, and I hope also in practice—*a development of the capacity for dialogue.*

May saw the talking aspect of therapy as essential, but at the same time he recognized that it is only one medium of dialogue. May cited a case reported by the Rogerian therapist Eugene Gendlin in which Gendlin was working with a schizophrenic: "Standing there next to him, looking up when he did, allowing him to move away and then moving up again, gradually dialogue became present," said May, and added: "The whole thing is a form of dialogue—the standing there, the moving away." In May's own experience, there are all kinds of blockages to dialogue in the beginning of therapy, characteristically, in the patients who came to see him, intellection and no feeling. Even the dreams of such patients illustrate the lack of dialogue. In order to build the capacity for dialogue, such patients have to risk relationships, and this entails a good deal of anxiety, experimentation, and probably failures along the way.[1]

## Medard Boss

It might seem strange to include the Swiss existential analyst Medard Boss among the existentialists of dialogue, since Boss derives from Heidegger, not Buber, and Heidegger accords the "between" only an ontic and not an ontological status. Boss does not modify Heidegger's *Mitsein* (being-with) in the direction of *Miteinandersein* (being-with-each-other), as does Ludwig Binswanger, who explicitly supplements Heidegger with Buber. Nor does Boss ever attain *in his theory* an encounter with persons or things in any really mutual way comparable to Buber's I–Thou relationship.

On the other hand, Boss is centrally concerned with therapy, as Binswanger is not. Also, whereas Heidegger emphasizes the person's own-most, non-relational, not-to-be-outstripped call to individualize the self down to its own *Dasein*, Boss emphasizes Heidegger's being-with, thus elevating it, in fact if not in theory, to an ontological status. Boss says of one's fellows that as human beings they are altogether different from things and are encountered as being-in-the-world even as I am. The fact that the world is one's world, according to Boss, does not stand in the way of one's existing with others and of one becoming immediately aware of

---

[1]The interview between Rollo May and Richard Stanton took place at May's home in Tiburon, California, on April 7, 1977. The passages quoted or paraphrased above are from Stanton 1978, pp. 136–139.

them as what they are. It is the essence of existence to be with others, and my world is necessarily one that one shares with others. "We never exist primarily as different subjects who only secondarily enter into interpersonal relations with one another," writes Boss. Rather "we are all out there in the world together primarily and from the beginning" (Boss 1969, p. 55).

Here Boss gives a more basically social interpretation of Heidegger than does Rollo May. The implication of this sociological approach to psychiatry is that "no psychopathological symptom will ever be fully and adequately understood unless it is conceived of as a disturbance in the texture of the social relationships of which a given human existence fundamentally consists" (Boss 1963, p. 56). How far this brings Boss in the direction of "healing through meeting" is shown by his quotation from "A Patient Who Taught the Author to See and Think Differently," the clinical vignette with which he opens his book *Psychoanalysis and Daseinsanalysis*:

> Toward the end of her last analytical session the patient asked her physician spontaneously, "Do you know what it was in your treatment which actually cured me?" Immediately she gave the answer herself: "First of all it was the simple fact that you were always available for me, that I could telephone you and come to you at any time, day and night, whenever I found it to be necessary. For a long time I did not believe that somebody actually would always be there for me. Slowly I learned to trust you, because dozens of experiences proved to me that you did not let me down. Only then I dared to live through you, so to speak, until I felt my own strength growing. Out of this trust in your reliability grew an increasing faith in the whole world, as I had never experienced before. Formerly I lived by my will power only, always pullling myself up by my boot strings till I was suspended in the air. The faith in you gave me the courage *to settle down inwardly to the very ground of my existence.* The second but equally important therapeutically efficient factor was your understanding of my paranoid delusions and hallucinations, your taking them seriously. Your knowledge of their genuine value and meaning enabled me to realize the wholeness of my own self and the oneness of myself and the world" (Boss 1963, p. 26).

Boss sees the human being as at every moment out in the world in relationship with what he or she encounters, even if that being is experienced as remote rather than near. From this sketch of relatedness Boss moves to relationship to a partner: "Love appears when being-together with a partner opens up an existence to hitherto unappropriated possibilities of relating to the world." From this standpoint, what Freud calls "transference," Boss describes as "always a genuine relationship between the analysand and the analyst." Despite the difference in their positions, "the partners disclose themselves to each other as human beings." No transfer of affect or empathy is necessary to explain an interpersonal relationship in which two persons disclose themselves immediately to each other. The patient's "transference love" "is love of the analyst himself, no matter how immature and distorted it may appear because of the limitations of perception imposed on the patient by his earlier relationship to his real father" (Boss 1963, pp. 123, 125).

Boss describes the Daseinsanalyst's attitude toward his patients as essentially what I shall put forward in "The Dialogue of Touchstones," the concluding chapter of this book. Respecting everything as a direct conveyor of meaning, the Daseinsanalyst "has no need to destroy what he actually sees and hears from the analysand and to replace it with assumed forces supposedly underlying the patient's behavior and perception." The Daseinsanalyst discards all labored psychoanalytic interpretations that might become obstacles to an immediate understanding between physician and patient. The analyst "will not try to persuade patients that much of what they feel and mean is only a cloak for opposite wishes and tendencies," thus avoiding giving the impression of devaluating their experiences. The analyst accepts and respects all the utterances and ways of relating of the patient and does not suggest that one kind of behavior is more real or fundamental than another (Boss 1963, p. 234f.).

The Daseinsanalyst must relate to others on the level where they are, and that means in most cases on the level of adults who have remained small children at the very core of their existence and who must be met on that same child-like level (Boss 1963, p. 242). Thus here, too, Boss places healing through meeting at the center of psychotherapy.

Boss seconds Freud in holding that the healing factor in psychoanalysis can never consist in allowing patients to live out all their instincts and impulses. Putting this in his own language, Boss asserts that one can attain true self-knowledge and authentic responsibility only if one becomes aware of and acknowledges as one's own all one's possibilities of relating to what one encounters. But Boss sharply differentiates that from the actual carrying out of these possibilities in one's relations toward partners outside the analytic situation. Here the context is the interpersonal, and there can be no self-realization without considering the welfare of those one encounters (Boss 1963, p. 254).

"There can be no psychoanalysis without an existential bond between the analyst and the analysand," writes Boss. This means that to imagine there can be analysis without countertransference, without involvement and response on the part of the analyst, is an illusion. The analyst can deny but cannot avoid having an emotional relationship with the analysand: even the objectifying attitude of indifference is a mode of emotional relating. What is more, for Boss, countertransference, like transference, is actually a genuine emotional interhuman relationship between the analyst and the patient, distorted though it may be (Boss 1963, p. 258).

In order for the emotional interhuman relationship between analyst and patient to be adequate, asserts Boss, the analyst must have "matured into the freedom of selfless concern for his patients." This "means that the analyst has all his own sensual and egotistical tendencies at his free disposal and can keep them from interfering secretly or openly with his genuine concern and selfless love for the patient." The analyst's sensitivity enables the analyst to carry out an "analysis of resistance." In this analysis, "the patient is tirelessly confronted with the limitations of his life . . . so that the possibility of a richer existence is implied" (Boss 1963, pp. 233–236; Boss 1973, pp. 434–438).

## Leslie Farber

One of the most significant contributions to our understanding of healing through meeting is the work of Leslie H. Farber. Under the influence of Buber, as well as of Kierkegaard and his former mentor Harry Stack Sullivan, Farber developed an original theory of "will and willfulness" as the center of psychiatric diagnosis and healing. Farber's approach to psychotherapy is essentially dialogical. At the same time, he has gone further than anyone in recognizing the terribly tragic limitations of healing through meeting to which Buber points in his dialogue with Rogers.

In *The Ways of the Will* and its overlapping sequel *lying, despair, jealousy, envy, sex, suicide, drugs, and the good life*, Leslie Farber distinguishes between a first and a second realm of the will, both of which are necessary in themselves and in their interdependence. The first realm of will moves in a direction rather than toward a particular object. By direction Farber does not mean an ideal goal, but rather a way interspersed with, yet not obstructed by, worldly detail and worldly objectives. It is an open way, the predominant experience of which is freedom. Since it is not a matter of immediate experience, and must be inferred after the event, Farber sees will of the first realm as unconscious in Buber's sense of the wholeness of the person underlying the split into physical and psychic. It exists in the hope of I–Thou, and I–Thou increasingly requires this first realm of will for its realization. Will stands in reciprocity with relation through life, but when will tries to do the work of relation or relation that of will, both will and relation are infringed. Memory and imagination within the first realm of will share in that realm's dialogical potentiality. "In fact, even in solitude these capacities seem to move in the direction of another human being."

Will of the second realm moves consciously toward a specific, utilitarian object. Our day-to-day existence could not be got through without this will, and our burgeoning technology owes everything to it. This second realm of will more readily permits direct phenomenological and psychological exploration, since it is a conscious will that is experienced during the event. Much of our education is accomplished under the dominion of this conscious, utilitarian will.

Farber stresses the interdependence of the two realms of will, even as Buber stresses the necessary dialectical alternation of I–Thou and I–It. The first without the second would result in a mysticism that betrays the appropriate objectifications the will is capable of; the second without the first would result in a rationalism that betrays the realities of the wholeness that makes existence possible. "To the degree the will of the second realm is misshappen, misapplied, or misdirected, the first realm will elude us, even as we willfully assert our proprietary claims over it" (Farber 1976, pp. 4–6).

As I–It becomes evil only when it seeks to dominate exclusively, and prevents the ever-new transmuting of It into Thou, so Farber's will of the second realm becomes "willfulness" only at the point where it seeks to do the work of the will of the first realm. We fall into willfulness, says Farber, when we succumb to the recurring temptation to apply the will of the second realm to those portions of life that not only will not comply, but also will become distorted under such coercion:

> I can will knowledge, but not wisdom; going to bed, but not sleeping; eating, but not hunger; meekness, but not humility; scrupulosity, but not virtue; self-assertion or bravado, but not courage; lust, but not love; commiseration, but not sympathy; congratulations, but not admiration; religiosity, but not faith; reading, but not understanding (Farber 1966, p. 15).

In willfulness, the will tries to do the work of the imagination. This applies to the therapist as well as the client. The therapist, because he knows that genuine listening is essential to true therapy, may try, in vain, to make himself listen. But listening is the work of the will of the first realm and becomes willfulness when it is taken over by the will of the second:

> In "Martin Buber and Psychoanalysis," I have suggested that listening requires something more than remaining mute while looking attentive— namely, it requires the ability to attend imaginatively to another's language. Actually, in listening we speak the other's words. It is not merely that listening does not respond to the constraints we impose, but that it withers as human possibility under will's dominion, as all of us realize who have tried to force our attention to an event, while our inclination struggled to look elsewhere (Farber 1976, p. 7).

As Farber develops his contrast between genuine will and arbitrary willfulness, the former emerges as an expression of real dialogue, the latter as an hysterical product of the absence of dialogue. In contrast to Freud, who sees hysteria as a product of repression, which can be cured by bringing the repressed material to consciousness, Farber defines hysteria as a disorder of the will that expresses itself in *willfulness*. "In willfulness the life of the will becomes distended, overweening, and obtrusive at the same time that its movements become increasingly separate, sovereign, and distinct from other aspects of spirit (Farber 1966, pp. 103, 20f.). This leads to that very failure of discretion and judgment, as well as imagination and humor, that Farber points to as the inadequacy of the schizophrenic in the world of *It* as well as in the relationship with the Thou.

Farber sees the origin of willfulness as the desperate need for wholeness. The proper setting of wholeness is dialogue. When this setting eludes us, "we turn wildly to will, ready to grasp at any illusion of wholeness (however mindless or grotesque) the will conjures up for our reassurance." This is a vicious circle, for the more dependent a person becomes on the illusion of wholeness, the less he is able to experience true wholeness in dialogue. "At the point where he is no longer capable of dialogue he can be said to be *addicted* to his will" (Farber 1966, p. 50). Willfulness, then, is nothing other than the attempt of will to make up for the absence of dialogue by handling both sides of the no longer mutual situation. No longer in an encounter with another self, he fills the emptiness with his own self, and even that self is only a partial one, its wholeness having disappeared with the disappearance of meeting. "This feverish figure, endlessly assaulting the company, seeking to wrench the moment to some pretense of dialogue, is the image of the eternal stranger: that condition of man in which he is forever separated from his fellows, unknown and unaddressed—it is the figure of man's separated will posing as his total self" (Farber 1966, p. 57).

In "Will and Anxiety" Farber defines anxiety, in conscious contrast to his teacher Harry Stack Sullivan, as a product of the separated, or isolated, will.

> By whatever name it is called, *anxiety is that range of distress which attends willing what cannot be willed*. In other words, anxiety can be located in the ever-widening split between the will and the impossible object of the will. As the split widens, the bondage between the will and its object grows, so that one is compelled to pursue what seems to wither or altogether vanish in the face of such pursuit (Farber 1966, p. 62).

The more stubbornly the will pursues its intractable goal, the more it becomes separate from those faculties of intellect and imagination that might objectify, divert, or dispel its bondage. The failure of meaning that characterizes anxiety stems from the withering of the will's goal in the face of the will's demands. In contrast to the customary distinction between fear as specific and anxiety as diffuse, Farber suggests that fear merges into anxiety when willing what cannot be willed takes over. At this point, the will itself comes to be experienced as impotent thrust, resulting in the helplessness and uncertainty that characterize anxiety.

Rather than call this "the Age of Anxiety," Farber calls it "the Age of the Disordered Will." We are enslaved, he says, by myriad varieties of willing what cannot be willed: to sleep, to read fast, to have simultaneous orgasms, to be creative and spontaneous, to enjoy old age. Above all, it is the *will to will* that makes anxiety so prominent in our time and explains the increasing dependence on drugs at all levels of our society. More important than their function in relieving anxiety is the illusion drugs offer of healing the split between the will and its refractory object. This illusion offers, briefly and subjectively, the appearance of a responsible and vigorous will. This is the reason, in Farber's opinion, why the addictive possibilities of our age are so enormous.

In his essay, "Martin Buber and Psychoanalysis," Farber (1966, Ch. 7) affirms that without meeting no successful treatment is possible. The "compulsive," "schizoid," or "hysterical" traits that therapist and patient have in common only indicate that both have an incapacity that hinders the meeting. Many of the disturbances that are seen as arising from "transference" are more correctly described as the striving for or retreating from the hope for a reciprocal relationship. Usually what we mean by transference is the very opposite of meeting, with its warmth, contact, and spontaneity. What is important, however, is to combine reciprocity or trust with truthfulness and proportion. These two can combine in a unique immediacy: meeting becomes truth. Such moments are entirely lacking in utility for ordinary goals of knowledge.

At the same time, Farber emphasizes that Buber's philosophy is based as much upon the necessary structures and categories of the world of It as the bringing of those structures and categories into the meeting with the Thou.

> The mistake is often made, especially with the schizophrenic, of overvaluing his lonely gropings toward the *Thou* and of underestimating his actual incompetence in the world of *It*, so that he becomes a tragic saint or poet of the *Thou*, martyred by the world of *It*.
>
> Once it is realized, however, that the *Thou* relation depends upon the world, of *It* for its conceptual forms or meanings, then psychosis can be seen as not only a failure of the *Thou*—of so-called personal relations. It is an equal failure of knowledge, judgment, and experience in the world of *It*. Whatever class the disorder falls into—whether it is marked by a recoil from relations, as in schizophrenia, or by a grasping at relation, as

in hysteria or mania—underlying its manifestations one can always find much ineptitude with people, much early failure to acquire the elementary tools of knowledge. . . . Without sufficient knowledge, memory, or judgment, every *Thou* invoked is apt to be a perilously shy and fleeting one. It recedes very quickly into its impoverished world of *It*, where there is little promise of return. And with each loss of the *Thou*, the schizophrenic is in special danger of retreating more permanently or deeply toward his far pole of alienation: into that *loneliness* of which both Sullivan and Fromm-Reichmann have written (Farber 1966, p. 148f.).

Farber describes this loneliness as a hopeless longing for the *Thou*, a despair that afflicts everyone at times "and overwhelms the more desperate ones we call psychotic." In this sense, the chatter by which we detain even an unwelcome guest at parting is no less a confession of the total failure of the wedding of minds than that even madder chattering by which the "manic" patient detains all humanity as his parting guest. "We strive wildly on the doorstep for one departing *Thou*." For the schizophrenic this often means that the longing for the Thou is accompanied by a fear of his loneliness being momentarily entered by a Thou and then leaving him all the more desolate and empty-handed when he returns to the vacant world of *It*. Unable to endure this possibility, he "exiles himself from both earth and heaven, and, with a surprising dignity, takes up his residence in limbo" (Farber 1966, p. 149f.). The sickness arising from lack of dialogue thus makes itself worse by striving in desperate or inadequate ways for the Thou or by fearing the loneliness that will follow the fleeting appearance of the Thou.

Farber is at his best in describing "the therapeutic despair" that continually threatens the psychiatrist who works with schizophrenia:

> As a quotidian affair stretching painfully through the years, the psychotherapy of schizophrenia has simply not been truthfully described. Reports not only give it an order and meaning that it does not possess; they also deprive it of the brutal tedium, exasperation, emptiness, futility—in short, the agony of existence in which dialogue is so fleeting as to be virtually nonexistent (Farber 1966, p. 167).

Chivalric legends and romantic accounts announced in conventional scientific prose cannot conceal "the pathos of two maddened human beings clutching at each other, whatever the pretext." The therapist cannot take refuge in silence, "that mirrorlike impassivity that is still considered a virtue in the treatment of neurosis." The therapist cannot deprive the patient of ordinary social responsiveness or answer the patient's silence with his own. "He is continually on guard against the double danger of silence and the fear of silence, which he knows can easily sour into a clotted self-consciousness to be relieved at any cost."

A treatment seen and reported in anecdotal terms will come to be practiced in these terms. "Any therapist who enters on his life with a schizophrenic expecting it to resemble the case reports is doomed, if not to premature despair, at least to more discouragement than necessary." Farber even suggests that the whole vocabulary of transference and countertransference, father-surrogates and mother-surrogates may have been developed to account for the fact that the therapist is so often forced, against his or her better judgment, to play the role of oracle or all-knowing authority! A good therapist must be able to imagine his or her own despair, as well as the patient's. "For the task of imagining the real [Buber's alternate phrase for "inclusion"] must include oneself, just as it includes those moments in which the other person cannot be vividly present to us" (Farber 1966, pp. 167f., 178–180).

Much of the reason for the absorption with countertransference on the part of those who treat schizophrenia lies in the nature of schizophrenia itself, which is a disorder consisting of a double failure in meaning and relation.

> Such civilized qualities as discretion, reticence, humor, judgment, and logic are poorly developed, if they are present at all . . . metaphorical thinking is morbidly deficient, causing the schizophrenic's understanding and perceptions, as well as his effort to communicate, to be uncomfortably literal (Farber 1976, p. 99).

In what sounds almost like a direct critique of the romanticizing of the schizophrenic at which Laing arrives in the last part of *The Politics of Experience*, Farber warns that if the therapist forgets the degree to which he has supplied meaning to a patient unable to provide any for himself, he may come to regard the schizophrenic as a "ragged oracle" with "the rare power to cut through the usual hypocrisies and pretensions of ordinary life, thereby arriving at some purely human meaning." On this reading, his illness becomes an appropriate response to the deceits and contradictions of the world in which he lives.

The very hunger for relation of the schizophrenic that the therapist rightly sees leads the schizophrenic to still further isolation in willfulness. Should relation be even fleetingly achieved, he dreads and is enraged by its loss. Both his attempts at relation and his repudiation of relation are expressions of his isolated will:

> In such an extreme state, much of his delusional and hallucinatory life will either reach for consummation, even glory, or else proclaim his repudiation of such a possibility with a web of corroborating, though

fantastic, details. . . . Willfully, then, the schizophrenic grasps at, and withdraws from, relation—sometimes simultaneously (Farber 1976, p. 102f.).[2]

Not until this willfulness of the schizophrenic is recognized can it be understood why the therapeutic life with schizophrenia is such a blood-curdling affair, full of screaming invective, brutal physical grappling, and all manner of obscenity. The therapist "may even come to count himself fortunate to have this semblance of relation, no matter how degraded, instead of none at all, which is his more frequent lot" (Farber 1976, p. 103f.).

One way out of the impasse of the disordered will may be despair, Farber suggests in "Schizophrenia and the Mad Psychotherapist." Despair may provide "the very conditions of seriousness and urgency which bring a man to ask those wholly authentic—we might call them tragic—questions about his own life and the meaning and measure of his particular human-ness" (Farber 1976, p. 94). When despair is repudiated, these questions may mark the turning to the inauthentic. This applies to the therapist too who *wills* relation. True relationship cannot be willed; it depends on honesty, imagination, tact, humor. "By contrast, the willful encounter . . . will have a special binge-like excitement, even though its center is hollow. Its intensity is of the moment." This drama of wills that passes for relation finally turns the therapist into "an apostle of relation who can no longer abide relation." As the therapist continues to will what cannot be willed, his human qualities progressively atrophy in favor of "those public, self-assertive gestures which are inauthentic to the person he might have become" (Farber 1967, p. 104f.).

Farber's implicit conclusion is that if patient and therapist alike are to have any hope of reaching real dialogue they must be willing to face the despair that occupies so central a place even in the attempt at healing through meeting:

It is when we stand stripped of every artifice and prop, every technical support of our profession, that we are closest to reality. And if it is only then, in the moment of extremity, that we approach genuine dialogue, genuine confirmation—the lack of which has driven us to this despair— so we may find the remedy concealed in the disease. It may be that only in such moments do we approach reality at all. It may be that at such moments the patient, too, is obeying such deep and elementary needs that it would be gratuitous to speak of pity and despair (Farber 1966, p. 182).

[2]On revelation in therapy as "lying" or deceit to recover a meaning that has been lost, see Farber 1976, pp. 206f., 211–220.

This despair must be distinguished from that pseudo-despair that leads to "the life of suicide." The very strategies of despair involved in the contemplation of suicide reveal a link to the life-outside-despair that despair is unable to sever. "Despair would not be so anguished a condition as it were it as wholly and hopelessly estranged as it believes itself to be" (Farber 1976, p. 82). Even if the life of suicide issues into actual suicide, this does not mean that the despair was as total as the despairer thinks. The man who commits suicide imagines he has made a bargain with death. Through death, he will be able to find the last and grandest expression of willfulness—"the dramatic representation of some uniqueness, some singularity of self with which life has seemingly so far failed to provide him, and of which his natural—un-self-engineered—death threatens to rob him." This ultimate perversion of dialogue is "a dream of the will—a despairing attempt to affirm the self in a form in which the self has never been and can never be" (Farber 1976, p. 83).

One of the most remarkable conclusions that Farber draws is that the genuineness of despair not only may lead the therapist to face the true situation in regard to his "dialogue" with his schizophrenic patient, but may even lead the patient to moments of pity for the therapist through which, for those moments at least, the patient transcends his schizophrenia and enters into dialogue. Thus, though the therapist may not demand that the patient sees the relationship from his point of view, it is possible with a schizophrenic that he may do so and that precisely here will lie the "healing through meeting" that takes place. Making use of Buber's concepts of presentness and confirmation, Farber suggests that only the therapist who is capable of arousing pity by becoming "present" for his patient will be able to help the patient. When the patient is able to make the therapist present, to "imagine the real" in relation to him, he becomes capable of pity for his friend's distress. "In response to the therapist's despair . . . the patient will often try to confirm the therapist's image of himself as therapist. And insofar as the therapist is sincerely dedicated to his work . . . this will also have the effect of confirming him as a fellow human being" (Farber 1966, p. 171).

# Chapter 8

# Gestalt Therapists

## Fritz and Laura Perls

The catch phrase "I and Thou, Here and Now" has long been a capsule definition of Gestalt therapy. Nonetheless, as Lynne Jacobs has pointed out, Fritz Perls' biological terminology of organism and environment is decisively different from Buber's philosophical, anthropological emphasis on the uniqueness of the human species. Jacobs thinks that Perls wrote his famous "Gestalt Prayer," with its even more famous line, "I do my thing," as a reaction to the push for "confluence," the symbiotic merging of personalities without respect for the boundaries of either, that he saw all around him.

> He made his point, and now that Gestalt therapy has learned his lesson, perhaps it can re-enter the world of mutuality, with the potential for growth and transcendence that exists when two individuals, fully responsible, allow their inmost selves to meet. . . . Therapists and patients alike have misinterpreted the notion of personal responsibility to mean that one should not allow oneself to be influenced or affected by another. Buber also emphasizes that no contact is possible except between separate, responsible persons. Yet his work emphasizes mutual influence, and is compellingly spiritual (Jacobs 1978, pp. 133f., 137).

The reason why Perls misinterpreted personal responsibility in this way was that he saw autonomy as the be-all and end-all of personal development, as his disciple Erving Polster himself has told me. "Maturation is the development from environmental to self-support," says Perls in one of his Gestalt lectures. For the therapist as well as the patient, Perls recognized that the alternation between contact and withdrawal is a healthy one and that the extreme of either is pathological. But in the end, I–Thou was for him a means to the end of autonomy, rather than a value in itself because autonomy was, to him, the final goal. In fact, both his personality and his methods were, in the highest degree, authoritarian.

In a dialogue between Laura Perls and myself on Buber and Gestalt therapy, Laura stated that for the last years of his life Perls was exclusively concerned with the It and not the Thou, that his purpose was demonstration of techniques, such as the "hot seat," and not dialogue. "Fritz fell back on what was comfortable. He was in the theater. He was a director. . . . What was very problematic in Fritz's approach was that he was not interested in the person as such but in what he could do with her. . . . Fritz was tremendous in therapy but he could not carry on the dialogue." What Laura Perls particularly lamented was that it was *this* aspect of Gestalt therapy that became most famous, so that Fritz Perls in the last years of his life is falsely taken by many as representative of Gestalt as a whole.

What impressed me most about Laura Perls in our dialogue was that she was witness not to the influence of Buber's thought on her approach to therapy but rather to his presence as she knew it when she met him in Germany. In this sense of the term "influence," she said that Buber and Tillich had more influence on her than any psychologist. "I find it nearly impossible to talk about how I do therapy," she said, "because it is so different with each person. Gestalt therapy is not a technique but a modality." For her what mattered was not technique, but rather style. What was important to her was not how she "did therapy," but rather how she was with people. In this she proved herself as dialogical as her husband Fritz, at least in his later years, was not. "What Buber called meeting we call contact," she said, "that is dialogue with the other as other. . . . Experience is on the boundary where you and I meet." Where Fritz set up autonomy as the highest value, she recognized that there is always interdependence. During the discussion after our dialogue, she agreed with a statement by Frieda Fromm-Reichmann concerning schizophrenics: "It is much more important the way you are than what you do." As an example, Laura Perls told of spending many sessions in total silence with a schizophrenic girl until finally she won her trust and her response. Thus, Laura's responsibility as a therapist made possible the other's response.[1]

Many of the writers in *Gestalt Therapy Now* agree with Laura Perls in rejecting artificial techniques in favor of genuine response. Some, like John Enright, explicitly reject the presumptuous and authoritarian tech-

---

[1] The dialogue between Laura Perls and Maurice Friedman was held before the Gestalt Therapy Institute, Los Angeles, February 22, 1979. I am indebted to Dr. Richard Hycner who attended the dialogue and took notes, which I have made use of.

nique of telling the patient, "You are trying to bore me," in favor of responsibly stating only what the therapist himself *knows* to be true—that he is finding it hard to listen. And many explicitly point to I–Thou and dialogue and, therefore by implication, healing through meeting, as central to Gestalt therapy. "The end point [of therapy] is reached when each can be himself while still maintaining intimate contact with the other," writes Arnold Beisser. The therapist "must remain his own man," avoiding being put off, frightened, or bored by the psychotic, writes Joen Fagan, "while also becoming enough involved with the patient's life-style to experience its problems and difficulties" (Fagan and Shepherd, eds. 1970, pp. 82f., 122, 79, 93). "The therapist's capacity for I–thou, here-and-now relationships is a basic requisite and is developed through extensive integration of learning and experience," writes Irma Lee Shepherd.

> The therapist's willingness to encounter the patient with his honest and immediate responses and his ability to challenge the patient's manipulative use of his symptoms without rejecting him are crucial. . . . The challenge to the therapist lies in discerning the fine line between overprotection and genuine acceptance of the patient's final wisdom in the moment (Fagan and Shepherd, eds. 1970, p. 234f.).

"The goal we set for the patients as they sit down together in a group or family is an I–thou relationship in which each person is aware, responsible, and direct in his own communications and listens as fully as possible to the other person as an equal," writes John Enright.

> The details of technique vary, but the strategy is always to keep a steady, gentle pressure toward the direct and responsible I–thou orientation, keeping the focus of awareness on the difficulties the patients experience in doing this, and helping them find their own ways through these difficulties (Fagan and Shepherd, eds., 1970, p. 116f.).

In discussing the central role of dialogue in Gestalt therapy, Vincent O'Connell makes an important distinction "between entering the person's world and wallowing with him in it." He sees allowing oneself to love as a step "into the liberty of the dialogue of limits, the life of community, the lived life." What is striking in this is his further distinction between "*speaking out* of the everyday" and "*sounding out* from the deep in oneself to the deep in the other."

> It is not until the conversation reaches the heart of the crisis at hand that the speaking out becomes the sounding out to each other. When this is a shared experience from both sides, it is the genuine dialogue that Martin Buber knew—the dialogue in sympathy wherein resolution and reconciliation become possible. . . . This is the work of the crisis, the work of the therapy: to transform ourselves with the other, and in this sounding out to meet him and know him. . . . We need dialogue, therefore, with

the other to complement and complete ourselves in our process of creative adaptation in community. The empirical fact is this; when we send out love, when we sound out to someone with whom there is conflict, bitterness, resentment, and unfinished situations . . . his heart is enabled to respond (Fagan and Shepherd, eds. 1970, pp. 250f., 255f.).

Lynne Jacobs, a fourth-generation Gestalt therapist, has pointed out the link between the here-and-now and the I and Thou:

If we attempt to hold onto any one moment, the liveliness vanishes and the cycle is interrupted. The excited intimacy of meeting someone's eyes becomes a dull staring. A momentary turning inward to touch our thoughts hardens into isolated, obsessional rumination (Jacobs 1978, p. 29).

She has also sensitively described the healthy dialectical alternation between the therapist-patient dialogue and the use of techniques. "Techniques must evolve organically from the I–Thou process," she asserts. "The important thing is that the dialogue predominate, and that deviations from the dialogue be used as information—to therapist and patient alike—on how they interfere with meeting, and what might be done to restore the dialogue." She recognizes, at the same time, that techniques are frequently misused because of the frustration of therapists when they feel stuck. In such cases, the technique no longer leads back to dialogue, but becomes instead a way to "make something happen" (Jacobs 1978, pp. 123, 134f.).

## Erving and Miriam Polster

In their discussion of "contact" in the middle third of their book, *Gestalt Therapy Integrated*, Erving and Miriam Polster offer us some meaningful intimations of the role of healing through meeting in Gestalt therapy. The Polsters begin their chapters on contact with a quotation from Martin Buber that sets the tone for their own dialogical approach to therapy:

Only the being whose otherness, accepted by my being, lives and faces me in the whole compression of existence, brings the radiance of eternity to me. Only when two say to one another with all that they are, "It is *Thou*," is the indwelling of the Present Being between them (Buber 1965).

Contact only takes place at the boundary and true contact never effaces the boundary: "Contact is not just togetherness or joining," write the Polsters. "It can only happen between separate beings, always requiring independence and always risking capture in the union." They recognize that in the moment of meeting a between comes into existence that is more than the sum of me and thee. They recognize the danger of engulfment: "In contacting you, I wager my independent existence," but they also recognize the necessity of taking this risk: "Only through the contact function can the realization of our identities fully develop." If I am experienced in full contact, then I can meet you "full-eyed, full bodied, and full-minded" and retain the sense of separateness at the boundary without the threat of overwhelming or being overwhelmed (Polster and Polster 1974, pp. 98f., 102f.).

Guiding people to recover their contact functions makes likely and even desirable intense interaction experiences in therapy. It also means substituting the present reality of dialogue for "transference" based on the past: "By making contact central, we have given up the traditional psychoanalytic concept of transference, where many therapy interactions were regarded only as distortions based on living in the past, having no current validity of their own." In place of transference there comes what Polanyi calls "indwelling" and Buber calls "inclusion," in which knowledge of the other is not an observation, but rather an encounter. The contact boundary is not the boundary of the self; it is the boundary between the selves. The therapist recognizes that when boundaries are rigidly set, the individual faces the double danger of explosion if the boundaries are expanded and emptiness and powerlessness if they are contracted. If such a person feels invaded or threatened while also experiencing striking back as outside the limits of his boundary, he may be unable to assimilate the emergency feelings that arise, with a resultant anxiety that may even lead to psychosis or suicide. (Polster and Polster 1974, p. 110f.). The sensitive therapist will be able to distinguish between persons who can safely expand their contact boundaries and those who cannot:

> There are some people who encourage others to explore their newness and to interact with them, and both of them grow thereby. There are others who remain closed off, allowing only minimal contact at the I-boundaries, maintaining separateness and permitting no growth. What more people need is to become experts, artists if you will, at sensing and creating environments where movement outside their present I-boundaries can be supported or in leaving or altering those environments where this seems impossible (Polster and Polster 1974, p. 115).

The Polsters point to persons who place some parts or functions of their bodies outside their sense of themselves, as a result of which they remain out of contact with important parts of themselves. They also understand that being willing to expand the contact boundary, whether in terms of the body functions or feelings of anger, love, or sadness, must also entail exposure of the person's previous *reluctance* to do so. This means that the first steps will necessarily be awkward and even exhibitionistic, since the person will lack the wholeheartedness to make possible pure, authentic spontaneity. A good therapist can tell the difference between the awkwardness and excesses of the exhibitionist phase and the grace and credibility of the spontaneous phase, but for the same reason, such a therapist will not nip the workthrough into spontaneity in the bud. "The therapy process, with its stimulation of new behaviors, is vulnerable to exhibitionism and with its emphasis on authenticity it is also critical of it" (Polster and Polster 1974, pp. 115, 124–126).

Like Arnold Beisser, with his paradoxical theory of change, the Polsters posit as a basic Gestalt principle accentuating what exists rather than merely attempting to change it. "Nothing can change until it is at first accepted; then it can play itself out and be open to the native movement towards change in life." Like the other Gestalt therapists discussed here, they stress, too, that contact episodes go beyond techniques so that the therapist experiences his or herself as a genuine participant in events. Because of their intensity and because they refer the participant back to his everyday life, these contact episodes have a heightened allegorical power to condense events that happen over periods of time into smaller units. The therapeutic contact is also representative in its teaching of skills that may be used in everyday life, in its arousal of the person, and in its development of a new sense of self (Polster and Polster 1974, pp. 150, 174, 184). The heightened dialogical quality of these representative events shows itself particularly clearly in arousal:

> Good therapists, whatever their theoretical home base, are exciting people. Their talk and their actions are incisive and stimulating. After being with them, one feels renewed and heartened for new developments long after the original contact was made. . . . The therapist's talent in making contact is his primary instrument for arousing the other person to use his own energies and to become emboldened to make changes (Polster and Polster 1974, p. 188).

The teaching of new skills, the power to arouse, and the change in one's sense of self all merge to make the therapy experience a spur to new living away from therapist or group. But the transition is laced with booby-traps: the protections and simplifications of therapy are missing in everyday life. For this reason, themes requiring resolution recur many times in therapeutic contact episodes, some reappearing over the entire lifetime of the individual. This is entirely consonant with the understanding of change as dependent not just upon a momentary breakthrough, but also upon a real expansion of the contact boundary:

> The impasse, the point at which the need to change meets a force which resists change with equal power, is repeatedly confronted until, bit by bit, the individual pushes out his own I-boundaries to include what had

formerly been unassimilable. The recurrence of themes represents the piecemeal exploration of psychologically unclaimed territory (Polster and Polster 1974, p. 194).

This expansion of the contact boundary applies equally to loving and hating. "To re-experience oneself as loving is to recover an aspect of full self-experience which is weak or absent in the everyday lives of many people we see." The therapist ought not to talk people out of their loving feelings, but to teach them, rather, that "to love someone does not mean we have to marry them, screw them, send them to college, invite them to parties, be with them always." Hatred is as central to the contact episode as loving because it, too, is a force born out of non-contact, which surges toward contactfulness. Hatred is a residue forming out of the accumulation of unexpressed feelings, words, or actions spawned by personal threat.

These feelings range from anger, rejection, and exclusion to suspicion, fighting, and alienation. "The special contacts which accompany hatred are so engrossing that if they are not faced in the therapy experience the potential for contact is seriously diminished."

The reservoir of excitement in hatred is so great that it threatens to engulf the individual. Therefore, the therapist must carefully order the pacing and timing of expressions of hatred to respect the integrity of the individual. "Pillow-hitting can be invalid when the therapist or the group, like a gang of cheerleaders, baits a blocked person into voicing his anger." It is also invalid when a person coerces himself into expressing anger by coming with that sole intention. It is not necessary to manufacture opportunities artificially for the flow of hostility; for there are more than enough genuine and natural ones! (Polster and Polster 1974, p. 199f.).

The therapist must be aware, of course, of the subtler manifestations of the hatred-based contact episode: "The boring talker, the point-misser, the late arriver, the obfuscator, the person unwilling to give an inch may all be deflecting their hostility so as to remain minimally contactful." The therapist can help such persons sharpen their focus and identify their feeling and its direction. The Polsters recognize that there is nothing essentially new or startling about the recognition of the importance of hostility in psychotherapy. "What is new is the concept of the contact boundary as the locus of restorative therapeutic action and the contact episode as the sequence of life events within which the restorative contact is established."

The understanding of the contact boundary and the contact episode may also illuminate schizophrenia and other forms of psychosis, as well as our defenses against them. "Deeply embedded in [the] human core is a reflexive dread of one's own madness." What makes this dread important is that it determines and permeates the contacts we are willing to permit.

All of us avert that contact that might threaten madness. The therapist must respect this fear of madness "in the development of the contact episode partly as a safety measure serving to retain the unity of the person and partly because fear of madness engenders a vigilance which unleashes a powerful anti-contact force" (Polster and Polster 1974, pp. 201–203).

Contact can lead to dialogue, but it is not in itself dialogue. Some part of contact, as the Polsters use it, touches on that mutuality within the ebb and flow of distancing and relating that characterizes dialogue at its most authentic. But precisely because we so desperately lack and need contact, the initial movement toward it is likely to be more an affair of the individual than of the interhuman, more I–It than I–Thou. Yet if this movement expresses itself in a genuine openness and reaching toward the other and meets with a response, it may flower into that mutual contact that stands at the heart of dialogue (Hycner 1985).

# Chapter 9

# Family Therapists

The primordial fact of family in human existence is given expression by Leslie Farber in his poignant essay, "Family Reunion":

> For the family is, indeed, inescapable. You may revile it, renounce it, reject it—but you cannot resign from it; you are born into it, and *it* lives within and through you, to the end of your days. This may be inspiring, it may also be very annoying; in either case it is humbling. . . . Families seem to have particular styles and themes that run through them in uncanny variation and repetition. . . . And however much the composition of the family may change, and the fates of individuals may alter, this thematic behavior seems to persist, almost as though it had a life of its own (Farber 1976, p. 227).

Farber sees the "family reunion" as a metaphor that may bring to a person's awareness realities of his or her existence that seldom penetrate consciousness because they are not directly perceived in experience. Through this metaphor, one can perceive one's own life as an arc that creates a tangible shape and is linked to a huge but still tangible network of interconnecting arcs. This is a perception beyond one's experience and almost beyond one's comprehension. Indeed, Farber defines a human being as a creature who is "born into a family, lives without and within it, colors and shapes it with his being . . . replenishes it with his children, and diminishes it . . . with his own death." The person at the family reunion who beholds the great chain of generations that contains and is contained by his own life "imagines his life taking its particular place in a vast, organic, historical continuity" (Farber 1976, p. 231f.).

When the family is thus understood, it is little wonder that it becomes the setting for healing through meeting *par excellence*!

In moving into the realm of healing through meeting, we must face the radical question of whether true healing, in the first instance, is not only *psycho*therapy, but also family, social, economic, and political therapy. The readjustment and integration of the intrapsychic sphere is the *by-product*, but the locus of true healing is the interhuman, the interpersonal, the communal, the social, the cultural, and even the political. To embark seriously on healing through meeting is to leave the safe shores of the intrapsychic as *the* touchstone of reality and to venture onto the high seas in which healing is no longer seen as something taking place *in* the patient. Although one hopes that the client becomes wholer in the process, and although the therapist has a special role as initiator, facilitator, confidant, big brother or big sister, and representative of the dialogical demand of the world, the healing itself takes place in that sphere Buber calls the "between." Nor can this healing be limited to the client alone or even to the relationship between therapist and client. To be real healing, it must eventually burst the bounds of *psycho*therapy and enter in all seriousness into the interhuman, the family, the group, the community, and even the relations between communities and nations. In his address to the Jungian Psychological Club of Zurich in 1923, "The Psychologizing of the World," Buber explicitly pointed to the problematic limits of the province of psychotherapy and the need that healing transcend that sphere:

> The sicknesses of the soul are sicknesses of relationship. They can only be treated completely if I transcend the realm of the patient and add to it the world as well. If the doctor possessed superhuman power, he would have to try to heal the relationship itself, to heal in the "between." The doctor must know that really he ought to do that and that only his boundedness limits him to the one side (Buber 1969, p. 150).

## Lyman Wynne

The transition to family therapy in the proper sense of the term occurred when therapists left the field of the *intrapsychic*, including the internalized family (what R. D. Laing calls the "family" in quotation marks), for direct work with the actual family (not in quotation marks). As Lyman Wynne has put it:

> Ever since Freud described the family constellation in terms of the Oedipal situation, the psychoanalytic process has included as one of its central tasks the untangling of the web of current and past family relationships. In individual psychoanalytic and psychotherapeutic treatment, the primary concern is, however, with the internalized, intrapsy-

chic representations of the patient's family relationships, rather than with the *direct* observation and study of actual, ongoing family transactions (Wynne 1965, p. 289).

Lyman Wynne gives us some very specific indications in his writings concerning family therapy with the families of schizophrenics. One difference in the approach of family therapy to the traditional intrapsychic approach of psychoanalysis is that in family therapy the approach is focused more on the *unnoticed but observable* rather than on the *unnoticed but inferable*. Wynne also includes the impact upon the therapist's own subjective experience as he comes into contact with the varied facets of the family. The motivation that brings family members into conjoint therapy is quite different from the motivation that brings individuals into group therapy, Wynne points out. Group therapy participants agree to meet together because of a wish for personal change; whereas in family therapy, the motivation is the web of troublesome relationship in which the members are entangled, with any desire for personal change being a bonus that may or may not be present. "This shared entanglement is the functional equivalent in family therapy of the individual inner distress which gives impetus to individual psychotherapy and conventional group therapy." One must also contrast the historical continuity of the family social organization and the discontinuity of the group therapy constellation (Wynne 1965).

In families in which the very possibility of emotional contact is regarded as unreal, very considerable therapeutic gains can ensue if the family therapist can start to uncover and help make tolerable their long-stifled, masked capacities for tenderness and affection toward one another. The family therapist must retain the capacity to be empathic with each member of the family and still be able to step back and reflect on overall transactions. It would be equally bad if he overidentified with particular family members or failed to appreciate, understand, and empathize with individuals in a particular family role. The recent trend in family therapy has been away from perceiving offspring as primarily victimized by their parents in favor of grasping the reciprocal nature of family relations. When families present "family-syntonic disorders," disorders that so fit the family system that they are not seen as disorders, the therapist can help to move them toward a community that confirms otherness by opening up closed-off issues.

A special problem in family therapy is that the verbal and nonverbal material available for clarification and interpretation rapidly outdistances what the family members are ready to allow into their awareness. "The family therapist needs to use all of his empathic capacities to understand the form in which the various family members are experiencing what is going on so that he does not leap ahead in ways which either are simply confusing to them or which provoke heightened defensive operations." In large or fragmented families, the use of co-therapists allows greater freedom, perspective, and resources. Even with co-therapists, however, the difficulty of bringing about genuine and lasting change in family patterns is far greater than the danger of unintentionally disorganizing them. *"Families have a staggering capacity to remain the same"* (Wynne 1971, pp. 184, 187, 190f.).

Family therapists are as prone as helpful family members to fall into the pattern of injecting meaning. "Helpfulness" is built into the roles of therapists who are expected to supply understanding about matters of which the patient is presumed to be unaware. This leads to that special hazard of being caught up in binding relationships that can neither grow nor be brought to termination and separation. The long training of psychotherapists in making helpful, "meaningful" interpretations all too easily fits into the pattern of injections of meaning. "In addition, whenever the therapist takes on an Olympian neutrality in which he makes pronouncements with a gentle air of compassion, genuine, reciprocal interchange and consensual validation are exceedingly unlikely."

Psychoanalytic "neutrality," on the other hand, can be experienced by the patient as *concealment* of meaning. Nonparticipant observation holds the patient at the psychological distance the observer prefers, leaving him feeling dependent and intrigued enough so that the likelihood of separation is reduced. From the standpoint of the schizophrenic patient, it is always a question whether the schizophrenic is engaged in the withholding of meaning or is enmeshed in a profound experience of meaninglessness rooted in the subculture of his family. This situation can make injection of meaning on the part of the therapist all the more tempting, since he feels under pressure to supply meanings when they seem to be lacking.

> In the psychotherapy of schizophrenics, the long and tedious hours in which little seems to be forthcoming from the patient inevitably leaves the therapist frustrated and anxious, often feeling useless and even degraded in relation to his role expectations of himself. The therapist is then prone to move in with elaborate speculations and inferences (Wynne 1971, p. 191).

But the dangers of concealment of meaning are equally great, leaving the therapist of the schizophrenic to walk on a "narrow ridge" between injection and concealment of meaning. The formalities of classical analytic practice are often wrongly understood to call for the withholding of meaning to an extreme degree, despite the evidence that Freud himself did not behave in such a nonparticipant manner. Schizophrenics who have little ability to observe themselves are apt to experience therapeutic neutrality as concealment and mystification. The "narrow ridge" between injection and concealment of meaning, as Wynne lays it out, is clearly healing through meeting:

> The first task of parents and therapists alike is to help establish a trustworthy relationship within which there can be reciprocal interchange, verbal and non-verbal. Then, and only then can failures of empathy, failures in sharing meaning, be checked out; steps to clarify misunderstandings and differences become possible (Wynne 1971, p. 192).

In his "reformulation" of the double-bind theory as it applies to therapy with schizophrenics, Wynne asserts that he feels less propelled than most of his therapist colleagues into trying to relieve anxiety and other symptoms quickly with either drugs or psychosocial interventions. If one lives with the anxiety produced by double binds and the circumstances that have induced it, valuable learning, which may forestall the endless, boring, and stultifying repetition of symptoms, may take place. In this connection, Wynne makes a valuable distinction between acute and chronic schizophrenics: "Acute schizophrenics have not yet given up in their efforts to find a solution to their problems and have not yet assumed, like the chronic schizophrenics, that the sharing of meaning is impossible and that unrelatedness is an enduring way of life." A therapist who is aware of this may hold back from those very drugs and other interventions that might push the acute schizophrenic into the hopelessness of the chronic one:

> Efforts to escape quickly from double binding situations, and therapeutic efforts to facilitate a quick escape, may forestall the opportunities to transform and enrich relationships. Despite the anguish which may be associated with the struggle, the rewarding opportunity for creative transformation of experience may be only possible by *not* escaping double binds for long periods of time. Creative passions, and even a certain zest and joy, may balance the inevitable pain and distress while one struggles to untangle double binds (Wynne 1976 p. 249f.).

In his recent monograph on the epigenesis of relational systems, Lyman Wynne gives indications of the stages of family development that have important implications for healing through meeting in family therapy. In striking parallel to what Erikson and others have put forward in theory of individual development, Wynne begins with the assumption "that relational processes within families and other enduring interpersonal systems follow one another in a certain developmental sequence." The four stages that Wynne sees as unfolding epigenetically in relational systems are:

1. *Attachment/caregiving*, complementary affectional bonding
2. *Communication*, sharing foci of attention and exchanging meanings and messages
3. *Joint problem-solving* and renewable sharing of tasks, interests, and activities
4. *Mutuality*, patterns of re-engagement, renewing and deepening each of the preceding modes of relatedness in a shifting pattern linked to the internal states of the participants and the external context (Wynne 1984, p. 300).

Throughout his deployment of these four epigenetic stages Wynne remains faithful to that double principle of distancing and relating that he found years before in Martin Buber's philosophical anthropology. This principle serves to give flexibility to the working of the stages in practice:

> The intensity of attachment/caregiving is strengthened by appropriately timed separation, whereas excessively prolonged and poorly timed separation can lead to detachment/rejection. . . . Also, temporary failures at joint problem-solving may serve as challenges leading to mastery, but, if excessively repeated, may lead to demoralized relational breakdown. . . . In relational systems, experiences of detachment/rejection, for example, are as essential to the further development of relatedness as are the experiences of attachment/caregiving (Wynne 1984, p. 301).

Wynne suggests that most life cycle changes in family role structure proceed inexorably regardless of the quality of relating of the participants with the result that the two are frequently out of synchrony. "If a family at the adolescent launching stage is still deeply enmeshed and emotionally overinvolved or is still communicating in an amorphous, fragmented, or constricted manner, problem-solving will be difficult indeed" (Wynne 1984, p. 307).

Wynne is particularly interested in communication and joint problem-solving because family therapists can directly help with these as opposed to attachment/caregiving and mutuality which must evolve on their own and cannot be aimed at directly without falling into what Farber calls willfulness. If communicating means a shared focusing of attention, leading to potentially shared meanings, it also means what Martin Buber calls "inclusion," or, in the language of R. M. Blakar, that Wynne quotes, "the individual's capacity to decenter and take the perspective of the other" (Blakar 1984, p. 44). An example of how one epigenetic process builds on another is the relation Wynne sees between attachment/caregiving and communication:

> When attachment/caregiving has not taken place, a shared cognitive and affective perspective cannot be well established. However, when

communication processes build upon attachment/caregiving, the participants draw upon abundant information that can be taken for granted (Wynne 1984, p. 307).

At the same time Wynne points out that mutuality does not necessarily or automatically emerge after the first three processes have developed. What it does do is "to draw upon accrued relational experience and skill from each of these stages in order to return selectively to whatever form of relatedness is appropriate to changing internal and external contexts" (Wynne 1984, p. 308). Wynne stresses again, as in his earlier work, that genuine mutuality means what we have called the "confirmation of otherness": It "not only tolerates divergence of self-interests, but thrives upon the recognition of such natural and inevitable divergence." Intimacy, on the other hand, Wynne sees historically as "more of a luxury than a developmental necessity in relational systems" (Wynne 1984, p. 309). What is more, "modern" couples are often so preoccupied with maintaining intimacy that they fail to give adequate priority to the necessities of day-to-day problem-solving. Therapists too, by neglecting what Buber called the "world of It," tend to prolong and promote pseudomutuality. Wynne sees intimacy as the subjective side of relatedness, the sharing of personal feelings, fantasies, and meaningful experiences in each of the four processes (Wynne 1984, pp. 309–312).

Wynne points to the usefulness of distinguishing between the "emotional bonding" found in attachment/caregiving and that found in mutuality and intimacy. "The epigenetic model has implications for identifying points of family impasses," Wynne concludes, "and for giving priorities to preventive and therapeutic interventions that are likely to be effective." Wynne emphasizes, in particular, "the desirability of strengthening joint problem-solving skills in therapy before mutuality and intimacy can be expected to stabilize" (Wynne 1984, p. 313f.).

# Ivan Boszormenyi-Nagy

The most decisive breakthrough to healing through meeting beyond the intrapsychic has been the work of Ivan Boszormenyi-Nagy. This work culminates in his contextual approach not only to intergenerational family therapy, but to all therapy as well.

From his understanding of family relatedness Boszormenyi-Nagy extracts some quite specific guidelines for family therapists, all of which fall within and contribute to a deeper understanding of healing through meeting. In order to exert a therapeutic influence, the therapist has to remain a discrete individual, thus impelling the family members to extricate themselves from their wishful symbiotic fantasies. Family therapists should guide, but not take over, real life decisions.

> They should help make sense out of the chaos; they should interpret where there is projecting, filibustering, denial of manipulations, and a variety of other resistance games. Finally, the therapists should reward the pursuit of mourning and serious exploration of the introjects by taking notice of these efforts as they occur. They must act as good parents through their incorruptible strength and their constructive empathy (Boszormenyi-Nagy and Spark 1973, p. 127).

Family therapists have to exemplify and *live* in trust and confidence in the frustrated and often hateful family atmosphere. In order to guide the family to a more meaningful marriage relationship for the parents and separation and meaningful marriages and parenthood for the offspring, they must remain open to deep, primary process clues in the context of an actual family drama, yet not selectively ignore defensive façades that resemble those of their own family. They must not be trapped into wanting to save one family member from another. At the same time, they must be alert to notice the variety of complex ways in which the partners are "grounded" in each other's personality. "As the family's style of interactions moves from symbiosis toward individuation, the capacity of the offspring for genuine encounter increases." In this process, the therapist and the family members gain mutual access to one another's unconscious dynamics, which may even reach a level of "psychotic involvement" or "therapeutic psychosis" (Boszormenyi-Nagy and Spark 1973, pp. 128–131, 134f.).

Even in individual therapy, Boszormenyi-Nagy points out, it is the relational context that produces the most significant changes. Coming to grips with issues involves the decision either to interrupt or to deepen the therapeutic relationship at each new point of resistance. This carries over to conjoint family therapy, which has the advantage of dealing with transference distortions in the relevant context of close real relationships in which alone certain fixated intrapsychic constellations can be reworked. In addition, the family therapist will design therapeutic goals in terms of the stage in which the *family* is fixated. "The autistically unrelated family may need a suffusion of trust." The therapist's expressions of anger or despair with the mistrusting members might even convey an inner belief in the existence of some goodness in life. Another central goal of family therapy is enabling children to obtain "workable" models for identification (Boszormenyi-Nagy and Spark 1973, p. 132f.).

Boszormenyi-Nagy sees the "invisible loyalties"—the fateful commitment and devotion that are important determinants in family relationships—as making for a deeper binding than the genuine I–Thou dialogue that is possible between those who are not related. My son is "a unique counterpart of my existential realm" whose meaning for me cannot be embodied by anyone else, for it is part of a multigenerational relationship system he and I share. Nor can talking *about* family relationships in group therapy or encounter groups take the place of actual family therapy, for it lacks "the pressure of relevance, which gives relational therapy its greatest leverage" (Boszormenyi-Nagy and Spark, 1973, p. 93).

This does not mean that the therapist does not play a part in the healing through meeting that takes place in family therapy. Family therapists must be open and expose themselves, and they must let this affect their relationships to their own families. "It is our conviction that growth in our personal life is not only inseparable from growth in our professional experience, but that it is our greatest technical tool" (Boszormenyi-Nagy and Spark 1973, p. 13). At the same time, "transference" in the family therapy system has a very different meaning than it has in individual therapy. Freud could speak of the patient's self-deception concerning the nature of the patient–doctor relationship as a cognitive error, a distortion in perception and attitudes. Family therapists, in contrast, are more interested in the existential implications of transference. Transferred attitudes and expectations carry the continuity of past, unresolved obligations and expectations of family legacies, and signify factual events. This means that positive transference to the therapist is not always possible or desirable, since it can amount to intrinsic disloyalty to the rejected parent. Aside from his efforts at redefining terms of a relational ethical dynamic, Boszormenyi-Nagy's goals of family therapy are best understood in terms of Buber's anthropology of *distancing* and *relating* as the two ontological movements fundamental to human existence. To Boszormenyi-Nagy, therapy can never stop with getting out the buried hostility toward parents, since that would inevitably lead to a violation of the universal legacy of filial loyalty, a rejection of the therapist, or a building up of guilt. "In our clinical experience, no one ends up a winner through a conclusion which predicates a hopelessly incorrigible resentment and contempt towards one's parent." In this sense, the term loyalty describes both the legacy (expectations) and its fulfillment.

> While conscious confrontation with one's hateful feelings amounts to progress, it does not represent a therapeutic end point. Unless the person can struggle with his negative feelings and resolve them by acts based on positive, helpful attitudes towards his parent, he cannot really free himself of the intrinsic loyalty problem and has to "live" the conflict, even after the parent's death, through pathological defensive patterns (Boszormenyi-Nagy and Spark 1973, p. 20).

Invisible loyalty means that frequently the outcome is the rejection and scapegoating of the spouse or the therapist in order to escape from the annihilating effect of victory over one's parents. "The cost of such victory would be guilt, shame, and a paradoxically binding loyalty, disowned, denied, yet paralyzingly adhered to at the same time" (Boszormenyi-Nagy and Spark 1973, p. 20). The positive goal of therapy is a dialectic between individuation and family loyalty, for the former cannot be achieved at the cost of simply severing family ties. Every step leading toward the child's true emancipation "tends to touch on the emotionally charged issue of every member's denied but wished-for everlasting symbiotic togetherness with the family of origin" (Boszormenyi-Nagy and Spark 1973, p. 21). The pathological expression of the failure to achieve this balance can coincide with what Murray Bowen calls the "undifferentiated ego mass" or what Boszormenyi-Nagy calls the "polarized fusion of roles," where instead of a genuinely antithetical dialogue of unique persons, people are symbiotically related through roles. Individual autonomy is not viewed mainly within the confines of ego strength and intrapsychic resourcefulness and effective adaptation, as in individual therapy, but is in a dynamically antithetic relationship with loyalty to the family of origin.

"In contrast with individual psychotherapy, family or relationship-based therapy proceeds step by step to remove deeper and deeper layers of *inauthentic loyalty definitions.*" The angry and resentful feelings expressed between the generations provide an opportunity to begin to break up what has been projected onto or attributed to the other person. The family therapist can encourage a mutual dialogue so that the aged parent (the grandparent) can reveal his own past, as well as current longings. When each generation is helped to face the nature of the current relationships, exploring the real nature of the commitments and responsibility that flows from such involvements, an increased reciprocal understanding and mutual compassion between the generations results. The grandchildren, in particular, benefit from this reconciliation between the generations; they are helped to be freed of scapegoated or parentified roles and they have a hope for age-appropriate gratifications plus a model for reconciling their conflicts with their parents. Any desperate, dramatic *acting-out* on the part of a child, Boszormenyi-Nagy points out, can always be considered by the therapist as a signal that the family as a whole is asking for help and as an indication of the necessity of working with the rest of the family and placing the responsibility for change primarily upon the adults (Boszormenyi-Nagy and Spark 1973, pp. 134, 224, 245, 376).

The child should be able to count on being loved and accepted by the family regardless of his earned merit. Yet at the same time, a capacity for meaningful contribution should be expected of every child (Boszormenyi-

Nagy and Spark 1973, pp. 83f., 87, 89). This also applies to a grown-up "child":

> Our concept of relational autonomy pictures the individual as retaining a modified yet fully responsible and sensitively concerned dialogue with the original family members. In this sense the individual can be liberated to engage in full, wholly personal relationships only to the extent that he has become capable of responding to parental devotion with concern on his part and with the realization that receiving is intrinsically connected with owing in return (Boszormenyi-Nagy and Spark 1973, p. 105).

In contrast to those family therapists who hold that the therapist must not judge, Boszormenyi-Nagy espouses a "multidirectional partiality" in which the therapist will be partial at one time to one member of the family and at another time to another, according to the relative merit of their sides. The family therapist must be strong enough to be included in the family system as present for each and every member, yet remain outside in the role of facilitator for emotional change and growth. In the beginning phase of treatment, it is essential that the family therapist try to establish some order of communication and to create an atmosphere of trust. Regardless of the family members' chaotic and provocative behavior toward the therapist, he has to maintain a sense of calm and reason. While being sympathetic and compassionate, he has to continuously hold them to increased understanding as well as modification of their infantile behavior, in order to help facilitate the growth process.

In the case of team therapy, the family therapists' capacity for relating to one another with openness and directness in facing intrateam conflicts and for revealing genuine concern and appreciation of one another's abilities provide the family therapy team with the strength to respond appropriately to different kinds of families and the multiple problems that they bring with them (Boszormenyi-Nagy and Spark 1973, p. 349). Above all, the family therapist must have that "inclusion" of which Buber speaks, by which the therapist "imagines the real," that is, experiences the patient's side of the relationship without losing his own. But there is also a demand that he places on the members of the family.

> The contract means that the therapist has to offer and actually make himself available as willing to help all members, whether they come to therapy sessions or not. In turn, he has to extract commitment for participation from all members of the family. He wants all those present to expose their opinions, needs, and wishes for help, and he tries to make sure that the messages of even the smallest child are being heard and responded to (Boszormenyi-Nagy and Spark 1973, p. 16).

Here we see multidirectional partiality at its most concrete.

In *Invisible Loyalties* (1973), Boszormenyi-Nagy calls for reciprocal justice and fair acknowledgment to rebalance the "merit ledger" between the generations. This can be done only through listening to each member's subjective construction of his accountability to the rest of the family. Boszormenyi-Nagy's touchstone of reality is not functional efficiency, but rather the intrinsic balances between hidden loyalty ties and exploitations. This leads, in turn, to what I call the "dialogue of touchstones," acknowledgment and exoneration in which each person's point of view is confirmed precisely through coming into dialogue with the opposing views of others. The goal of Boszormenyi-Nagy's family therapy is not the community of affinity, or like-mindedness, but what I call the "community of otherness."[1] In marriage, it is not just two individuals who join, but rather two quite different family systems of merit. If one does not intuitively perceive this, one marries the other only in fantasy, as the wishfully improved re-creation of one's own family of origin. Each mate may then struggle to coerce the other to be accountable for those of his or her felt injustices and accrued merit that comes from his or her family of origin. By improving their reciprocal loyalty exchange with their families of origin, Boszormenyi-Nagy's family therapy helps husband and wife relate to each other and to their children.

Thus, confirmation in the dialogue of touchstones leading to the community of otherness is both the way and the goal of Boszormenyi-Nagy's family therapy. "Personal exploitation is measurable only on a subjective scale which has been built into the person's sense of the meaning of his entire existence" (Boszormenyi-Nagy and Spark 1973, p. 81). Being confirmed is not a matter of the *quality* of the world's goods that one gets, but rather of "a reality-based or action dialogue, which is more than the sum total of two persons' subjective experiences" (Boszormenyi-Nagy and Spark 1973, p. 82). The concept of reality-testing in Freudian psychology is a comparatively monological one, in which the patient is either reality-bound or subject to distortion. This means, as Ronald Laing has pointed out, that the psychiatrist determines what is "normal" and invalidates the experience of the patient. And it means, as Boszormenyi-Nagy has stressed, that "the psychotherapist, together with his patient, develop what is normal and implicitly invalidate the experience and needs of all partners to the patient's close relationships."[2]

In a 1979 summation of "contextual therapy," Boszormenyi-Nagy (1981) further elaborates the multidirected partiality of the family therapist as "an actively structuring and guiding principle that leads to an

---

[1]See Friedman 1972; Friedman 1974, Chapter 19; and Friedman 1983, Chapter 13.
[2]Letter from Ivan Boszormenyi-Nagy to Maurice Friedman, June 21, 1974.

elicitory rather than prescriptive or judgmental intervention." The therapist guides the family members to the multilaterality of fairness in which one person's being heard or being held accountable makes it easier to hear others or to let oneself be called to account. Thus, the therapist helps them take the first steps toward engagement in a mutuality of trust and trustworthiness. "The lack of trustworthiness in one's relational world is the primary pathogenic condition of human life." The therapist can address this problem of eroding trust by eliciting every family member's own responsible review of his or her side of mutual entitlements and indebtedness.

Boszormenyi-Nagy's definition of the goal of contextual therapy, "rejunction," is essentially identical with Buber's call to overcome existential guilt and re-establish the dialogue with the world through repairing the injured order of existence:

> The goal of contextual therapy is rejunction, that is, 1) an acknowledgment of the principle of equitable multilaterality, 2) an ethically definable process of re-engagement in living mutuality, and 3) a commitment to fair balances of give-and-take. In other words, family members explore their capacity for reworking stagnant imbalances in how each of them uses the other and in how they are available to each other. The courage they invest in the review and repair of inadvertent relational corruption and exploitation yields returns in therapeutic resources, the chief among them being: earned trustworthiness (Boszormenyi-Nagy 1981).

The balance of relational fairness depends on a relatively equitable investment of trust in caring mutuality; for trustworthiness is the fundamental resource of family therapy.

Boszormenyi-Nagy differentiates between both the traditionally neutral or impartial therapeutic stance and the generalized notion of empathy, on the one hand, and the multidirected partiality that requires sequential, transitory siding "against" someone, on the other. In order to be able to side with the merit of now one, now another family member, the family therapist must have the capacity for an "as if" participation in the merit of the relational position of each and every family member. "Even more important, perhaps, is the need to hear hidden and unspoken aspects of exploitation and victimization, especially as they affect small, dependent children." At the same time, the family therapist must keep in mind that it is unfair and unwise to make a parent concede his or her role as a victimizer without considering the parent's own past victimization as a child. The therapist must be sensitive to the signals that a family member makes that he or she is not ready for assuming relational accountability without first receiving more evidence of the therapist's empathic concern. Having sided with the parents in their past roles as victimized and potential victimizers, the therapist will also find it easier to be partial to the child without the risk that implicit disloyalty becomes the price of the child's therapeutic progress (Boszormenyi-Nagy 1981).

Although at times Boszormenyi-Nagy may have seemed to transpose dynamic psychology, with its hidden determinants, onto the broader stage of the family, he cautions the contextual therapist against reifying and unduly personifying transactional-systemic patterns as the ultimate sources of an impersonal "family malfunction" or "pathology." "These patterns are epiphenomena of the underlying multiple self–other dynamics, ultimately regulated by the ethics of the quality and symmetry of trust investments and balances of fairness." He also cautions against a mere prescriptive rearrangement or "restructuring" of family transactions; for this restructuring may risk long-range disloyalty and a newly found, passive dependence on the therapist. Rather, the therapist must become a consultant for the catalysis of a living give-and-take of a more equitable kind (Boszormenyi-Nagy 1981).

In contrast to traditional psychology and psychodynamic literature, which generally underemphasizes the self's investment in concern and caring for others, in contextual therapy the therapist must have the conviction that caring about the partner's justified merits enables the one who cares to move toward autonomous individuation and growth:

> By investing appropriate new initiatives of trust, he increases his entitlement to acknowledgement of his acts of filial devotion, and to the pursuit of his own autonomous goals, *e.g.*, to forming peer relationships. Consequently, his moves toward autonomy become progressively liberated from encumberment with an immobilizing guilt born of disloyalty (Boszormenyi-Nagy 1981).

Through its trust-building strategies, contextual therapy is able to internalize the therapist's concern for fairness and trustworthiness, mobilize the resources of fair reciprocity via an examination of intermember accountability, differentiate between the unchangeable fact of shared rootedness and the vicissitudes of such emotional attitudes as love or hate, realistically rebalance stagnant interindividual ledgers, revise and rework invisible loyalties, correct invalid ethical substitutions, deparentify children, and transform passively dependent attitudes into actively accountable initiative and planning. Among the advantages of contextual therapy is the fact that its ethical emphasis is universally applicable to the human condition and that its "language" of fairness versus unfairness is accessible to uneducated people, as well as to people of high educational or social status.

The exploration of balances of entitlement and indebtedness is a highly effective intervention with many cases of depression, as well as in patients with impulses toward suicide and self-sacrificial behavior. Instead of focusing on an effort to fight pathology or impose "change" in the service of social conformity, contextual therapy makes use of the resources of responsibility and trust inherent in hidden relational investments. "It also helps to produce more reliable, lasting therapeutic change by staving off the development of existential guilt over symptomatic improvement with its implications of disloyalty." Finally, through its multidirected partiality, the contextual approach prevents the handing down of pathology to future generations and serves the present generation's concern for the survival of their offspring (Boszormenyi-Nagy 1981).

In another recent article Boszormenyi-Nagy and his close associate, Barbara Krasner, describe contextual therapy as "trust-based therapy," which they characterize in turn as a radical departure from the traditional medical or psychological individual perspectives in the direction of "concern, trustworthiness, adversariness, exploitation and fair mutuality between family members." They emphasize that the personal uniqueness of family members is just as much a concern of contextual therapy as their personally exchangeable "systemic" roles. This uniqueness includes a person's relatedness to his or her multigenerational roots, with their specific racial, religious, and ethnic facets. A trust-based therapy regards signs of striking mistrust as potential resources for building trust. It also sees trust as a necessity for the acceptance of periods of transitory unfairness, which are unavoidable in any relationship.

The therapeutic significance of the lifelong implications of parent–child relationships has been grossly disregarded by classical family therapy, Boszormenyi-Nagy and Krasner claim:

> Who lived for them, who wanted them, who was available to them and who made material and relational investments in them are fundamental factors in their attitudes toward the world. The fact of roots and legacies in common represents a non-substitutive bond among people that not only outlasts physical and geographical separations from families of origin, but also influences the degree to which offspring can be free to commit themselves to relationships outside of their original ties, including marriage and parenthood of their own. The long term legacies of parental accountability are inescapably weighty (Boszormenyi-Nagy and Krasner 1980).

The therapists' overt concern with relational responsibility growing out of these legacies leads them at once into depth dimensions of relationship, including guiding family members through the most heated, direct, and controversial aspects of their relationship—their responsibility for trustworthiness. Like the Hasidic notion of serving with the "evil" urge, trustworthiness enables ego strength to invest itself in controlling one's tendencies toward an exploitative misuse of close relationships. "From the perspective of contextual therapy, the fairness of the balance of give-and-take in relationship is a more sensitive and more accurate measure of reality distortions than is the insight-oriented self-reflection of one individual."

Boszormenyi-Nagy and Krasner see multidirected partiality as a strategy that begins a constructive process of trust building, one requiring therapeutic courage to side temporarily *against* family members as well as with them, but one that also protects the therapist against countertransference reactions. Building trust makes possible the recognition and reworking of long-standing balances of unfairness in the legacies of parents, thus freeing them from defensive and retributive behavior and freeing their offspring from being overburdened by them and condemned to a similar fate. Building trust includes a respect for equitability on every member's own terms, an integrity of give-and-take in relationship, a mutuality of consideration, and a capacity for re-distributing the returns that reside in joint accounts of trust investments.

As various family members turn to the therapist for help, he himself becomes a major, if interim, recipient of their trust investments. The therapist can inject his own regard for accountability and integrity into the family's relationships and can elicit responsible attitudes that may lead to a more genuine dialogue among them. He proceeds on the conviction that trustworthiness follows earned merit rather than power, that children should not be forced to guarantee age-inappropriate nurturance to their parents or be used as unilateral, captive investors in their parents' depleted accounts of trustworthiness. But the therapist cannot function indefinitely as a primary source of trustworthiness for his patients or his own resources become depleted as he becomes a captive of their expectations that he supply hope, trust, dependent support, limitless empathy, and one-sided partiality. Thus, what is central to Buber in *I and Thou*—learning to meet others and hold one's ground when one meets them—is central to Boszormenyi-Nagy's family therapy.

Boszormenyi-Nagy characterizes contextual therapy as a major recasting of the approach that he took in *Invisible Loyalties*. If this is indeed the case, it is even more in the direction of healing through meeting. "Contextual therapy assumes that the leverages of all psychotherapeutic interventions are anchored in relational determinants," write Boszormenyi-Nagy and David Ulrich, co-authors of a massive monograph, *Contextual Family Therapy* (Boszormenyi-Nagy and Ulrich 1981). Whether one or several persons are present, the goal of contextual therapy is a responsible treatment of intermember issues of fairness and trust on the part of both participant and therapist. The multilaterality of the relational ethical dynamic precludes the use of the term "patient," but, in contrast with the systemic view, it retains interest in each individual's subjective vantage point. Here a distinction must be drawn between those therapies that use transference, that is, substitutive relational contexts, and those that offer assistance within the participants' original relational context.

Defining moves toward trustworthy relatedness as "rejunctive," moves away from it as "disjunctive," and "relational stagnation" as familial disengagement from concern about fairness, Boszormenyi-Nagy and Ulrich posit the existence of a reservoir of trust out of which the child can initiate repayment of trust toward the parents. When the parents maintain a balance of fairness, the child's basic loyalty commitment is reinforced, but even when they do not, the child's response can provide the leverage needed to obtain a rejunctive move from the parents. Exploitative parents draw on the child to help make up for what they dissipate through infinite overpayment to the generation preceding them and, though existentially guilty, they feel very little guilt. As the child gains in growth and power, on the other hand, he or she becomes increasingly accountable for taking action to preserve the ledger balance.

The true give-and-take nature of the ledger is shown by the fact that a parent who persistently declines to claim an entitlement and persists in a pattern of overpayment may create as much developmental detriment as one who constantly demands too much. The child who has no access to direct knowledge of the multigenerational ledger remains vulnerable and may "buy into" the expectation that the debt to the parents is an endless one that takes priority over every other human concern. On the other hand, the child who shoplifts or who refuses to eat (anorexia) may be making an intrinsic contribution by forcing into the open an issue of human balance.

Boszormenyi-Nagy and Ulrich hold that the "revolving slate" aspect of invisible filial loyalties is the chief factor in family and marital dysfunction because the grown child of the stagnant family will be unable to weigh what is fair in relationships to spouse and children and will manifest this disengagement through frigidity, indifference, or even cruelty. Liberation from this revolving cycle of destructive action can take place only through the discovery of resources of trustworthiness; the damage to parentified children is not the reversal of roles, but rather the unilateral depletion of the child's trust resources. Even the seemingly well sibling who appears to have escaped the pathogenic system may be caught in a guilt-laden commitment to overavailability in which he or she may take care of the entire family's needs for reason and organization, allowing the others to enjoy regressive gratifications.

After the therapist has helped the family members of the formerly stagnant family to develop trust bases, he can encourage autonomy in problem-solving in which such transitions as adolescence, separation, marriage, and death demand new commitments and new freedom of choice. The therapist's efforts to re-open issues of trust with such families may provoke responses of rage or despair all the more intense because they are experienced *in vivo* rather than in the substitute context of the therapeutic transference.

As trust deepens, the therapist can be more openly confronting, offering concrete behavioral options toward achieving the goals of re-engagement and rejunction. But whether working with several family members or an individual, the context of overall balance of fairness remains the same. "We do not, for example, seek to restore a school-phobic child to functioning without regard for the mother who may decompensate if the child leaves the house." Since the focus of contextual therapy is on the original, rather than the substitutive therapeutic context, it is not essential to deal with derivative symbolic materials, and since it is on multilaterality, it is not necessary to ask, "What are your needs?" which can become a bottomless pit. As family members become more multilaterally fair, they change and improve the nature of their entitlement, thus standing up for themselves in a different and deeper way than the more common individualistic approach. "This strategy is especially effective with persons whose ego functions show little strength."

Contextual therapy includes in its own way concern for age-appropriate power and role structures in the family members. "When an honest statement from one member becomes ammunition for his victimization, the therapist moves at once to block this disjunctive effort." The therapist sets family members the task of defining issues that have depleted trust among them and helps each member clarify his position to prevent the dialogue from breaking down. "But if the therapist steps in to make the point for a person, the therapist may feel relief while the work stops." The therapist assesses the interindividual ledgers of the family as the dialogue unfolds, but he does not explain their accounts to the family members. He balances siding with one family member with the demand for accountability from that person. Above all, he helps the offspring in their task of exonerating the parents through dispelling "the cloud of shame, blame, and implicit contempt that hangs over the parents' lives and thus envelops the children too."

Ivan Boszormenyi-Nagy distinguishes the "context" of contextual therapy from "the obvious fit of any individual into transactional systems":

> It is the *ethics* of the personal *sides* of human existence that is the most important aspect of our relational context. This includes each person as a unique center of his universe, rather than regarding him as an item of feedback corrections or escalations. It deals with ethical balances between family members even before they get inundated by guilt and

judgmentalism. It deals with the ethics of relational options of several persons at a time. It is not *the* individual and his surroundings.[3]

Liberation from the revolving cycle of destructive action takes place only through discovery of resources of trustworthiness. Contextual therapy helps in such discovery not only through bringing family members into genuine dialogue with one another, but also through teaching them to stand up *against* guilt and *for* their own entitlements. The enhancement of the family's dormant resources for trustworthiness requires mutuality of effort among members through which they become more multilaterally fair and in so doing change and improve the nature of their own entitlement. Here, too, meeting others and holding one's ground go together: "This is a different and deeper way of standing up for one's self."[4]

The culmination of Boszormenyi-Nagy's family therapy, in its most recent formulation, is opening up people's capacity for extending due caring to each other, in accordance with relational responsibility, especially as it concerns posterity, giving family members an opportunity for positive position taking, eliciting responses through responsible dialogue, and giving priority of consideration to the vulnerably exposed children.[5]

One question that we might raise concerning contextual therapy has to do with the distinctive priority role that it ascribes to legacy-based, parent–child relationship over peer-level dialogue. The great service of contextual therapy is that it corrects the individualism of intrapsychic and analytical therapy and with it such romantic and illusory notions as that a relationship should be judged only by the degree to which it fulfills the individual "needs" and realizes the individual potentialities of each of its members, or that when two people marry, they marry each other and not their families as well. What Freud did for the field of psychoanalysis, Boszormenyi-Nagy has done for family therapy: Boszormenyi-Nagy has uncovered the *invisible* loyalties and the equally hidden multigenerational family ledger of merit that have been overlooked. At the same time, we must remember that the "invisible loyalties" often represent the pathology of the family as well as its potential health. The emphasis upon the vertical, multigenerational dimension of relationship is necessary, in part, because the partners in marriage bring their family of origin into their new relationships. Without realizing it, they tend to place their mates within the old family system or, what amounts to the same thing, to see them as the magic helpers that will save them from their family system.

Marriage, as Buber has said, means "the acknowledgement of vital, many-faced otherness." Otherwise it is not a true marriage. Each marriage

---

[3]Letter from Ivan Boszormenyi-Nagy to Maurice Friedman, June 17, 1980.
[4]Ivan Boszormenyi-Nagy and David N. Ulrich (1981). *Contextual Family Therapy.*
[5]Based on a letter from Ivan Boszormenyi-Nagy to Maurice Friedman, June 27, 1984.

ideally means bringing not only the individual partners but also their families, their family systems, and their multigenerational ledgers of merit into genuine dialogue. When this is *not* done, the new family becomes stagnant and the progress of the childen toward their rightful autonomy becomes impossible. Thus the healthy ongoingness of the generations not only is not impeded by the dialogue with otherness, it is made possible by it. This dialogue is, in the first instance, on the peer level: one's mate is one's peer and, what is more, does not come from one's family of origin. In the second instance, it also extends to the dialogue between the mates and the parents of their spouses, on the one hand, and their own children, on the other. If it is traditionally difficult to relate to one's in-laws as one's family, it is, in fact, no less difficult to relate to one's children in their real otherness and uniqueness and to avoid that trilogy of binding, delegating, and expelling to which Helm Stierlin has pointed as three of the ways in which parents deny children their existence in their own right and seek instead to subordinate them to an imposed family system (Stierlin 1974).

# Part II

# CONFIRMATION AND HEALING THROUGH DIALOGUE

# Chapter 10

# Confirmation and the Development of the Person

Mutual confirmation is essential to becoming a self—a person who realizes his uniqueness precisely through his relation to other selves whose distance from him is completed by his distance from them. We do not exist as self-sufficient monads that only secondarily come into relationship with one another, any more than we are mere cells in a social organism. We exist as persons who need to be confirmed in our uniqueness by persons essentially other than ourselves.

> The basis of man's life with man is twofold, and it is one—the wish of every man to be confirmed as what he is, even as what he can become, by men; and the innate capacity in man to confirm his fellow men in this way. That this capacity lies so immeasurably fallow constitutes the real weakness and questionableness of the human race; actual humanity exists only where this capacity unfolds.
>
> . . . . . . . . . . . . . . . . . . . . . . . . . . . . . . . . . . . . . . . . . . . . . . . . . . . . . . . .
>
> Sent forth from the natural domain of species into the hazard of the solitary category, surrounded by the air of a chaos which came into being with him, secretly and bashfully man watches for a Yes which can come to him only from one human person to another (Buber 1966, pp. 67f., 71).

We live in an ever flowing interchange. If we can confirm ourselves, it is only because we have been confirmed by others, and if others can confirm us, it is only because we can accept being confirmed by them. To be confirmed we must be made present by the other as the persons we are. This confirmation takes place neither out of selfishness—because it is to the interest of the other to do so—nor out of altruism—because the other selflessly sets herself or himself aside to minister to our needs—but out of the fundamental reality of the partnership of existence. We do not have to choose between the individual and society, solitude and togetherness. Rather we have to hold the tension of being at one and the same time separate and together, ever more deeply in dialogue and, just as a result, ever more fully unique.

Carl Rogers illustrates this ever flowing interchange and the interrelation of dialogue and uniqueness in his own most recent statements on confirmation:

> When I am not prized and appreciated, I not only *feel* very much diminished, but my behavior is actually affected by my feelings. When I am prized, I blossom and expand, I am an interesting individual. In a hostile or unappreciative group, I am just not much of anything. People wonder, with very good reason, how did he ever get a reputation? I wish I had the strength to be more similar in both kinds of groups, but actually the person I am in a warm and interested group is different from the person I am in a hostile or cold group.
>
> Thus, prizing or loving and being prized or loved is experienced as very growth enhancing. A person who is loved appreciatively, not possessively, blooms and develops his own unique self. The person who loves nonpossessively is himself enriched. This, at least, has been my experience (Rogers 1980, p. 23).
>
> A finely tuned understanding by another individual gives the recipient a sense of personhood of identity. Laing (1965) has said that "the sense of identity requires the existence of another by whom one is known." Buber has also spoken of the need to have our existence confirmed by another. Empathy gives that needed confirmation that one does exist as a separate valued person with an identity (Rogers 1980, p. 154f.).

This mutual confirmation of human beings is most fully realized in what Martin Buber calls "making present," an event that happens partially wherever persons come together, but in its essential structure, only rarely. Making the other present means to "imagine the real," to imagine quite concretely what another person is wishing, feeling, perceiving, and thinking. One, to some extent, wills what the other is willing, thinks what he is thinking, feels what he is feeling. The particular pain I inflict on another surges up in myself until paradoxically we are embraced in a common situation. This event is not complete until he knows himself made present by me and until this knowledge induces the process of his inmost self-becoming. "For the inmost growth of the self is not accomplished, as people like to suppose today, in man's relation to himself, but . . . in the making present of another self and in the knowledge that one is made present in his own self by the other."

True confirmation means that I confirm my partner as this existing being, even while I oppose him as the person that I am. To confirm him in this way I need the aid of "imagining the real." This is not intuitive perception, in the ordinary sense of the term, but rather a bold swinging into the other that demands the intensest action of my being. Here the realm of my act is the particular real person who steps up to meet me, the person I seek to make present in all his wholeness, unity, and uniqueness. I can only do this as a partner, standing in a common situation with the other, and even then one's address to the other may remain unanswered and the dialogue may die in seed.

We have in common with every thing the ability to become an object of observation, writes Buber in *The Knowledge of Man*. But it is the privilege of man, through the hidden action of his being, to be able to impose an insurmountable limit to his objectification. Only as a partner can a human being be perceived as an existing wholeness. To become aware of a human being means to perceive his wholeness as person defined by spirit: to perceive the dynamic center that stamps on all his utterances, actions, and attitudes the tangible sign of oneness. Such an awareness is impossible if, and so long as, the other is for me the detached object of my observation; for he will not thus yield his wholeness and its center. It is possible only when he becomes present for me.

The essential problematic of the sphere of the between, writes Buber, is the duality of being and seeming. The person dominated by being gives himself to the other spontaneously without thinking about the image of himself awakened in the beholder. The "seeming man," in contrast, is primarily concerned with what the other thinks of him, and produces a look calculated to make himself appear "spontaneous," "sincere," or whatever he thinks will win the other's approval. This seeming destroys the authenticity of the life between person and person and with it the authenticity of human existence, in general. The tendency toward seeming originates in man's need for confirmation and in his desire to be confirmed falsely rather than not to be confirmed at all. "To give in to this tendency is the real cowardice of man," writes Buber; "to withstand it is his real courage."

This distinction between "being man" and "seeming man" enables Buber to substitute for the older notions of man's being good or bad by nature a more modern realization: even though some persons appear to be entirely determined by seeming, it is only the successive layers of deception that give the illusion of individuals who are seeming men by their very nature. "I have never known a young person who seemed to me irretrievably bad," writes Buber. "Man is, as man, redeemable."

We need to be confirmed in our uniqueness, yet we need to be confirmed by others who are different from us. This is not a paradox so long as genuine interhumanness stands at the center of human existence; for our very existence as selves originates in and perseveres through the interhuman. But other persons, including our parents, are not always willing to confirm us in our uniqueness. We cannot become ourselves without other people who call us to realize our created uniqueness in response to our life tasks. Many of us, unfortunately, have experienced "confirmation" of a very different nature, confirmation with strings attached. Many of us are, in effect, offered a contract that reads: "We will confirm you only if you will conform to our model of the good child, the good churchgoer, the good student, the good citizen, the good soldier."

Once we have bought that bargain, and most of us buy it more or less, we are placed in an impossible double bind. As long as we are confirmed in this way, we know somewhere in our heart of hearts, even though we forget it consciously, that it is not *we* who are being confirmed, but rather the role that we are acting in order to please significant others. Yet if we try to rebel against this pseudo-confirmation and break out of it, the other half of the contract goes into effect. We have, without knowing it, internalized the proposition that if we do not act this way, we *cannot* be confirmed because we are not lovable. As a result, we isolate ourselves far beyond the power of those significant others to do so. This is the paradox at the heart of all conditional confirmation.

Now we are able to see why "inclusion," or "imagining the real," lies at the heart of confirmation. No one can confirm us through empathy—because they do not give of themselves thereby—or through identification—because they miss us in our uniqueness and filter through only what is like themselves. They can confirm us only if they bring themselves in their uniqueness into dialogue with us in ours and confirm us while holding in tension the "overagainstness," and, if necessary, even the opposition that comes out of this unique relationship between two unique persons. If, instead, they offer us conditional confirmation, a "contract" whereby we are confirmed only according to our good behavior, then, as we have seen, the confirmation that we receive becomes at best problematic.[1]

---

[1]For a full-scale discussion of the problematic of confirmation, see Friedman 1983, chapters 5–8.

# Chapter 11

# Disconfirmation and "Mental Illness"

*Sequential evolution of mutual validation occurs in its most intense form in family life. Once the validation process goes off the track, we have emotional and psychological disturbance. Then we have a lifelong problem. One cannot be validated except by some one whom one validates. It is a mutual escalation process.*

Saul L. Brown, M.D., Director of Psychiatry,
Cedars Sinai Medical Center, Los Angeles

If confirmation is central to human and interhuman existence, then it follows that disconfirmation, especially in the earliest stages of life, must be a major factor in psychopathology, or what is popularly miscalled "mental illness." Instead of finding the genesis of neurosis and psychosis in frustrated gratification of drives, à la Freud, we shall find it more basically and more frequently in disconfirming situations in the family that impair the child's basic trust. "One can hypothetically assume that if the parent is prematurely lost as a component of the child's identity delineating ground," writes Ivan Boszormenyi-Nagy, "a fixated bottomless craving for trust becomes his permanent character trait" (Boszormenyi-Nagy 1965, p. 120). Nagy's hypothesis is confirmed at length by the theories and clinical practice of Heinz Kohut, Harold Searles, Ronald Laing, Helm Stierlin, and Carl Rogers.

## Harold Searles

Harold Searles focuses on the world of the schizophrenic and tries, through understanding it, to discern a path that might lead to healing. Searles, like Kohut, traces the genesis of psychopathology to disconfirmation. But Searles sees this disconfirmation more in terms of the place of the child in the family rather than in terms of the introjection of significant mirroring and/or idealized others.

Searles sees the child's identity as coming into being in response to the pressures of other family members and the role they assign the child. When the child has no well-established, developing identity in the family, no single predominant and consistent family role from which to view himself and the outer world, then he no longer feels his own inner reality to be that of a single, living human entity and his family-world is rendered chaotic and ambiguous. This ambiguity extends to his perceptions themselves; "the child cannot build up realistic perceptions except insofar as there is a reliable, mutually trusting emotional climate in which he knows where he stands with each of his parents—knows who he is to them, and knows that he is loved and accepted by them." Though this *could* be further refined to Kohut's mirroring and idealized parents, it is significant that Searles' language is interpersonal, whereas Kohut's remains intrapsychic. In Searles, the relationship itself is emphasized; in Kohut, it is what each person *is* that is important first of all with the relationship more a secondary derivative.

In the families of schizophrenics, there is so little trustful, leisurely sharing of one another's thinking that the child has little time and emotional security for weighing perceptions before meanings must be imposed upon them. The child must react to perceptions quickly, confirming emotional prejudices and superego standards derived from parental indoctrination. The child is not free to do otherwise, for he is given to feel that the only alternative to oneness with the parent is total isolation, craziness. He must often choose between the parent's world-view and his own senses that present contradictory data. Such a child is placed in a double bind not only between parent and himself, but also in the way he is viewed by other family members:

> His family-role as regards perception is deeply *conflictual*, for on the one hand, the other family members, themselves striving to become whole, integrated individuals, implicitly react to him as the *spokesman for* their own dissociated personality aspects, and hence unwittingly encourage him to be aware of personality traits, and interpersonal processes, in the family which they are dissociating; but on the other hand, they react to him as being crazy to the extent that he functions as an individual who *is* aware of these aspects of the reality of the family-world around him (Searles 1967, p. 122f.).

These double binds lead to severe distortions in which the schizophrenic either feels meaninglessly unrelated to the components of the world around him or so fused and blended with them that, again, perception and meaning are not achieved. In extreme cases, what are essentially inner, emotional changes are experienced as perceptual changes in the surrounding world. Searles gives the example of a woman he worked with for many years who felt her own existence as highly discontinuous, dissociated (pushed out of conscious awareness) much that she did, and had the delusion that she had many "doubles" who did what people attributed to her. She also saw others as doubles: "She could not realize that I was the same person but in a different mood, a different combination of feelings, than she had ever seen me in before, or the same person but one toward whom she was having a new combination of feelings."

Faced with such chaotic perceptional experience, the paranoid attempts to arrange it in some artificially imposed, delusional order, such as a Communist or Mafia plot. That he experiences the plot as centering upon himself is a reaction to his being most deeply threatened lest he be as insignificant, as outside of everyone else's awareness, as they are to him. The disconfirmation that the schizophrenic individual experiences leaves him with far more intense, and intensely conflictual, feelings outside his awareness than the healthy person, while at the same time he has far less capacity to face and integrate such feelings (Searles 1967, pp. 123–125).

In his essay, "The Patient as Therapist to His Analyst," Searles extends disconfirmation as the genesis of mental illness to the specific disconfirmation or perversion of the need the infant feels to be a therapist to his mother. In certain tragic circumstances, the child fails to become a truly human individual. Instead he becomes a "symbiotic therapist, whose own ego-wholeness is sacrificed throughout life in a truly selfless devotion, to complementing the ego-incompleteness of the mothering person, and of subsequent persons in his life who, in his unconscious, have the emotional meaning of similarly incomplete mothers." Ironically, it is the patient's nascent capacity for love and for the development of mature human responsibility that impels him to this martyr-like role. It does not matter whether this striving is seen as "selfish" or "altruistic," since what we are dealing with here is the vain attempt to change a vicious circle of relationship into a good one:

> The patient's therapeutic striving is to function as mother to his biological mother (the latter's ego development in regard to her own mothering effort, being fixated at, or having regressed to, an infantile level) so as to enable her to become sufficiently integrated and mature that she will become able to function truly as a mother to the patient (Searles 1975, p. 137).

Searles sees the family–environment warping of the infant's therapeutic strivings as a *major* source of *all* psychopathology. The failure of the psychotic to become an individual human self, in particular, is explicable primarily through the fact that his own individuation is postponed in the service of his functioning symbiotically as therapist to one or another of his family members, or to all collectively in a family symbiosis. Or he may bear an unconscious, lifelong guilt at having failed in his therapeutic effort to enable his ego-fragmented mother to become a whole and fulfilled mother to him. We might say that he has been needed and used by one or another member of the family, but in such a way as to *dis*confirm him as a person in his own right. Disconfirmation may come equally through not being *allowed* to help others. "The lack of opportunity for and recognition of reparative activities can greatly encourage psychotic states of mind," Searles quotes M. Milner, and, to much the same effect, E. Singer: "Those concerned with the origins of psychopathology and with efforts to rekindle emotional growth must give serious attention to the possibility that the most devastating of human experiences is the sense of uselessness" (Searles 1975, pp. 149, 98f., 145, 148).

# R. D. Laing

Ronald Laing also sees psychopathology as originating in disconfirmation within the family, but Laing, like Farber and Jourard, deals with confirmation explicitly in Buber's terms. Laing sees the mother's failure to respond as threatening the individual with the loss of his self, for "a necessary component in the development of the self is the experience of oneself as a person under the loving eye of the mother." Laing, very much aware of the "contract" with strings attached of which we spoke in the last chapter, quotes one schizophrenic patient, Joan, as saying:

> Everyone should be able to look back in their memory and be sure he had a mother who loved him, all of him; even his piss and shit. He should be sure his mother loved him just for being himself; not for what he could do. Otherwise he feels he has no right to exist. He feels he should never have been born (Laing 1965, p. 172).

Although the mother mediates the world to the infant in the first place, Laing does not think exclusively of schizophrenogenic mothers, but rather of schizophrenogenic families. Such families may disconfirm the person precisely by confirming a false self-system. Julie complained about being smothered and not being allowed to live as a person when she was, in fact, the family's favorite, was given everything, and was encouraged to grow up. Only it was her false self and not her true one that was confirmed. Although the husband and wife could agree on nothing else, they maintained a collusion in accepting Julie's false self as good and rejecting every other aspect of her as bad. What Laing outlines for us amounts to a real denial of the other's touchstone of reality and with it of any possibility for a "dialogue of touchstones":

> The most schizophrenogenic factor of this time was . . . the complete absence of anyone in her world who could or would see some sense in her point of view, whether it was right or wrong. . . . Julie was not simply trying to preserve her existence, she was trying to achieve existence. . . . The common family senses accorded her no existence. Her mother had to be right, totally right. When her mother said she was bad, Julie felt this as a murder. It was the negation of any autonomous point of view on her part. . . . The existential truth in Julie's delusions was that her own true possibilities were being smothered, strangled, murdered (Laing 1965, p. 192f.).

In *Self and Others*, Laing points out that even when a person puts himself into his acts and the acts seem to have some point, the person can experience emptiness and futility if he is accorded no recognition by the other and if he feels he is not able to make any difference to anyone. Laing, like Buber, recognizes that rejection can be confirmatory if it is direct, not tangential, and grants significance and validity to the action that evokes it. Like Lyman Wynne, Laing finds many families in which there is little genuine confirmation, and pseudoconfirmation prevails. It is not outright neglect, but rather the unwitting subtle and persistent disconfirmation or the active confirming of a false self that leads to schizophrenia. "*Someone in a false position feels guilt, shame, or anxiety at not being false.*" Julie's mother regarded the passive listless "thing"-Julie as normal, while reacting to spontaneity with anxiety and attributions of badness or madness (Laing 1971, pp. 83, 99–102).

Laing analyzes "collusion" in terms of Buber's understanding of the "seeming" person who makes a false bid for confirmation and thereby renders the interhuman inauthentic:

> Two people in relation may confirm each other or genuinely complement each other. Still, to disclose oneself to the other is hard without confidence in oneself and trust in the other. Desire for confirmation from each is present in both, but each is caught between trust and mistrust, confidence and despair, and both settle for counterfeit acts of confirmation on the basis of pretense. To do so *both* must play the game of collusion (Laing 1971, p. 108f.).

"Seeming" persons who are in collusion are not hiding their "true" selves, for neither has arrived at any genuine realization of herself or himself or of the other. Such mutual pseudoconfirmation may also, of course, lead to conflict when peoples' wishes do not dovetail. Each wishes the other to "mother" him and puts the other down for not doing so. The one does not *project*, using the other as a hook to hang projections on.

Rather he strives to induce the other to become the very *embodiment* of projection. If the other does not go along with this collusion, the other feels guilty. If he does go along, however, he becomes estranged from his own self. When two people collude, each embodies a fiction that the other desires, thus confirming the other in the false self that he is trying to make real. "The ground is then set for prolonged mutual evasion of truth and true fulfillment" (Laing 1971, pp. 109–111).

The paranoid, in contrast, occupies a much lonelier position. Though in his delusions of persecution he is the center of everyone else's world, he is tormented and preoccupied with the thought that he never occupies first place in anyone's affection. The other is there, but *he* is not there to the other. He lives not so much in his own world, but rather in the empty place he supposes he does *not* occupy in the *other's* world. "Unable to experience himself as significant for another, he develops a delusionally significant place for himself *in the world of others*" (Laing 1971, pp. 136–138).

Much of what Laing writes about "mystification" in *The Politics of Experience* is an extension of this understanding of disconfirmation in its various forms. Laing sees the family as a "protection racket": behind all the mutual back-scratching and esteem-, status-, support-, protection, and security-giving and -getting lurks the terror of not being confirmed. The end result is Marcuse's "one-dimensional man"; for the family's function of repressing Eros induces a false consciousness of security; denies death by avoiding life; promotes respect, conformity, and obedience; and induces a fear of failure and a respect for work and for "respectability." Laing illustrates at length how this inducement works through his discussions of attributions in *The Politics of the Family*. Whether the attribution is badness or prettiness, the structure is the same: The parents impose their points of view on the child and make the child feel guilty for having thought otherwise (Laing 1967, p. 64; Laing 1972, p. 122).

## Helm Stierlin

The German family psychiatrist Helm Stierlin has enriched our understanding of what we have called the "contract" and what Laing calls the false self system through his distinction between three types of disconfirmation that lead to pathology and delinquency: the "bound child," the "delegated child," and the "expelled child." The "bound child" is given the implicit message that he dare not venture out from the family system. Parents, faced with their own developmental crisis, attempt to tie their children ever more closely to themselves and to the "family ghetto" and to delay or prevent the children's separation at all costs.

In his discussion of "cognitive" or "ego" binding, Stierlin resumes some of the themes of double binding, attributions, and mystifications that one sees in the work of Wynne and Laing and, implicitly, in Searles:

> Cognitive—or "ego"—binding . . . implies devious communications which mystify, interfere with the sharing of a common focus of attention, and disaffirm one's own or the other's messages. Such devious communications strain and unsettle the partner in the dialogue and they throw this dialogue off the track. . . . They violate his or her "cognitive integrity"; they wound him; they cause him to lose trust in his inner signposts, in his perceptions of himself and others, and in his most basic feelings. Such feelings—for example, feelings relating to our loving or being lovable—are always vulnerable to contrary attributions—i.e., to assertions that the person does not "really" feel this way or that he is only covering up, deceiving himself, etc. For these experiences cannot be confirmed by ordinary logic, by simple proof or disproof, or by recourse to an impartial arbitrator. To be validated, they must be subjectively asserted yet also be shared and exposed. But such sharing and exposure imply vulnerability to the violence of a cognitive binder (Stierlin 1974, p. 42f.).

If we substitute the words "confirm" and "disconfirm" for "validate" and "invalidate" in the above paragraph (which Stierlin himself does at one point), we shall recognize what a vivid illustration such cognitive binding is of disconfirmation as the root of psychopathology.

Stierlin relates the delegating mode of interaction between parents and children to unresolved ambivalence and conflict in the parents in their own developmental crisis. They themselves alternate between consolidating existing relations and jobs and making new starts that take them out of the family orbit. They turn to their children with conflicting expectations, binding them and sending them out. The delegated child must take it upon himself to cope with parental ambivalence and makes himself into *their* reconciling agent, always at the expense of his own genuine growth and separation. The very adolescents who seem to flaunt their rebellion by taking drugs, defying authorities and conventions, being sexually promiscuous, and running away, are, in fact, the most loyal and compliant of children. They are responding to their parents' covert expectations, and their conflicts are conflicts of loyalties and of missions with which their parents burdened them, whether those missions are to act out the parents' libidinal desires or to atone for the parents' bad conscience.

Among the "missions impossible" Stierlin cites are embodying and actualizing a parent's grandiose ego ideal of achievement, fame, beauty, or vitality and embodying and externalizing the badness and craziness that a parent, in his innermost self, feels and fears to be his fate. This latter mission often arises from parents who, haunted by the shadow of mad relatives, delegate a child to become the mad family member in an attempt to control, contain, and neutralize this feared and ever-present madness in themselves (Stierlin 1974, pp. 51f., 132f., 182f.).

Helm Stierlin has written a psychobiography of Hitler as a delegated child who was fulfilling his mother's desires to escape her position as a servant who has become the father's second wife, but is still treated essentially as a servant. Another well-known example of the delegated child is found in Bud Schulberg's book *What Makes Sammy Run* (1941), which portrays the movie magnate Samuel Goldwyn. Goldwyn's parents were both immigrants, and the father was unable to win a successful place in the economy and culture of his new country. The mother, as a result, transferred her interest to the son, who was to make up to her for the father's lack. If one were to ask Samuel Goldwyn why he worked so hard all his life, he would say it was strictly for himself or perhaps for his wife and children. In actuality, he was running for his mother. The crucial element in the third mode of interaction, expelling, is that the parents, in trying to solve *their* crises and in seeking new starts in life via partners, jobs, or emotional investments, come to view their adolescent children as hindrances. They rebuff and neglect their children, letting them run loose and leaving them to themselves so that they constantly get the message: "You are expendable, the earlier you leave home the better." This is the child who becomes a casual runaway and, in many cases, a suicide. There are also mixed cases, such as the so-called chronic schizophrenics who are sent away to mental hospitals and are maximally alienated from their parents, yet stay maximally bound to them at the same time.

Stierlin also subsumes Kohut's observations on narcissism in *The Analysis of the Self* (1971) under the expelling mode. The parents of such children are cold and depriving, as a result of which the children grow up in an interpersonal vacuum devoid of parents, warmth, care, and concern. Although the children are provided with a stable home and material comforts, they have no sense of self-importance. Their excessive dread of being found insignificant turns all their endeavors into one relentless quest for the confirmation of their (inwardly doubted) importance. They often display an autonomy and creativity that enables them to recruit ever new admirers to confirm their importance. Yet no one so much as they illustrate the problematic of confirmation, since each fresh success and each new admirer offers them only temporary respite from their own inward doubts of their having importance. Their seeming grandiosity covers over an inner vacuum (Stierlin 1974, pp. 66f., 136f., 154f.).

# Carl Rogers

Carl Rogers' discussion, "Ellen West—and Loneliness," affords us an excellent summation of the correlation between disconfirmation and "mental illness":

> In some of the most significant moments of life, she [Ellen West] was made to feel that her own experiencing was invalid, erroneous, wrong, and unsound, and that what she *should* be feeling was something quite different. Unfortunately for her, her love for her parents, especially her father, was so strong that she surrendered her own capacity for trusting her experience and substituted theirs, or his. She gave up being her self . . . "I scream but they do not hear me." Ellen's words ring in my ears. No one *did* hear her as a person. Beyond her childhood years—and perhaps not even then—neither her parents, nor her two analysts, nor her physicians ever seem to have respected her enough to hear her deeply. They did not deal with her as a person capable of meeting life, a person whose experiencing is trustworthy, whose inner feelings are worthy of acceptance. How, then, could she listen to herself or respect the experiencing going on within her?
>
> "I am isolated. I sit in a glass ball, I see people through a glass wall. I scream, but they do not hear me." What a desperate cry for relationship between two persons. She never experienced what Buber has called "healing through meeting." There was no one who could meet her, accept her, as she was (Rogers 1980, pp. 173–175).[1]

---

[1] See also Rogers 1980, pp. 211, 226.

# Chapter 12

# Confirmation in Therapy

If disconfirmation or the absence of confirmation lies at the root of much psychopathology, then confirmation lies at the core of healing through meeting. Healing through meeting, in Buber's terms, is that therapy that goes beyond the repair work that helps "a soul which is diffused and poor in structure to collect and order itself," to the essential task—"the regeneration of an atrophied personal center." This is particularly clear in the "loving fight" through which, Stierlin holds, mutual liberation can occur in the conflict between the generations. Such a "loving fight" is characterized, first, by the two parties striving to differentiate and to articulate their differing needs and interest and bringing these into an ongoing communication and relatedness. Second, it is characterized by a deepening awareness of the parties' interdependence and mutual obligations, and, third, by promoting each party's repair work. This makes possible a three-dimensional liberation that, ideally, can include the parents' parents and the children's as yet unborn children (Stierlin 1974, p. 181f.).

Much of what we shall have to say about Harold Searles' approach to confirmation in therapy we shall reserve for our chapter, "The Dialogue of Touchstones," to which subject he has made an especially significant contribution. Here we shall look only at the conclusions he draws from his thesis that the patient is, and needs to be recognized as, a therapist to his analyst. "The more ill a patient is," writes Searles, "the more does successful treatment require that he become, and be implicitly acknowledged as having become, a therapist to his officially designated therapist, the analyst." It is only insofar as the patient can succeed in his therapeutic striving toward the therapist that he can become sufficiently free from guilt and sufficiently sure of his worth that he can become more deeply a full human individual. "Individuation has become free of its connotation of murderous dismembering, or lethal abandonment of the mother for whom the patient has not only been made to feel responsible, but whom the patient has genuinely loved and wanted to somehow make whole and fulfilled." Conversely, the analyst's failure to recognize the long-repressed therapeutic striving in the patient accounts, more than any other interpersonal element in the treatment, for the patient's unconscious resistance to the analytic process (Searles 1975, pp. 96, 99, 149).

Ronald Laing focuses on brilliant analysis and diagnosis and has little to say about actual confirmation and healing through meeting. He does offer a few poignant examples in one chapter, "Confirmation and Disconfirmation," of *Self and Others*. In a session with a 25-year-old schizophrenic woman, who sat at a distance from him without moving or speaking, his mind drifted away to thoughts of his own. In the midst of these, he heard her say in a very small voice, "Oh please don't go so far away from me." It was clear to Laing that the most important thing for him to do at that moment was to confirm the fact that she had correctly registered his actual withdrawal of his "presence."

> There are many patients who are very sensitive to desertion, but are not sure of the reliability, much less validity, of their own sensitivity. They do not trust other people, and they cannot trust their own mistrust either (Laing 1971, p. 104f.).

The other example that Laing gives is that of a nurse who gave "a somewhat catatonic, hebephrenic schizophrenic patient" a cup of tea. On taking the tea, this chronically psychotic patient said to the nurse, "This is the first time in my life that anyone has ever given me a cup of tea." To Laing, this becomes the very symbol of confirmation in therapy. The "schizophrenic" is often so labeled because he is *very* sensitive to not being recognized as a human being, because he has a great need to give and receive love. For such a person, the real giving of a cup of tea can be the confirmation of his existence as a human being, a person of meaning and worth. All too often cups of tea are given because one wants to show off or one wants to get something out of the other.

> It is the simplest and most difficult thing in the world for *one person*, genuinely being his or her self, *to give*, in fact and not just in appearance, *another person*, realized in his or her own being by the giver, *a cup of tea*, really, and not in appearance (Laing 1971, p. 106f.).

Practically everything that Carl Rogers has written about therapy can be seen as confirmation of the disconfirmed or unconfirmed self of the client. Sidney Jourard, who follows Rogers in many respects, is even more explicit about the centrality to therapy of confirmation and healing through meeting. Jourard sees himself as confirming his client through his *intention*—"the wish that the one who is the other for the therapist should experience his freedom, should be and become himself." This commitment transcends the therapist's loyalty to any automatized technique or theoretical orientation. At the same time, it leaves room for technique as an art to be learned from a teacher, "an *idiom* in which one expresses an initial therapeutic intent."

Jourard's focus, when he encounters a patient suffering from the confining and crippling effects of childhood privations and trauma, is not to pursue the roots of "pathology" with the patient but rather to wonder how it would be possible to mobilize his despairing spirits so that he might transcend the present circumstances which he has let grind him down. For Jourard, the central factor in "iatrogenic wellness" is "the strength of the *healer's* faith in the potentials of the sufferer to transcend the limiting conditions of his existence." From this standpoint, trust and hope are not *contributors* to healing, but rather are themselves the indication that a *total* organismic healing, or reintegration process, has been set in motion (Jourard 1968, pp. 57–59, 68).

For Jourard, confirmation is an act of love through which one acknowledges the other as one who exists in his own peculiar form and has the right to do so. Such acknowledgment transcends both the concept that the therapist has of the client's being and the client's own previous concepts and presentations of himself. Thus the therapist's confirmation enables the client to grow:

> My suspension of my preconceptions of his being invites him to let go while he is in my presence. He can drop yesterday's self-presentations, commitments, interests and goals, and explore the possibilities of new ones. He can weep, regress, enter into himself while he is with me, and feel assured that I am waiting, perhaps with a hand holding his, until he emerges to tell me who he is. And I confirm him, at each instant of the journey, as being the one he is—John searching; John in despair; John emerged, with new goals and values (Jourard 1968, p. 123f.).

In the course of his seminars at the Washington School of Psychiatry, Martin Buber threw out some hints concerning confirmation in therapy and its relation to healing through meeting. In the time of the strongest transference, the patient needs, in his unconscious, to give himself up into the hands of the therapist so that contact may occur. The therapist's openness and willingness to receive whatever comes is necessary in order that the patient may trust existentially. A certain very important kind of healing—existential healing—takes place through meeting rather than through insight and analysis. This means the healing not just of a certain part of the patient, but also of the very roots of the patient's being. The existential trust of one whole person to another has a particular representation in the domain of healing. So long as it is not there, there will be no realization of this need to give up into the hands of the therapist what is repressed. Without such trust, even masters of method cannot effect existential healing.

The existential trust between therapist and patient that makes the relationship a healing one in the fullest sense of that term implies confirmation, but of a very special sort. Such confirmation does not replace transference. But when meeting is the decisive factor, it changes its meaning and dynamic. Everything is changed in real meeting. Confirmation can be misunderstood as *static*. I meet another—I accept and confirm him as he now is. But confirming a person *as he is* is only the first step. Confirmation does not mean that I take his appearance at this moment as being the person I want to confirm. I must take the other person in his dynamic existence, in his specific potentiality. In the present lies hidden what can *become*.

This potentiality, this sense of his unique direction as a person, can make itself felt to me within our relationship, and it is that I most want to confirm. In therapy, this personal direction becomes perceptible to the therapist in a very special way. In a person's worst illness, the highest potentiality of this person may be manifesting itself in negative form. The therapist can directly influence the development of those potentialities. Healing does not mean bringing up the old, but rather shaping the new: It is not confirming the negative, but rather counterbalancing with the positive (Friedman 1966, p. 38f.; Buber 1969, pp. 169–173).

Buber's insistence that confirmation is not static, but rather is a confirmation of the potentialities hidden in the worst illness of the patient touches on the issue that arose in the dialogue between Buber and Rogers concerning the difference between *accepting* and *confirming*. Carl Rogers, as we have seen, tends to equate acceptance and confirmation. True acceptance, he holds, means acceptance of this person's potentialities as well as what he is at the moment. If we were not able to recognize his potentiality, Rogers says, it is a real question whether we could accept him. If I am accepted exactly as I am, he adds, I cannot help but change. When there is no longer any need for defensive barriers, the forward-moving processes of life take over. It is precisely this assumption—that the processes of life will always be forward-moving—that Buber questions, and this leads him to a distinction between affirmation and confirmation that Rogers does not make:

> Every true existential relationship between two persons begins with acceptance. . . . I take you just as you are . . . in this moment, in this

actuality. . . . Confirming means . . . accepting the whole potentiality. . . . I can recognize in him, know in him, more or less, the person he
has been . . . *created* to become. . . . And now I not only accept the
other as he is, but I confirm him, in myself and then in him, in relation to
this potentiality that . . . can now be developed . . . can evolve . . . can
answer the reality of life. . . . "I accept you as you are" . . . does *not*
mean "I don't want you to change," but . . . "I discover in you just by
my accepting love . . . what you are meant to become" (Buber 1966,
p. 181f.).

Buber goes on to say that in working with a problematic man he must
sometimes help him against himself, for because of this problematic, life
has become baseless for him.

What he wants is a being not only whom he can trust as a man trusts
another, but a being that gives him now the certitude that "there *is* a soil,
there *is* an existence. The world is not condemned to deprivation,
degeneration, destruction. The world *can* be redeemed. *I* can be redeemed because there is this trust." And if this is reached, now I can help
this man even in his struggle against himself. And this I can only do if I
distinguish between accepting and confirming (Buber 1966, p. 183).

Rogers, as we have seen, moves somewhat in the direction of this
distinction by putting "congruence" ahead of "empathic understanding"
and "unconditional positive regard" in his list of what is essential to good
therapy. Yet congruence is only half the picture. It means I must confirm
you as what I am and not what you or I might expect or wish me to be. It
does not yet mean that I may *struggle with* and *oppose* you precisely in
order to *confirm* you. Sidney Jourard suggests that Rogers, who speaks of
the atmosphere in which a person can grow, has himself discovered that
it is not enough just to be a wonderfully permissive and "reflecting" individual.

To confirm the other as the one he is and invite him to take the
freedom to reveal and be whoever and whatever he is means the therapist
must also grant himself the same freedom to be and to respond as the very
person he is. It also means that even while one stands back and lets the
other's being "happen" and disclose itself in its reality and authenticity,
one meets him as oneself, recognizing that "often the most direct confirmation is to take a stand in opposition to the disclosure of the other." Even
this meeting in opposition confirms for the other that he is the one he is.
"It lets him know that he exists" (Jourard 1968, pp. 74, 122f.).

The therapist can also help the patient grow, Jourard claims, through
challenging him and encouraging him to attempt new projects. If the
therapist's concept of the patient's being is one that encompasses more
possibilities in his behavior than he himself has acknowledged, if his

concept of the patient's being is more inclusive and accurate than the patient's concept of his being, and if he lets the patient know from moment to moment how he *truly* experiences him, then the patient can compare this with his own experience of himself and his own self-concept. The therapist "may thus insert a thin edge of doubt into the crust" of the patient's self-concept, helping to bring about its collapse so that he might re-form it. "In fact, this is what a loving friend, or a good psychotherapist does" (Jourard 1968, p. 122).

Viktor Frankl seems to imply a similar distinction between acceptance and confirmation when he says that the loving person not only sees the essential traits and features in the beloved person, but also sees what is potential in him, what is not yet actualized but yet ought to be actualized. By making the beloved aware of what he can be and of what he should become, the loving person makes these potentialities come true (Frankl 1970, p. 113f.). The Gestalt therapist Vincent O'Connell comes close to this understanding of confirmation when he writes: "I have also learned that, for me at least, the fitting response is honest and loving anger (when it comes), since in that anger there is intimate involvement and a call to the person" (Fagan and Shepherd, eds. 1970, p. 251f.).

The beginning of all human relationships and, therefore, of all helping, healing, therapeutic relationships, is "I accept you as you are." But that does not mean I confirm everything you do just because you do it. That would be putting aside the reality of the relationship, the reality of myself as a person confronting you. It is not that I judge you from above or that I moralize at you. Yet our very relationship is a demand on you as on me. I have to come to you from where I am in my uniqueness. I cannot make myself a cipher in order to help you. To confirm the other is only possible within the relationship itself, insofar as the other can communicate his self or her self to you and you can experience both his and your own side of the relationship.

The therapist may have to wrestle *with* the patient, *for* the patient, and *against* the patient. He is not only concerned with the person he is at that moment, but also with his becoming what he or she is called to become. The therapist may have "unconditional positive regard" for the patient, if it is congruent with his relationship to the patient, in the sense that he does not offer confirmation with strings attached: "You must become the sort of person I want you to be if you want me to help you." But this cannot mean that whatever the patient does the therapist will regard positively. He cannot do that and be a person and he cannot do that and be a healer or a helper to the patient.

I had a student the first year I taught at Sarah Lawrence College, whom I could not understand why they kept in school. She came to my office every week for an individual conference, sat in my chair with her feet on my desk, got red in the face, and never said a word! Toward the end of that year—her sophomore year in college—she decided she wanted to do something for me and wrote a philosophy paper on Kant and Hume that I truly felt to be on a graduate level. All the faculty, from the president and dean down, laughed at me. They had not read the paper, and most of them were not trained as philosophers, but they thought they had this student pegged as incapable of serious work. The same night this student took an overdose of sleeping pills and would have died had not some other instinct led her to alert someone so her stomach was pumped out. The reaction of my colleagues was that they should throw her out of school. "How can you do that now," I protested, "when you have kept her all year without good reason?" I insisted on her staying and won the battle.

The next fall, this same student took an individual study course with me. Halfway through she said, "I really don't want to do what I was going to do. I want to change it to something else." "Fine," I said. At the end of the quarter she said to me, "I haven't got a paper for you, but I will write you a letter telling you about the paper that I shall write." Again I said, "Fine," and I gave her credit for the quarter's work. After she had received the credit, she announced that she now wished to switch to my colleague Helen Merrell Lynd and study with her. To this, too, I replied, "Fine," but I added, "You have to write the paper for me." Not only this student, but a number of faculty began pressuring me, including her "don," a psychology faculty woman whose newborn twins this student threatened to drown in the bathtub. "I am getting closer and closer to the subway trains in New York City," this student said to me. "Which is more important to you, that paper, or my life?" "It is you who wants the credit," I answered. "Which is more important to you, the credit or your life?"

She finally did write the paper for me, as the second part of a paper she wrote for another faculty member. What is more, I was the only member of the faculty with whom she kept in contact for a number of years after her graduation when she went on with a fellowship to a graduate school in psychology and became a clinical psychologist. If I had allowed her to get away with her blackmail, I should not have been confirming her as a person or even, if I thought in those terms, as a "sick" person in need of therapy. I could only help heal her by holding my ground and being faithful to my side of the dialogue, while trying to understand her side from within.

Even if the other is "dead wrong," he still has his own point of view, his own existence, which cannot be removed from him. Real confirmation cares enough about the other person to wrestle with him, for him— confirming him even while opposing him. It does not presume, but it cares, and this caring often means a contending within the dialogue with him. Hans Trüb helps us to understand the meaning of confirmation in therapy through his conception of the two stages. In the first stage, as we have seen, the person who comes before the therapist is the person who has been unconfirmed, disconfirmed by the world. That person needs a confidant, a big brother or a big sister, someone who will understand, not with analytical categories, but through his eyes, someone who really hears and who "imagines the real" while he is listening. That is an important part of the healing process, but that alone cannot heal. That is perhaps one of the limitations of "receptive listening" and "unconditional positive regard." Part of the sickness lies in the fact that, because of this nonconfirmation, the person has withdrawn from active dialogue with his family, his friends, and his community.

At some point, therefore, the therapist must enter a second stage in which he helps the client resume the interrupted dialogue with the community. He does this by placing on the client the demand of the community— not from above, but rather by really standing his ground as the person he or she is *and* by representing and bearing the community values that he or she embodies. Without that second stage—not replacing, but combined with the first stage—there can be no real healing.

The same is true of the approach to real, or existential, guilt. It is not enough for the therapist to help to call people to account in terms of their self-betrayal or even their guilt toward their family or the therapist himself. The calling to account must, at the same time, be a calling back into the interrupted dialogue with the community. This is not a matter of wallowing in guilt, but rather of a creative response, a spontaneity that, in the end, forgets to be concerned with oneself and says, "I can go forth in a new situation and really meet it, really be present to it, even though I did not in the past."

The question remains, of course, as to what is the right admixture at any time of the two stages—the therapist as confidant and the therapist as bearer of the genuine demand of the community who helps the patient return into dialogue with the community. There is no formula that tells the therapist how much time to spend in the one stage and how much in the other. Both stages must probably be there at every moment, but the right proportion between the two at any one time is a matter of tact and art and real listening. It is also a matter of "grace"—of allowing something to come to one and allowing oneself to respond and to discover what is called for in each situation through just this openness and response. There are persons who could be severely injured by a premature placing upon them of the demand of the community, just as there are persons who could be severely injured if the therapist never reached that stage.

The two stages that Trüb points to as an essential part of healing through meeting can help us understand a good deal about the problematic of confirmation. This problematic includes the fact that the therapist values the other enough to treat him or her as a human being, and not just as a sick person. This care means helping the other to reach the place where he or she can enter into dialogue, first with the therapist and then with the other persons in his or her life. It also means allowing the other to go back and forth—not placing upon the other some abstract moral demand that will not allow the other to regress, when he or she must, to the stage of one whose need is for comfort, consolation, and understanding. True confirmation is not "empathic understanding" alone or even "inclusion" alone; it is also struggle and demand. In the end, moreover, it is not something that the therapist *does* to the patient, but rather an event that takes place *between* them, one that helps the patient go back into the world to give and receive confirmation in the mutual interaction with others.

An important link between Trüb's two stages, as between confirmation and healing through meeting, is the "dialogue of touchstones," which we shall discuss in Chapter 18. It will deepen our understanding of confirmation and the dialogue of touchstones if we first take a fuller and more systematic look at a number of aspects of healing through meeting, all of which have already been touched on: the unconscious, dreams, guilt, mutuality, empathy, and inclusion.

Chapter 13

# The Unconscious as the Ground of the Physical and the Psychic

"Each school of depth psychology possesses its own unconscious," wrote Viktor von Weizsäcker. Dialogical psychotherapy too has important implications for the unconscious.

Freud, Jung, and the whole psychoanalytic world have assumed without further ado that the unconscious is a mind or a psychic reality that contains ideas capable of being repressed and capable of being brought to consciousness through Freudian transference to the therapist or through Jungian encounter with the shadow. Only this unexamined assumption can explain their uncritical transference of psychologism from the conscious to the unconscious and their failure to recognize—not theoretically, but rather in their approach to dreams and unconscious "materials"—that if the unconscious is really unconscious, we may know its effect, but we can never know it or its contents except as they are shaped and elaborated by the conscious.

The reason Freud found it necessary to postulate an unconscious was the powerful evidence he accumulated by way of dreams, slips of the tongue, and the whole roster of what he called "the psychopathology of the everyday." Although Freud held the unconscious to be something that one really does not and cannot know, he still characterized it as "psychic," rejecting out of hand those who wished to equate "psychic" and "conscious" and those who held that the unconscious is the epiphenomenal residue of somatic, physiological occurrences out of which the psychic proceeds. "The unconscious is the truly real psychic," Freud wrote. "Every psychic act begins as unconscious." Freud even stressed that we should not make the difference between conscious *I* (the ego) and unconscious *It* (the id) too strong, since the I is a particular differentiated part of the It.[1] Freud distinguishes between the preconscious, which is not noticed but can be known, and the unconscious, which cannot be known because of repression. Freud saw the unconscious as containing more than repressed material, however. He saw unconscious energy as an unbound primary process, which has no relationship to reality and does not know the principles of contradiction or time (Ellenberger 1970, p. 512).

Although the major emphasis in Freudian psychoanalysis is upon bringing to light repressed material from the unconscious, there are some aspects of Freud's view of the unconscious that lend themselves to healing through meeting. Freud held that the analyst should allow his own unconscious activity to operate as freely as possible and suspend the motives that usually direct his attention. The analyst must take care not to substitute a censorship of his own for the selection the patient has forgone. Training analysis was meant to get rid, as far as possible, of the conscious prejudices and the unconscious defenses of the analyst. But, as Laplanche and Pontalis have stressed, Freud demands more than this.

> The desired goal would appear to be actual direct communication between one unconscious and another: the analyst's unconscious has to relate to the emerging unconscious of the patient as a telephone receiver is adjusted to the transmitting microphone. This is what Theodor Reik was later to describe figuratively as listening with the third ear (Laplanche and Pontalis 1973, p. 44f.).

In the view of Theodor Reik and his followers, the countertransference becomes the mark of the depth of empathic communication. For Freud and most psychoanalysts, the essential part of the psychoanalytic dialogue continues to take place at an ego-to-ego level. Yet Freud attested to the direct communication between one unconscious and another on the basis of his own experience as an analyst:

> Everyone possesses in his own unconscious an instrument with which he can interpret the utterances of the unconscious in other people.
> The *Ucs.* of one human being can react upon that of another, without passing through the *Cs.* This deserves closer investigation, especially with a view to finding out whether preconscious activity can be excluded as playing a part in it; but, descriptively speaking, the fact is incontestable.[2]

---

[1]Based on a manuscript in Martin Buber's handwriting in a folder entitled "Das Unbewusste" in the Martin Buber Archives, The Jewish and National University Library, The Hebrew University, Jerusalem, Israel.

[2]Sigmund Freud, "The Disposition to Obsessional Neurosis" (1913i), G.W., VIII, 455; S.E., XII, 320; Sigmund Freud, "The Unconscious" (1915e), G.W., X, 293; S.E., XIV, 194, quoted in Laplanche and Pontalis 1973, p. 44 *n.*

In contrast to Freud, Jung holds that the unconscious has an autonomous course of development complementary to consciousness and is the seat of the universal primordial images he calls archetypes. Actually the archetypes proper are numinous, life-like centers of psychic energy, contentless universals that are normally latent and unconscious, whereas it is only the archetypal images that are manifested to consciousness and filled with specific content. Jung's concept of the shadow differs from Freud's idea of repression in that it is the negative side of a person of which that person is unaware, but which he could be conscious of if he honestly wanted to (Ellenberger 1970, pp. 705–707).

In general, Jung follows Freud in regarding the unconscious as psychic. The collective unconscious represents the objective psychic for Jung, the personal unconscious, the subjective. At one point, Jung's recognition that the archetypes cannot with certainty be described as psychic leads him to a glimpse of that unity of the physical and psychic that, we shall see, stands at the heart of Buber's approach to the unconscious:

> The archetype signifies a sphere which, on the one hand, demonstrates no characteristics of the physiological and, on the other hand, cannot in the last analysis be spoken of as psychic, although it manifests itself in a psychic way. But physiological happenings act thus without one being able to describe them therefore as psychic. Although there is no form of existence that is not mediated to us exclusively through the psychic, one cannot explain everything as merely psychic (Ellenberger 1970, p. 462).

Jung cautions us not to confuse the archetypal representations with the archetype itself, which he sees as "a psychic factor, belonging to the invisible, ultraviolet part of the spectrum," and is, as such, a transcendent, "psychoid" reality incapable of becoming conscious.[3]

Martin Buber has suggested that the unconscious may really be the ground of personal wholeness before its elaboration into the physical and the psychic. Freud, he holds, and after him, Jung, have made the simple logical error of assuming that the unconscious is psychic since they wished to deny that it was physical. They did not, Buber holds, see this third alternative and with it the possibility of bursting the bounds of psychologism by recognizing that the division of inner and outer that applies to the psyche and the physical need not apply to the unconscious. Here, in contrast, there might be direct meeting and direct communication between one unconscious and another.

> Most psychological schools, especially that of Jung, assume that there is a nonphenomenological yet psychical reality. This means the assumption of a rather mystical basis of reality. . . . The assumption of a psyche

---

[3]C. G. Jung, "Der Geist der Psychologie" in *Eranos Jahrbuch* XIV (1946), pp. 425, 427, 449, 460–462, quoted in Martin Buber, "Das Unbewusste."

that exists as something exists in space should be either a metaphor or an entirely metaphysical thesis about the nature of being for which we have no basis at all in experience. Freud remained in the last instance a radical physiologist. Jung dealt wrongly with the problem, and Freud did not deal with it at all. . . . Freud does not speak explicitly of the psyche but of what is "psychoate." He never defines it. Freud was a simplificator, just as in the social field Marx was before him, i.e., one who places a general concept in place of the ever-renewed investigation of reality. A new aspect of reality is treated by the simplificator as the solution of one of the riddles of being. Fifty years of psychotherapeutic thought have been based on this dangerous manner of thinking. Now this period is at an end (Buber 1969, p. 157).

In his 1952 essay, "Healing through Meeting," Buber throws out a hint concerning the nature of "the unconscious," which is nowhere elaborated in his other writings:

The sphere in which this renowned concept possesses reality is located, according to my understanding, beneath the level where human existence is split into physical and psychical phenomena. But each of the contents of this sphere can in any moment enter into the dimension of the introspective, and thereby be explained and dealt with as belonging to the psychic province (Buber 1969, p. 139).

In March and April of 1957, Buber conducted seven private seminars for the Washington School of Psychiatry, three of which dealt with the unconscious, a subject on which Buber had devoted much study and thought and which he originally intended to write up as a group of essays for the mature statement of his philosophical anthropology, *The Knowledge of Man.*

Freud, said Buber in these seminars, fell into the logical fallacy of declaring the unconscious to be psychical as the alternative to the view of his opponents, who held that because the psyche is conscious the unconscious must be physiological. Francis Schiller, for example, characterizes the unconscious mind as "an extrapolated concept rather than a thing in itself" and identifies it with physiological events.[4] To recognize that the unconscious is *not* only physiological does not necessarily mean that it is *only* psychical; yet Freud and all those who followed him in the various schools of psychiatry have held this to be the case. As revolutionary as Jung's differences from Freud are, he too puts the unconscious into the *psychical* category, and so does all modern psychology.

The *physical* and the *psychical* represent two radically different modes of knowing: that of the senses and that of the "inner sense." Pure psychic

---

[4]Francis Schiller, "Consciousness Reconsidered" in *Rational Mind, Unconscious Mind, and Brain, Psychosomatic Medicine,* XI, quoted in Buber, "Das Unbewusste."

process is not to be found in the physical. Our memory retains the process, to be sure, but by a new process in time. Physiology deals with things that are to be found, psychology with things that are not to be found. The psychic is pure process in time. In order to grasp the physical as a whole, we need the category of space as well as time. But for the psychic we need time alone. There are meeting points between the physical and the psychical—conscious ones—but we must distinguish between these two articulations of the unconscious.

The assumption that the unconscious is either body or soul, physical or psychical, Buber reiterated, is unfounded. The unconscious is a state out of which these two phenomena have not yet evolved and in which the two cannot be distinguished from one another. The unconscious is our being itself in its wholeness. Out of it the physical and the psychical evolve again and again and at every moment. The unconscious is not a phenomenon. It is what modern psychology holds it to be—a dynamic fact that makes itself felt by its effects, effects the psychologist can explore. But this exploration, as it takes place in psychiatry, is not of the unconscious itself, but rather of the phenomena that have been dissociated from it. Modern psychology's claim that there are unconscious things that influence our life and manifest themselves in certain conscious states is one that Buber, in contrast to Sartre, Binswanger, and other phenomenologists, does not contest. But we cannot, he reminds us, say anything about the unconscious in itself. It is never given to us. The radical mistake that Freud made was to think that he could posit a region of the mind as unconscious and at the same time deal with it as if its "contents" were simply repressed conscious material which could be brought back, without any essential change, into the conscious.

Dissociation is the process in which the unconscious "lump" manifests itself in inner and outer perceptions. This dissociation, in fact, may be the origin of our whole sense of inner and outer. The conscious life of the patient is a dualistic life, as he knows it; his objective life is not dualistic, but he does not know this life. A person can have, to some extent, the consciousness of the coming together of his forces, his acting unity, but he cannot perceive his unity as an object.

If the unconscious is not of the nature of the psychic, then it follows that the basic distinction between the physical and the psychic as "outer" and "inner" does not apply to the unconscious. Yet Freud, holding that the unconscious must be simply psychical, places the unconscious *within* the person, and so do all the schools that have come after Freud. As a result, *the basis of human reality itself comes to be seen as psychical rather than interhuman, and the relations between person and person are psychologized.* Freud's notion of making the conscious unconscious and the unconscious conscious means that there are repressed elements that the patient puts down into Acheron and that the therapist later induces him to bring out into the open. Buber's understanding of the relation between conscious and unconscious is radically different:

> If the unconscious is not something psychic that can be preserved in the underground but just a piece of human body and soul existence, it cannot at all again be raised as it was. We do not have a deep freeze which keeps fragments, but this unconscious has its own existence. It can again be dissociated into physical and psychic phenomena, but this means a radical change of the substance. This radical change can be accomplished by the patient with the supervision, help, and even initiative of the therapist (Buber 1969, p. 166).

The concept of "transference" changes radically if we no longer mean by it making the unconscious conscious, but rather the elaboration of elements that are dissociated from the unconscious. If the aim of therapy is to bring up something that is lying in the underground of the unconscious, then the therapist is only a kind of midwife. But if this work means the real and sometimes radical change of the substance, then transference eminently implies a certain influence of the therapist on the very act that is taking place. The patient *feels* as if he were discovering something that is going on, which is essentially the same as what is contained in his soul in unconscious form. "This is a mistake of the patient," said Buber, "induced by the relation between him and the therapist." Actually the patient brings up what he senses is wanted of him, something that is the product of his relationship with the therapist.

> I would ask the therapists of the world to examine anew the nature of this unique transference relationship. . . . No other relationship produces such strange phenomena. The responsibility in this new concept is shared and is not only up to the therapist (Buber 1969, p. 166).

Since the material that the patient brings forth in therapy is made and produced rather than simply brought up from the unconscious, the responsibility of the therapist is greater than has usually been supposed. "In the last ten years or so," Buber said in the course of the 1957 seminars, "I have the impression of a certain change in psychotherapeutic practice in which more and more therapists are not so confident that this or that theory is right and have a more 'musical,' floating relationship to their patients. *The deciding reality is the therapist, not the methods.*" Although no doctor can do without a typology, he knows that at a certain moment the unique person of the patient stands before the unique person of the doctor. He throws away as much of his typology as he can and accepts the unforeseeable happening that goes on between therapist and patient.

The usual therapist imposes himself on his patient without being aware of it. What is necessary is the conscious liberation of the patient from this unconscious imposition of the therapist—leaving the patient really to himself and seeing what comes out of it. The therapist approaches the patient, but he must try to influence him as little as possible, that is, the patient must not be influenced by the general ideas of the therapist's school of psychology. "It is much easier to impose oneself on the patient than it is to use the whole force of one's soul to leave the patient to himself and not to touch him. *The real master responds to uniqueness.*"

If the unconscious is that part of the existence of a person in which the realms of body and soul are not dissociated, then *the relationship between two persons would mean the relationship between two nondivided existences.* Thus the highest moment of relation would be what we call unconscious. (More precisely, the unconscious and the conscious are integrated in the spontaneity of personal meeting.) The unconscious should have, may have, and indeed will have more influence in the interhuman than the conscious. In shaking hands, for example, if there is a real desire to be in touch, the contact is not bodily or psychical, but a unity of one and the other. There is a direct contact between persons in their wholeness, of which the unconscious is the guardian.[5]

If the unconscious is the guardian of personal wholeness, then how are we to understand the unconscious of the divided person, the person with whom, above all, Freud dealt in his therapy and from whom he extrapolated his theory of repression of censored ideas into the unconscious? Leslie H. Farber, who himself has explicitly adopted Buber's understanding of the unconscious in his books *The Ways of the Will* and *lying, despair, jealousy, envy, sex, suicide, drugs, and the good life,* has suggested to me that Buber uses the unconscious in two different ways. From my discussion with Farber on this point, I think he meant that sometimes Buber uses the unconscious as the wholeness of the person prior to its elaboration into the physical and the psychic and sometimes he uses it as closer to Freud's sense of an unknown sphere that, in the divided person as in the whole, has real effects on the conscious life, which can be known even though it cannot be known in itself.

Buber did not deny repression, but he denied it the central, immutable place in human nature that Freud gave to it. Though he did not speak of this in his Washington seminars, he did express his views on the Freudian concept of repression in connection with his discussion of Max Scheler's anthropology in "What Is Man?," the first formal statement of Buber's own philosophical anthropology:

---

[5]The above pages are based on Section 8 of my "Introductory Essay" (Friedman 1966) to Buber 1965b, pp. 33–38, in which I paraphrase my notes on Martin Buber's seminars on the unconscious and dreams for the Washington School of Psychiatry, 1957.

Though these categories have general validity, the central position which Freud gives them, their dominating significance for the whole structure of personal and communal life, and especially for the origin and development of the spirit, is not based on the general life of man but only on the situation and qualities of the typical man of to-day. But this man is sick, both in his relation to others and in his very soul. The central significance of repression and sublimation in Freud's system derives from analysis of a pathological condition and is valid for this condition. The categories are psychological, their dominating power is pathopsychological. . . . Only if the organic community disintegrates from within and mistrust becomes life's basic note does the repression acquire its dominating importance. The unaffectedness of wishing is stifled by mistrust, everything around is hostile or can become hostile, agreement between one's own and the other's desire ceases, and the dulled wishes creep hopelessly into the recesses of the soul. . . . Now there is no longer a human wholeness with the force and the courage to manifest itself. For spirit to arise the energy of the repressed instincts must mostly first be "sublimated" . . . spirit . . . can mostly assert itself against the instincts only by convulsive alienation. *The divorce between spirit and instincts is here*, as often, *the consequence of the divorce between man and man* (Buber 1965, p. 196f., italics added).

It is Hans Trüb who has best spelled out the implications of this approach to the unconscious for healing through meeting. Repression, instead of being a basic aspect of human nature or an inescapable manifestation of civilization and its discontents, becomes the early denial of meeting, and its overcoming means the re-establishment of meeting, the breakthrough to dialogue:

*The unconscious touched by us has and takes its origin from that absolute "no" of the rejected meeting behind whose mighty barrier a person's psychic necessity for true meeting with the world secretly dams itself up, falls back upon itself, and thus,* as it were, *coagulates into the "unconscious."*
Because of the unconsciousness of the images we are delivered up passively to the might of the reality of the real; by means of analysis, by making the images conscious, we are capable of meeting this reality of the world steadily. . . . Introspective analysis does not open up for us a world which has to compete with reality; it does not open up for us another reality *as a world* in which one might be able to live. Rather it puts us in possession of the *world of images* with which alone we are truly enabled to meet the one and only real world . . . when we summon the person as person, we seek something which is in him from the beginning and yet disappeared in his youth. What is meant by the unconscious is precisely the personal element which is lost in the course of development . . . which escapes consciousness (Trüb 1952, pp. 96, 98f. 103f. in Friedman, 1973, p. 504).

The American psychologist Sabert Basescu strikes a note similar to Trüb's in his recognition of the part that volition and personal choice play in the formation of the unconscious:

> Most often, unconscious content is seen to be the consequence of childhood repressions. I think it is also the consequence of conscious choices. That is, the ways in which one chooses to structure his or her world influences the nature of one's unconscious experience. What is unconscious is a function of the self and its projects and is determined by them. Unconsciously determined behavior is a result of prior choice and commitment. In that sense, the unconscious influences consciousness and consciousness influences the unconscious. Psychoanalysis has traditionally concerned itself with the former, not the latter. . . . I try to emphasize the latter (without neglecting the former) . . . (Basescu 1977, p. 162).

In the light of both Buber's and Trüb's discussion of repression and its origin in the turning away from or failure of dialogue, we are in a position to deal more precisely with what we said above about the second type of consciousness as an unknown sphere that has real effects on the conscious life. In the relatively whole person, this unconscious would have a direct impact, not only on the conscious life, but also on others, precisely because it represents the wholeness of the person. In the relatively divided person, on the contrary, the unconscious itself has suffered a cleavage so that not only are there repressed materials that cannot come up into consciousness, but what does come up does not represent the wholeness of the person but only one of the fragments.

If we follow this logic, Freud's man would turn out to be the divided and sick modern person who has become alienated from any community in which he or she has confidence and trust. This would also turn out to be an oversimple picture, since we would have to differentiate not only between the unconscious and preconscious, as Freud does, but between the various fragments of the divided self that may dwell separately in the unconscious, even when this term is used in the Freudian sense of what is not accessible to consciousness because of repression.

This would open the way for the understanding of the phenomenon of multiple personalities, such as Sybil, who had sixteen personalities, fifteen of which knew nothing about the others, but one of which knew all about the rest. It would also open the understanding of gradations between the "whole person" and the "divided person." No one is ever whole once and for all. Rather, wholeness is a continually achieved and reachieved personal reality that is always confronted with the task of accepting what is brought to it by the address of the world as well as bringing into personal wholeness the surging and possibly conflicting emotions aroused by that address. On the other hand, even the most severely divided person, like Sybil, is not totally unaware on some level of the other parts of the self. As one moves to greater wholeness, one's unconscious would increasingly reflect and guard that wholeness.

As the unconscious of the relatively whole person is the very ground of meeting and an integral part of the interhuman, the unconscious of the relatively divided person is the product of the absence or denial of meeting. From this we can infer that the overcoming of the split between the repressed unconscious and the conscious of the divided person depends on healing through meeting. This includes such confirmation as the therapist can summon from the relationship with the client to counterbalance the "absolute no" of the meeting rejected or withheld in childhood.

# Chapter 14

# Dialogue with Dreams

At the beginning of his essay "Dialogue," under the heading "Original Remembrance," Martin Buber tells us of a recurring dream that is itself a powerful intimation of the role that dreams play in the life of dialogue:

> Through all sorts of changes the same dream, sometimes after an interval of several years, recurs to me. I name it the dream of the double cry. Its context is always much the same, a "primitive" world meagerly equipped. I find myself in a vast cave, like the Latomias of Syracuse, or in a mud building that reminds me when I awake of the villages of the *fellahin*, or on the fringe of a gigantic forest whose like I cannot remember having seen.
>
> The dream begins in very different ways, but always with something extraordinary happening to me, for instance, with a small animal resembling a lion-cub (whose name I know in the dream but not when I awake) tearing the flesh from my arm and being forced only with an effort to loose its hold. The strange thing is that this part of the dream story, which in the duration as well as the outer meaning of the incidents is easily the most important, always unrolls at a furious pace as though it did not matter. Then suddenly the pace abates: I stand there and cry out. In the view of the events which my waking consciousness has, I should have to suppose that the cry I utter varies in accordance with what preceded it, and is sometimes joyous, sometimes fearful, sometimes even filled both with pain and with triumph. But in the morning recollection it is neither so expressive nor so various. Each time it is the same cry, inarticulate but in strict rhythm, rising and falling, swelling to a fulness which my throat could not endure were I awake, long and slow, quiet, quite slow and very long, a cry that is a song. When it ends my heart

stops beating. But then, somewhere, far away, another cry moves towards me, another which is the same, the same cry uttered or sung by another voice. Yet it is not the same cry, certainly no "echo" of my cry but rather its true rejoinder, tone for tone not repeating mine, not even in a weakened form, but corresponding to mine, answering its tones—so much so, that mine, which at first had to my own ear no sound of questioning at all, now appear as questions, as a long series of questions, which now all receive a response. The response is no more capable of interpretation than the question. And yet the cries that meet the one cry that is the same do not seem to be the same as one another. Each time the voice is new. But now, as the reply ends, in the first moment after its dying fall, a certitude, true dream certitude comes to me that *now it has happened*. Nothing more. Just this, and in this way—*now it has happened*. If I should try to explain it, it means that that happening which gave rise to my cry has only now, with the rejoinder, really and undoubtedly happened.

After this manner the dream has recurred each time—till once, the last time, now two years ago. At first it was as usual (it was the dream with the animal), my cry died away, again my heart stood still. But then there was quiet. There came no answering call. I listened, I heard no sound. For I *awaited* the response for the first time; hitherto it had always surprised me, as though I had never heard it before. Awaited, it failed to come. But now something happened with me. As though I had till now had no other access from the world to sensation save that of the ear and now discovered myself as a being simply equipped with senses, both those clothed in the bodily organs and the naked senses, so I exposed myself to the distance, open to all sensation and perception. And then, not from a distance but from the air round about me, noiselessly, came the answer. Really it did not come; it was there. It had been there—so I may explain it—even before my cry: there it was, and now, when I laid myself open to it, it let itself be received by me. I received it as completely into my perception as ever I received the rejoinder in one of the earlier dreams. If I were to report with what I heard it I should have to say "with every pore of my body." As ever the rejoinder came in one of the earlier dreams this corresponded to and answered my cry. It exceeded the earlier rejoinder in an unknown perfection which is hard to define, for it resides in the fact that it was already there.

When I had reached an end of receiving it, I felt again that certainty, pealing out more than ever, that *now it has happened* (Buber 1965, pp. 1–3).

Healing through meeting means the concrete unfolding in therapy of the "ontology of the between." In terms of the preceding chapter, it means specifically the discovery of the implications of our understanding of the unconscious for the dream-work that the client carries out in dialogue with the therapist. In every school of therapy, in fact, there is a correlation between the view of the unconscious and the understanding and interpretation of dreams. The correlation goes both ways, of course. One of the milestones on Freud's road to the understanding of the unconscious was his *Interpretation of Dreams.*

According to Ellenberger, Freud's approach to dreams contained four innovations:

> The first is his model of the dream with its distinction of manifest and latent content and its specific pattern of being lived simultaneously in the present and the remote past. The second is Freud's contention that the manifest content is a distortion of the latent content, resulting from repression by the censor. . . . Freud's third innovation was the application of the free association as a method for the analysis of dreams, and the fourth was the introduction of systematic dream interpretation as a tool of psychotherapy (Ellenberger 1970, p. 493).

In his *Interpretation of Dreams,* Freud asserts that what we remember of dreams is, in the first place, mutilated by the unfaithfulness of our recollection, which appears to a large extent to be incapable of preserving the dream and has perhaps lost the essential pieces of its content. But in the second place, everything indicates that our memories of the dream are not only fragmentary, but also are untrue and falsified. Indeed, some authors hold that everything of order and connection that we use to recollect the dream is actually read into it! Freud quotes Nietzsche's saying that in the dream an ancient piece of humanity lives on to which we have barely any direct access.

Freud claims that there are persons who are fully aware of the fact that they are asleep and dreaming and are even able to direct their dreams. "One such dreamer, for example, was dissatisfied with the turn a dream was taking, interrupted it, and, without waking up, began it again in order to continue it in a different direction." This is almost exactly what Buber reported of himself during the seminars for the Washington School of Psychiatry! "The interpretation of dreams is the *via regia* to the knowledge of the unconscious in the life of the soul," Freud wrote. The most complicated and most correct processes of thought, to which one cannot deny the name of psychic happenings, may occur without penetrating to the consciousness of the person. In the face of this, Freud asks what role remains in our representation to the once all-powerful consciousness through which we interpreted everything else. His answer is, "nothing other than a sense organ for the perception of psychic qualities."[1]

---

[1]Sigmund Freud, *Die Traumdeutung* (cited after the London edition II/III), pp. 516f., 554, 613, 616f., 620, quoted in Buber, "Das Unbewusste."

Freud's mistrust of our memories of dreams is shared by many others. The French philosopher Henri Bergson states that the imagination of the sleeper who awakes adds something to the dream, modifies it retroactively, and fills in the holes, which may be considerable. Harry Stack Sullivan makes an even stronger disclaimer:

> One never, under any circumstances, deals directly with dreams. It is simply impossible. What one deals with in psychiatry, and actually in a great many other aspects of life, are recollections pertaining to dreams; how closely, how adequately these recollections approximate the actual dreams is an insoluble problem, because as far as I know there is no way to develop a reasonable conviction of one-to-one correspondence between recollection of dreams and dreams themselves. . . . In most of the dreams that the patient feels more or less compelled to report, one frequently encounters massive evidence of security operations that have gone into action on awakening. Although the fragments of these dreams which are reported might be very helpful if they could be preserved in meaningful detail, they have quite insidiously and unwittingly been moved into great textures of dramatic action in which everything which met the real utility of the dream has been almost hopelessly confounded into what Freud called secondary elaboration (Sullivan 1953, pp. 331–333).

The German philosopher and psychologist Ludwig Klages has provided us with a bridge to the dialogical understanding of dreams in his book on the consciousness of dreams. "What we touch on in the completed dream," writes Klages, "can no longer be called subject and object." Klages sees the meaning of the dream as the destruction of time. Not only does something not remain the same with the lapse of time, but even in the same time it can be both one thing and another. In the dream the logic of identity and the concept of fact disappear. When one seeks to capture the dream, it melts away. In the dream we no longer find ourselves in the flux of time where every now incessantly flees into the past. Rather we found ourselves in an ever enduring present with an unbounded, moving non-point, and we find ourselves even as little in a space which it takes time to measure. Rather we exist in an unbounded here. Only the person who has fully taken in the fact that the dream space is essentially dissimilar to waking space and dream time from waking time can undertake to interpret the contents of dreams with any hope of success.[2]

A still more important bridge to the dialogical understanding of dreams is Rollo May's phenomenological study, "The Dreams of Susan." The original state of the infant, May suggests, is not unconsciousness but a

---

[2]Ludwig Klages, *Vom Traumbewusstsein*, pp. 22, 32, 39, 43, quoted in Buber, "Das Unbewusste."

generalized awareness out of which consciousness and unconsciousness develop as a by-product of the differentiation of self and world and the emergence of language and the capacity to use symbols. The split in consciousness inherent in the differentiation between subject and object involves the capacity to postpone or deny awareness of potentialities. In fact, May defines the contents of the unconscious as "the potentialities for awareness and experience which the individual is unable or unwilling at that time to actualize."

From this approach to the unconscious it follows that every dream situation has within it some crisis that is the occasion for the person's having the dream on this particular night. "Every dream has within it some decision, latent, repressed or contradictory as this may be." The incentive for dreaming is the need to re-mold one's relationship to the world in the face of some conflict, anxiety, bafflement, or fork in the road. Thus to May the unconscious experience *itself* is intentional, moving toward meaning. This is a meaning the patient must experience rather than explain. The dream symbol and myth unites feeling, willing, and thinking in a totality of meaning that "grasps" us. May also goes along with Freud and Jung in the belief that there are symbols that have such deep biological and cultural roots, like those related to birth and death, that they may well be universal. But he emphasizes more than they do the importance of the way in which the given individual relates to a universal symbol. To understand the individual we must understand "how he uniquely selects, forms, and re-creates a universal symbol." One example May gives is the mirror, which stands in Susan's dreams for an intersubjective world with no people in it, a world in which others exist only in terms of reflections, only in reference to "How do I look?" (May 1968).

In his seminars for the Washington School of Psychiatry, Buber questioned whether we know or *have* dreams at all. What we possess, rather, is the work of the shaping memory that tells us of the dreamer's relation to the "dream," but nothing of the dream in itself. Buber also questioned the notion of the "content" of dreams and with it Freud's whole theory of repression:

> We are inclined to think the rhythmical recurrence of dreams is analogous to the conscious state of the soul. Yet we cannot compare a dream to any other phenomenon. In the dream itself it seems we have a certain feeling of consciousness. Its relation to consciousness in psychic life is a real problem. . . . Sometimes when I am waking I make a violent effort to detach myself from the world of dreams and enter the common world of man (Heraclitus) (Buber 1969, p. 159).

Another question that Buber raised was that of the identity and nonidentity of the dream-object with the object in waking life. In dreams, the order and hegemony of waking life is suspended in favor of continuity and connection of a very different nature.

> A psychological theory of the dream is made terribly difficult by the fact that the dream is not given us as an experience or an object of investigation or something that can be compared with the conscious. In my old age I have not arrived at a state of equanimity about the dreams I have every night. Freud dealt with it as self-understood. The Taoists never ceased to think about the problem of dreams. The dream is a problem really neighboring on that of death. Shakespeare's comparison is not metaphorical, for both are unknown by their very nature. We think we know the dream of our shaping memory, but there is a substrate that eludes us (Buber 1969, p. 159f.).

Buber's report of his own dreams strikingly bears out Klages' observations on the great difference between the space and time of waking and that of the dream:

> In the dreams that we remember there is sometimes an interposition of spaces, meaning that here things are going on and here other things, not intermingling. Here there are, so to speak, two planes, two space dimensions going on, one in the face of the other. Even more curious are appearances in time. I once had a dream in which at one moment I walked forward and a wind was blowing into my face, and I said to myself in the dream, "Ah, this is the other time." I felt not only the one line of time going on from birth to death, but also as if there were another line of time coming toward me, striking me. In reflection I thought, "Oh, this is the same thing with space as with time." In dreams there is a connection between things entirely different from that of waking, but it exists. There was a time in my life when I knew very much of dreams and then less and less, so now it is only remembering (Buber 1969, p. 163).

Buber also reported on how he succeeded in guiding the dream while asleep and on that basis concluded that there is a certain moment of will in the dream though not felt as such in the dream:

> A certain dream went on until in a moment I felt in the dream, "It is not as it should be—what now?" As if I were writing a story and thought of changing it. From this moment on the same scene occurred again and again with some variants. Finally, I succeeded in changing the last scene and it went on. This recurred many times (Buber 1969, p. 163).

There is, in conscious life, an ordering force. Each morning anew when we awake a power begins to make us act and live in a common cosmos. Nothing of this kind happens in dreams. They have a certain continuity and connection of their own, but we cannot understand this connection or compare it to that of the waking world. The dreamer, so long as he is dreaming, has no share in the common world and nothing, therefore, to which we can have access. The existential analyst Medard Boss contests Heraclitus' statement that only the waking have a common world by pointing to the fact that in dreams we are seldom alone and that 85 percent of our dreams include other people. In so doing, Boss misses the essential difference between relationships in the waking world and those in dreams. Dreams are the residue of our waking dialogues. Not only is there no real meeting with otherness in our dreams, but even the traces of otherness are greatly diminished. This does not mean, as Jung and Fritz Perls hold, that every person in the dream is really ourselves. But we cannot speak of dream relations as if they were identical with relations to persons in waking life.[3] What we can say is that having set the dream over against us, thus isolated, shaped, elaborated, and given form as an independent opposite, we enter into dialogue with it. From now on it becomes one of the realities that addresses us in the world, just as surely and as concretely as any so-called external happening.

"There are two kinds of therapists," Buber asserted at the Washington seminars, "one who knows more or less consciously the kind of interpretation of dreams he will get; and the other, the psychologist, who does not know. I am entirely on the side of the latter, who does not want something precise. He is ready to receive what he will receive. He cannot know what method he will use beforehand. He is, so to speak, in the hands of his patient." One cannot interpret poetry by the same methods one interprets a novel, and still less can one interpret the dreams of one patient by the same methods one interprets the dreams of another. A person is a better therapist if, in the interpretation of dreams, he is not a Freudian, Jungian, or Adlerian, but rather is guided by what the patient brings to him. The therapist must be ready to be surprised. From this type of "obedient listening," a new type of therapist may evolve—a person of greater responsibility and even greater gifts, since it is not so easy to master new attitudes without ready-made categories (Buber 1969, p. 167f.).

---

[3]Medard Boss, *Der Traum und seine Auslegung* (1955), p. 97. Quoted in Buber, "Das Unbewusste." See also Buber 1965b, Chapter 4.

# Chapter 15

# Paradoxes of Guilt

One of the most important contours of dialogical psychotherapy, as of all psychotherapy, is the therapist's approach to guilt. Freud saw guilt as repressed from conscious awareness, and dreams as the royal road to guilt, as to the unconscious in general. Buber, although not denying the existence of repressed neurotic repressed guilt, went beyond Freud in positing the existence of an "existential guilt" attached to events that are accessible to the conscious mind, but that have lost their character of guilt because of our attitude toward them. The dialogical therapists must be ready to deal with that attitude in quite specific ways.

To Freud, guilt was the product of the introjection of the harsh superego. As such, it was identical with societal and parental taboos, at best, or the neurotic fixation of these processes, at worst. Although Freud did not imagine that one could overcome guilt entirely, he looked on it as something to be modulated, insofar as possible, in favor of what might allow the individual more happiness. Guilt to Freud, therefore, was a built-in part of the psychic and social system, but was inherently extrinsic as far as values go.

There is nothing paradoxical in all this. From the standpoint of healing through meeting, in contrast, guilt is doubly paradoxical. It is paradoxical, first, in that healing through meeting necessarily implies the existence of a real, existential guilt, which, however, is usually confusedly intermingled with neurotic and/or merely social guilt. It is paradoxical, second, in that the predominance of neurotic guilt in our culture and the traumatized response to it on the part of many individuals makes it difficult to discuss real guilt without evoking the same reactions of acquiescence or rejection that are triggered by neurotic guilt.

The common order of the world that we build up through our common speech and the centrality of human existence as "We" are basic to Martin Buber's distinction, in "Guilt and Guilt Feelings" (*The Knowledge of Man*, 1966), between "groundless" neurotic guilt—a subjective feeling within a person, usually unconscious and repressed—and "existential" guilt—an ontic, interhuman reality in which the person dwells in the truest sense of the term. The analyst, writes Buber in "Healing through Meeting," must see the illness of the patient as an illness of his relations with the world. True guilt does not reside in the human person, but rather in his failure to respond to the legitimate claim and address of the world. Similarly, the repression of guilt and the neuroses that result from this repression are not merely psychological phenomena, but rather events between persons (Buber 1969, pp. 140–142).

Existential guilt, continues Buber, is "guilt that a person has taken on himself as a person and in a personal situation." Certainly there is purely social and even neurotic guilt derived from a set of mores and taboos imposed upon the individual by parents and society and incorporated into an internalized "superego." But there is also real guilt, guilt that has to do with one's actual stance in the world and the way in which one goes out from it to relate to other persons. Real guilt is neither subjective nor objective. It is dialogical—the inseparable corollary of one's personal responsibility, one's answerability for authenticating one's own existence, and by the same token, for responding to the partners of one's existence, the other persons with whom one lives. Where there is personal responsibility, there must also be the possibility of real guilt—for failing to respond, for responding inadequately or too late, or for responding without one's whole self.

Such guilt is neither inner nor outer. One is not answerable for it either to oneself alone or to society apart from oneself, but to that very bond between oneself and others through which one again and again discovers the direction through which one can authenticate one's existence. If a relation with another cannot be reduced to what goes on within each of the two persons, then the guilt one person has toward a partner in a relationship cannot be reduced to the subjective guilt he feels. "Existential guilt," writes Buber, "occurs when someone injures an order of the human world whose foundations he knows and recognizes [at some level of his being] as those of his own existence and of all common human existence." Hence, existential guilt transcends the realm of inner feelings and of the self's relation to itself.

The order of the human world that one injures is not an objective absolute, whether of Platonic ideas, society, or the church, hence something that we may see as purely external and alien to ourselves, however much we must submit ourselves to it. It is the sphere of the "interhuman" itself, precisely those We's that we have built in common in family, group, and community and to which our own existence belongs in the most literal sense of the term. Although we may not recognize what it means to injure an "order of the human world," everyone knows quite well how, through acts of omission or commission, attacking or withholding oneself, one may injure one's family, one's group of friends, one's community, one's colleagues, or one's fellow employees. The sphere of the interhuman and the guilt that arises in it cannot be identified with the taboos and restrictions of any particular culture and society. "The depth of the guilt feeling is not seldom connected with just that part of the guilt that cannot be ascribed to the taboo-offence, hence with the existential guilt."

Guilt is an essential factor in the person's relations to others: it performs the necessary function of leading one to desire to set these relations to right. It is actually here, in the real guilt of the person who has not responded to the legitimate claim and address of the world, that the possibility of transformation and healing lies. The therapist may lead the person who suffers from existential guilt to the place where that person can walk the road of illuminating that guilt, persevering in one's identification of oneself as the person who, no matter how different from what one once was, took on that guilt, and, insofar as one's situation makes possible, restoring and repairing "the order of being injured by one through the relation of an active devotion to the world" (Buber 1966, Ch. 6).

"Original guilt consists in remaining with oneself," writes Buber in criticism of the German existentialist philosopher Martin Heidegger. If the being before whom this hour places one is not met with the truth of one's whole life, then one is guilty. Primal guilt is not found in our relation to ourselves, but rather by becoming aware of the life in which we are essentially related to something other than ourselves.

By the same token, real guilt could not be limited to the guilt that the existential psychoanalyst Medard Boss, following Heidegger, sees as arising from failing to fulfill one's indebtedness to Being through realizing one's potentialities:

> If you lock up potentialities you are guilty against (or *indebted to*) what is given you in your origin, in your "core." In this existential condition of being indebted and being guilty are founded all guilt feelings, in whatever thousand and one concrete forms and malformations they may appear in actuality.[1]

One's potential uniqueness may be given, but the direction in which one authenticates one's existence is not; one discovers it in constantly renewed decisions in response to the demand of concrete situations. When we are

---

[1]Quoted in May 1958, p. 53.

guilty, it is not because we have failed to realize our potentialities, which we cannot know in the abstract, but rather because we have failed to bring the resources we find available to us at a given moment into our response to a particular situation that calls us out. This means that we cannot be guilty *a priori* to any ideal conception of the self, but only in relation to those moment-by-moment chances to authenticate ourselves that come to us in the concrete situation. Our potentialities cannot be divorced from the discovery of our personal direction, and this comes not in the meeting of a person with oneself, but rather with other persons. The order of existence that one injures is one's own order, as well as that of the others, because it is the foundation and the very meaning of one's existence as self.

The denial of "the depth of existential guilt beyond all mere violation of taboo" is what Freud sought to accomplish through relativizing guilt feelings genetically, writes Buber in "Guilt and Guilt Feelings." It is characteristic of that "advanced" generation for which "it now passes as proved . . . that no real guilt exists; only guilt-feeling and guilt convention." This denial amounts to a crisis not only in the life of modkern man, but also of man as such, for "man is the being who is capable of becoming guilty and is capable of illuminating his guilt."

One part of this crisis is the denial of real guilt. Another is the complex and confused intermingling of real and neurotic guilt even when real guilt is not denied. This makes it a very delicate and subtle matter for both therapist and client to sort out the strands and know which at any given instant is which. The clinical psychologist A. David Feinstein offers a helpful suggestion for the approach to this sorting out:

> Identifying whether a patient is suffering from a neurotic or existential guilt is complicated by the fact that the two often combine and interact. Existential guilt may begin to lift once its meaning has been grasped, but accompanying neurotic guilt may already have been engaged. For instance, enjoying favorable circumstances in a world where many are suffering invites existential guilt when you are in some fundamental way denying your calling in relation to the human community. If you were also programmed to decrease your sense of selfworth whenever you get the bigger piece of the pie, neurotic guilt will also be present. If both forms are thus engaged, it can be therapeutically useful to separate the informative aspects of the existential guilt from the punishing qualities of neurotic guilt. . . . Once this has been recognized and changes are made but guilt persists, counseling that challenges such guilt becomes appropriate.[2]

---

[2]A. David Feinstein, "Self-Responsibility in Illness and the Issue of Guilt" (unpublished). Much of Feinstein's article is based on this present chapter, which Feinstein saw in manuscript form.

Still another part of the crisis is the difficulty of distinguishing when it is oneself as a person that is called to account and not allowing others to lay "guilt trips" on one that one cannot and ought not to own.[3]

What can the therapist who is committed to healing through meeting do in the face of these paradoxes of guilt? One answer to this question is that given by Ivan Boszormenyi-Nagy in his book *Invisible Loyalties*. Hans Trüb, Leslie Farber, Ronald Laing, and Sidney Jourard, as we have seen, make explicit use of Buber's understanding of confirmation and of the primacy of meeting, or dialogue, in their approach to therapy. Only Boszormenyi-Nagy, to my knowledge, has built his therapy on the further reaches of Buber's philosophical anthropology—his understanding of the "essential We," the common world built by the common "speech-with-meaning" and the existential guilt that arises from the injury to this common world (Buber 1966, Chs. 4 and 6).

According to Boszormenyi-Nagy, the patient cannot solve his problems with his family, as so many traditionally oriented psychoanalysts recommend, just by moving away from home and becoming independent or by bringing to consciousness his feelings of hatred for his parents. A mass escape from filial obligations through fear of responsibility can infuse all human relationships with unbearable chaos, Boszormenyi-Nagy says. The individual can become paralyzed by amorphous therapeutically inaccessible existential guilt. By the same token, "the true measure of human emotion is not the intensity of its affective or physiological concomitant, but the relevance of its interpersonal context." Boszormenyi-Nagy follows Buber in distinguishing between relationships that are merely functions of individual becoming, normalcy, adaptation, and perspective and relationships that are ontological in the sense that they have a reality, accountability, meaning, and value in themselves. This leads Boszormenyi-Nagy to forceful and repeated emphasis on Buber's distinction between *intrapsychic guilt feelings* and *interhuman existential guilt*.

> The therapist who wants to liberate the patient from his concern for or guilt-laden loyalty to members of his family may succeed in removing certain manifestations of psychological guilt, but may at the same time increase the patient's existential guilt. Buber distinguished between guilt feelings and existential guilt. The latter obviously goes beyond psychology: It has to do with objective harm to the order and justice of the human world. If I really betrayed a friend or if my mother really feels that I damaged her through my existence, the reality of a disturbed

---

[3]This touches on the problematic of guilt, to which I have devoted most of a chapter in the book that lays the groundwork for this one, namely, Maurice Friedman, *Contemporary Psychology: Revealing and Obscuring the Human* (Pittsburgh: Duquesne University Press, 1984), pp. 167–175.

order of the human world remains, whether I can get rid of certain guilt feelings or not. Such guilt becomes part of a systemic ledger of merits and can only be affected by action and existential rearrangement, if at all (Boszormenyi-Nagy and Spark 1973, p. 184).[4]

However valuable its contribution to the understanding of man as a closed system, any psychodynamic theory that confines itself to the motivation of the individual can be potentially socially destructive in its failure to meet the demands of our age for being aware of and responding to the needs of others. What makes a family perspective on justice particularly essential is the fact that some persons will never face or even recognize the injustice they have inflicted upon others except through the penalty their children and grandchildren pay. The family therapist focuses on a specific existential dimension that is being avoided, denied, and eroded in our age: the accounts of the justice of the human world. The family therapist must act in terms of a transgenerational bookkeeping of merits, an invisible systemic ledger of justice that resides in the interpersonal fabric of human order or the "realm of the between."

The therapist must distinguish between the person-to-person exploitativeness of nongiving or nonreciprocal taking and the structural exploitation that originates from system characteristics that victimize both participants at the same time. An imbalance between two or more partners in relationships registers subjectively as exploitation by the other. Moreover, an individual can be "caught" in existential guilt through the actions of others as one inherits a place in the multigenerational network of obligations and becomes accountable in the chain of past traditions. The less one is aware of these obligations, the more one will be at the mercy of these invisible forces (Boszormenyi-Nagy and Spark 1973, pp. 8, 55–58, 60f., 67).

Boszormenyi-Nagy sees the modern illusion of replacing rather than mitigating retributive justice with humanity as a great hypocrisy, which is a threat to the dynamic fiber of society itself. "Whereas an individual's *guilt feelings* can be understood without a consideration of the other members' feelings and reactions, the underlying existential guilt cannot." Therefore, the question of justice cannot be reduced to a matter of individual forgiveness or love, as so many imagine. What is more, "in not holding the innocent child accountable for the father's sins or the parents for their child's transgressions, we may overlook actual but hidden forces of complicity which reside in the family system."

The family therapist discovers that "past relational accounts which cannot be settled through self-reflecting analysis, transference resolution,

---

[4] I refer to Boszormenyi-Nagy alone in the text because he is the author of the main theoretical chapters of *Invisible Loyalties*.

and insight can actually be resolved through interpersonal initiative and corrective action, often in a three generational context." Personal exploitation is measurable only on a subjective scale that has been built into the person's sense of the meaning of his entire existence. The family therapist must deal with the subjective measure of exploitation of each member of the family system. "By opening up the door to rebalancing of merits through action, the process of therapy may reverse the accumulation and perpetuation of loaded, unsettled accounts which could otherwise prejudice the chances of future generations" (Boszormenyi-Nagy and Spark 1973, pp. 69, 78–81).

Buber's and Boszormenyi-Nagy's concept of "the just order of the human world" is a dialogical one. However pathological it may be, the unique experience of each of the persons in the family is itself of value: it enters into the balance of merit and into the dialogical reality-testing—the "dialogue of touchstones." The scapegoater in the family can be looked upon as needing help and the scapegoat as a potential helper; for the former is taking an ever heavier load of guilt on himself and the latter is accumulating merit through being loaded on by others. Justice is, for Boszormenyi-Nagy, "a personal principle of equity of mutual give and take which guides the individual member of a social group in facing the ultimate consequences of his relationships with others" (Boszormenyi-Nagy and Spark 1973, p. 61). The climate of trust that characterizes a social entity is the sum total of the subjective evaluations of the justice of each member's relational experiences within what Boszormenyi-Nagy calls the "revolving slate" of the historically formed merit ledger. The trust-worthiness of relationships depends on earned relational merit.

> We believe that the "interhuman" realm of justice of the human world is the foundation of the prospects of trust among people. . . . Attempts at denying or escaping from such accounting constitute a major dynamic of every relationship system. While such escape may be necessary temporarily for the person's autonomous explorations, it must be uncovered and faced if the social system is to remain productive of healthy growth (Boszormenyi-Nagy and Spark 1973, p. 148).

Insight alone—the confrontation with the merit ledger—is only the preface to the task of actively balancing relationships. In *The Knowledge of Man*, Martin Buber sees the overcoming of existential guilt as taking place through the three stages of illuminating that guilt, persevering in that illumination, and repairing the injured order of being by re-entering the dialogue with the world. In exact parallel, Boszormenyi-Nagy sees knowledge of the self and increased assertiveness as finding their place in the context of the accounts of fairness and justice in close relationships. No matter how vindictive a person may feel, the therapeutic goal must ultimately be focused on mutual clarification and reconstruction in order to provide the adult child and his parents with the opportunity to break the destructive chainlike patterns of relationship that may have continued for several generations.

The injustice of the parentification of children by their parents can only be redressed if one first goes back to the relationship of the parents to their family of origin and does something about constructive repayment of indebtedness there. Thus, as a therapeutic goal, by exonerating their parents, children extend to them an especially needed, primary form of inherent, residual acknowledgment. The family therapist must help the children obtain release from their captive victimization. In order to accomplish this, however, it is first necessary that the adults' own unmet dependency needs and unresolved negative loyalty ties, based on unjust treatment and exploitation by their families of origin, be recognized and worked through—whenever possible with the families of origin themselves. In many cases, even the terminal illness of the grandparent offers the opportunity for repayment of obligations and subsequent emotional liberation of all three generations from guilt. "We believe that the major avenue toward interrupting the multigenerational chain of injustices goes via repairing relationships, and not through the dichotomy of either magnifying or denying the injury done to particular members" (Boszormenyi-Nagy and Spark 1973, p. 95). One of the great opportunities of Boszormenyi-Nagy's three-generational approach lies in the possibility of rehabilitating the member's painful and shameful image of his parents through helping the member understand the burdens laid on his parents by their families of origin.

By opening up the door to rebalancing merits through action, the process of family therapy may reverse the accumulation and perpetuation of loaded, unsettled accounts that prejudice the chances of future generations. This applies even to the so-called "paranoid."

> If a human being has been too deeply hurt and exploited to be able to absorb his wounds, he is entitled to a therapeutic recognition of the reality of his wounds and to a serious examination of the others' willingness to repair the damage. Only through such a "concession by the world" will he be prepared to reflect on the possible injustice of his own actions to others. . . . The badly hurt paranoid person should be given an extra chance, at least to the extent that the unfair balance of his justice is recognized. Whereas the reality of each member's early exploitation is anchored in the family's multigenerational ledger, each individual family member's sense of suffered injustice becomes his life-long programming for "emotional distortions," a psychological reality (Boszormenyi-Nagy and Spark 1973, p. 91).

Justice, like trustworthiness, characterizes the emotional climate and the underlying existential ledger of a relationship system. Both concepts lie beyond the realm of individual psychology, and both lead to a reexamination and redefinition of the theories of projection, reality-testing, fixation, displacement, transference, change, ego strength, and autonomy. From the standpoint of the relationship system, paranoia, for example, may be a partly reality-based state of mind. Although it may be an overreaction to this particular person, it still grows out of a real ethical imbalance of the past. This redefinition of traditional psychological terms also leads Boszormenyi-Nagy to insight into the application of his dynamic of justice to the larger society as a whole. The "generation gap" is not one of communication, but rather of justice, Boszormenyi-Nagy claims. "Retributory projection on all parent-like persons might be an important component of the hostility that exists between youth and the older generation in any culture." Healing through meeting goes over here in all explicitness to the "Caring Community" that confirms otherness. "The greatest cultural task of our age," writes Boszormenyi-Nagy, "might be the investigation of the role of relational, not merely economic justice, in contemporary society. And the greatest gap in our social science pertains to the denial of the psychological significance of retributive social dynamics" (Boszormenyi-Nagy and Spark 1973, pp. 66, 74).

After reading *Invisible Loyalties* a highly competent family psychiatrist commented: "The whole aim of psychotherapy has been to get rid of guilt, and now Nagy wants to bring it back in!" This comment, I suspect, grows out of and illustrates all three paradoxes of guilt. It seems likely that this psychiatrist was not familiar with the notion of existential, or real, guilt, in the first place. Second, in his practice I am sure that he has been so occupied with the neurotic guilt that he encounters that even if he had encountered existential guilt he would be more concerned about the neurotic and would have difficulty in distinguishing the one from the other. Third, even if the first two suppositions were not true, his clients would undoubtedly be so hung up on neurotic guilt that he would hesitate to introduce any notion of real guilt for fear of triggering off unhealthy reactions on their part. For him, therefore, Boszormenyi-Nagy's position would not constitute an adequate answer to our question, "What can a therapist committed to healing through meeting do in the face of the paradoxes of guilt?"

I believe that here Hans Trüb can come to our aid. Trüb experienced a crisis as a therapist from his denial of *ethos* and with it real guilt in favor of a higher "spiritual" plane to which he wished to bring his patients. After his crisis, Trüb concluded that the acceptance of real guilt is the beginning of responsibility, and responsibility is what enables the person whose relationship with the community has been ruptured to reenter into dialogue with the community. But Trüb also recognized, as we have seen, that this rejunction with the community, to use Nagy's phrase, has to take place in two stages: First, the therapist has to realize that the person before him is someone who has been rejected and disconfirmed by the community, someone who stands in need of the understanding and confirmation that a confidant and big brother or big sister can give. Only later, after the therapist has succeeded in giving the patient the confirmation he has been denied, does the therapist enter the second state and place upon the patient the demand of the community in order to help the patient renew the dialogue with the community that has been injured or destroyed.

Placing the demand of the community does not mean any moralizing from above. It means connecting the hour of therapy with real life so that the client can recognize in the therapist a really other person who himself has real ties to the community and stands within it. Trüb's two stages are remarkably parallel, indeed, to the comfort and demand that the Hebrew prophet brought to the community of Israel in order to bring it back into dialogue with God. One part of that message was the recognition of real guilt, but another was the promise and renewal of dialogue:

> For a brief moment I forsook you,
> but with great compassion I will gather you.
> In overflowing wrath for a moment
> I hid my face from you,
> but with everlasting love I will have compassion on you. . . .
> For the mountains may depart
> and the hills be removed,
> but my steadfast love shall not depart from you,
> and my covenant of peace shall not be removed,
> says the Lord, who has compassion on you. (Isaiah
> 54:7–10)

Trüb's two stages cannot be applied mechanically. Only out of the dialogue itself will the therapist know when to bring comfort and when to place demand and when, perhaps, a combination of the two. Some persons may be so injured that it is hardly possible to reach the second stage, in which the full reality of healing through meeting can take place. Here the therapist not only needs all the wisdom and tact he can summon, but also the courage to address and the courage to respond of existential trust. All these will only have meaning, moreover, if they take effect within the act of inclusion in which the therapist makes the patient present and, through a bold imaginative swinging, experiences his side of the bipolar relationship.

There still remains one aspect of our paradox that neither Boszormenyi-Nagy nor Trüb has adequately dealt with. That is the fact that in our culture there is such a strong conditioning of guilt that most people are simply triggered by the term and *cannot* make the distinction between real and neurotic guilt. In the face of this fact, the therapist has a simple expedient, one which will probably also help him too, since he is a part of the culture. That is, at certain times and in certain cases, not to use the word "guilt," but instead to speak of responsibility in its relation to response and to help the patient to see the extent to which it is his own existence that is injured when the common order of existence is injured by him. This too cannot be moralizing from above, but only a part of sensitive dialogue and dialectic between therapist and patient.

In the end, the paradox of guilt must be understood in the broader context of the problematic of confirmation and the "dialogue of touch-stones" that can, more than anything, lead to healing through meeting.

# Chapter 16

# The Problematic of Mutuality

As soon as healing through meeting is made the focus of therapy, the question inevitably arises as to how much mutuality is possible and desirable between therapist and patient. This is a question that begins on the far side of the terminology of transference and countertransference. In its original usage by Freud, transference implies the projection by the patient upon the analyst and countertransference implies the projection by the analyst upon the patient. Whether one regards countertransference negatively, as Freud did, or positively, as Jung did, it is still largely an intrapsychic matter, even as is transference. The problematic of mutuality, in contrast, has to do with the real interhuman relationship between therapist and patient and with the extent to which that relationship can be fully mutual.

Freud prescribed a mirrorlike impassivity on the part of the analyst, who should himself be analyzed, who should not reciprocate the patient's confidences and not try to educate, morally influence, or "improve" the patient, and who should be tolerant of the patient's weakness. In practice, however, Freud "conducted therapy as no classical Freudian analyst would conduct it today," writes Janet Malcolm in *Psychoanalysis: The Impossible Profession*, shouting at the patient, praising him, arguing with him, accepting flowers from him on his birthday, lending him money, and even gossiping with him about other patients! Among Freudian analysts today, the analyst generally confines himself to listening to the patient, offering sparse interpretations of the unconscious meaning of his communications. This behavior is so neutral that it invariably provokes anger and may even lead the patient to terminate. "He does not give advice," reports Janet Malcolm, he does not talk about himself, he does not let himself he provoked or drawn into discussions of abstract subjects, he does not answer questions about his family or his political preferences, he does not show like or dislike of the patient, or approval or disapproval of his actions. His behavior toward the patient is as neutral, mild, colorless, self-effacing, uninterfering, and undemanding as he is able to make it, and as it is toward no one else in his life—with the paradoxical (and now absolutely predictable) result that the patient reacts with stronger, more vivid and intense personal feelings to this bland, shadowy figure than he does to the more clearly delineated and provocative figures in his life outside the analysis. On this paradox . . . the analysis is poised, and it may as easily founder as take off. If the patient sees the analyst as a cold, callous person of limited intelligence and unbounded tactlessness, he may decide to quit the analysis (Malcolm 1981, p. 37f.).

Sandor Ferenczi, one of Freud's early followers, departed from this neutrality and impassivity in favor of giving a nursery care, or management of regression (D. W. Winnicott) to very sick patients, including one whom he saw anytime, day or night, and took with him on his holidays. Even Anna Freud, in 1954, called for the recognition that in analysis two real people of equal adult status stand in a real personal relationship to each other. It is the neglect of this side of the relationship, and not just "transference," that causes the hostile reactions analysts get from their patients. In 1961 in *The Psychoanalytic Situation*, Leo Stone expressed concern lest the analyst's unrelentingly analytic behavior subvert the process by shaking the patient's faith in the analyst's benignity. A failure to show reasonable human response at a critical juncture can invalidate years of patient, skillful work, Stone declared (Malcolm 1981, pp. 133, 40, 42).

The problem of mutuality cannot be understood, we have suggested, within strict limits of orthodox psychoanalysis, since it cannot relegate the relationship between therapist and patient to one of pure "transference" and "countertransference." Sidney Jourard's books, *The Transparent Self* and *Disclosing Man to Himself*, are helpful in setting the groundwork for this problem, since Jourard was influenced both by Carl Rogers and Martin Buber and found no conflict between the two in his own approach to mutuality. Jourard places Buber's I–Thou relationship, or "dialogue," at the center of therapy, which implied to him that he must share himself as he is with his patient: *"I can come closest to eliciting and reinforcing authentic behavior in my patient by manifesting it myself."* Jourard counsels the therapist to hear out his patient, but at the same time maintain his separate identity. The therapist's spontaneity and honesty invites that of the patient: "Self-disclosure begets self-disclosure." The heart of the I–Thou relationship, to Jourard, is abandoning all attempts to shape his patient's behavior according to some predetermined scheme. Therapy is not a setting in which the therapist *does* things to a patient, but rather "an honest relationship gradually developing into one of I and Thou; a dialogue, in which growth of both parties is an outcome." Jourard agrees with Rogers that good listening reinforces further self-disclosure by the patient, but he also testifies that over the years he has come more and more to supplement such listening by "giving advice, lecturing, laughing, becoming angry, interpreting, telling my fantasies, asking questions—in short, doing whatever occurs to me *during* the therapeutic session in response to the other person."

This does not mean *full* mutuality to Jourard, any more that it does, in fact, to Rogers. He trusts what comes out of him in response to a patient, but he still checks this by common sense or judgment, and he limits it to an openness of himself *in that moment.* He finds this transparency, or "congruence," to use Rogers' term, totally consonant with Buber's dictum that in a real dialogue one cannot know *in advance* how one will respond. If he does not want to answer a question, he tells this to the patient honestly and directly. If he is angry, worried, or anxious, he lets it be known. The result of this transparency is that the patient "will come to know him *as he is during the hours together.* (One need not tell the patient about one's life outside the therapy hour, unless one wishes.)" Such honesty and spontaneity corrects the patient's transference misperceptions and makes the therapist's responses unpredictable and therefore unmanipulable by the patient. The patient's distrust is gradually relieved, and the therapist "provides the patient with a role model of authentic being with which he can identify." Such authenticity on the therapist's part may mean that the therapeutic relationship changes the therapist as much as the patient (Jourard 1971, pp. 141f., 144–151).

In *Disclosing Man to Himself*, Jourard reaffirms all these emphases upon mutuality in the therapist–patient relationship. As the therapist grows in the capacity for dialogue, he becomes more wholehearted in his "invitation to terrified, self-concealing people to disclose themselves as they are." "A therapist, himself a rehabilitated phony, invites the patient to try the frightening rigors of the authentic way, first with the therapist and then with others." Jourard not only makes the I–Thou relationship the center of healing, but also sees it as the *sine qua non* for any good interpersonal relationship between therapist and patient, "where the influencer is as vulnerable and open as the one to be influenced": "*Only* within such a mutually open relationship can the therapist maximally present his therapeutic influence, *at the risk, incidentally, of being demoralized or sickened by the patient*" (italics added). "No technique will work when I and thou are not thus open."

This often includes for Jourard some form of physical contact to expedite the arrival of this mutual openness and unreserve. Holding hands with a patient, putting an arm around a shoulder, giving a hug, all may be of value within the context of an unfolding dialogue. "I believe we are a nation of people who are starved for physical contact (Jourard 1968, pp. 23, 61–65). At the same time, Jourard recognizes that authentic self-disclosure that is blind to the other and does not imagine the real will be therapeutically harmful. He lost several male patients because he assumed that they could "take it." He was being sensitive to his own authentic being and not theirs:

> If I had not been so smug or blind, I would have kept my mouth shut for five or six sessions until I got to know who they were. I wasn't responding to who they were; I was responding to this *autistic image* I had of who they were. They very effectively told me, by leaving, that I wasn't treating *them* at all (Jourard 1968, p. 80f.).

In the name of the I–Thou relationship, Jourard has gone considerably further than Carl Rogers toward espousing full mutuality between therapist and patient. Yet Buber found questionable even the degree of mutuality that Rogers put forward in the dialogue with him—one that, at that time, had more to do with listening than with response, "unconditional positive regard" and "empathic understanding" than "congruence."

Martin Buber, as we have seen, suggests that there are times when the therapist must put aside his professional superiority and his method and meet the patient as self to self. Yet in his 1957 dialogue with Carl Rogers, Buber would not accept Rogers' insistence that the relationship between therapist and patient should be seen, within the relationship itself, as fully mutual. To understand Buber's stance on this issue, we must look again at what he has written concerning "inclusion," in particular the "normative limitation" of inclusion in the therapy situation. In friendship and love, "inclusion," or experiencing the other side, is mutual. In the helping relationships, however, it is, Buber says, necessarily one-sided. The patient cannot equally well experience the relationship from the side of the therapist or the pupil from the side of the teacher without destroying or fundamentally altering the relationship. This does not mean that the therapist is reduced to treating his patient as an object, an It. The one-sided inclusion of therapy is still an I–Thou relationship founded on mutuality, trust, and partnership in a common situation, and it is only in this relation that real therapy can take place. If "all real living is meeting," all true healing also takes place through meeting.

If the psychotherapist is satisfied to "analyze" the patient, "i.e., to bring to light unknown factors from his microcosm, and to set to some conscious work in life the energies which have been transformed by such an emergence," then, says Buber in his 1958 Postscript to *I and Thou*, he may be successful in some repair work. At best he may help a soul that is diffused and poor in structure to collect and order itself to some extent. But the real matter, the regeneration of an atrophied personal center, will not be achieved. This can be done only by one who grasps the buried latent unity of the suffering soul with the great glance of the doctor, and this can only be attained in the person-to-person attitude of a partner, not by the consideration and examination of an object.

A common situation, however, does not mean one that each enters from the same or even a similar position. In psychotherapy, the difference in position is not only that of personal stance, but also of role and function, a difference determined by the very difference of purpose that led each to enter the relationship. If the goal is a common one—the healing of the patient—the relationship to that goal differs radically as between therapist and patient, and the healing that takes place depends as much upon the recognition of that difference as upon the mutuality of meeting and trust.

> In order that he may coherently further the liberation and actualization of that unity in a new accord of the person with the world, the psychotherapist, like the educator, must stand again and again not merely at his own pole in the bipolar relation, but also with the strength of present realization at the other pole, and experience the effect of his own action . . . the specific "healing" relation would come to an end the moment the patient thought of, and succeeded in, practising "inclusion" and experiencing the event from the doctor's pole as well. Healing, like educating, is only possible to the one who lives over against the other, and yet is detached (Buber 1958, p. 133).

The issue that arose in the dialogue between Buber and Rogers is a subtle one, to do justice to which we must look at what each of the two said. Rogers began with a description of his own approach to therapy and ventured that it was, as he himself had often written, an I–Thou relationship:

> I feel that when I'm being effective as a therapist, I enter the relationship as a subjective person, not as a scrutinizer, not as a scientist. I feel, too, that when I am most effective, then somehow I am relatively whole in that relationship. . . . To be sure there may be many aspects of my life that aren't brought into the relationship, but what is brought into the relationship is transparent. There is nothing hidden. Then I think, too, that in such a relationship I feel a real willingness for this other person to *be what he is.* I call that "acceptance." I don't know that that's a very good word for it, but my meaning there is that I'm willing for him to possess the feelings he possesses, to hold the attitudes he holds, to be the person he is. And then another aspect of it which is important to me is

that I think in those moments I am able to sense with a good deal of clarity the way his experience seems to him, really viewing it from within him, and yet without losing my own personhood or separateness in that.

Then, if in addition to those things on *my* part, my client or the person with whom I'm working is able to sense something of those attitudes in me, then it seems to me that there is a real, experiential meeting of persons, in which each of us is changed. I think sometimes that the client is changed more than I am, but I think both of us are changed in that kind of an experience (Buber 1966, p. 169f.).[1]

It is not surprising that Buber characterized what Rogers had said as "a very good example for a certain moment of dialogic existence," for there are here present all the elements Buber himself emphasizes: meeting the other as a partner and not as an object, experiencing the patient's side of the relationship without losing one's own, bringing oneself as a whole person, accepting the other as the person he is in his otherness. It is important to note that in this description Rogers does not, in fact, claim total mutuality. He, as therapist, sees the patient from within, whereas the patient's inclusion is limited to sensing something of the therapist's attitude toward him and does not touch on the therapist as a person with problems of his own.

Buber suggested that in this situation, which the therapist and the patient have in common, it is, from the point of view of the therapist, a sick person coming to him and asking for a particular kind of help. Rogers objected that if he looked at the patient as a "sick person," he would not be able to be of real help to him. Buber discarded the word "sick," but retained the description of the situation as one in which the person comes to the therapist for help and insisted that this makes an essential difference in the role of therapist and patient:

He comes for help to you. You don't come for help to him. And not only this, but you are *able*, more or less, to help him. He can do different things to you, but not help you. And not this alone. You *see* him, just as you said, as he *is*. He cannot, by far, cannot *see you*. Not only in the degree, but even in the kind of seeing. You are, of course, a very important person for him. But not a person whom he wants to see and to know and is able to. He is floundering around, he comes to you. He is, may I say, entangled in your life, in your thoughts, in your being, your communication, and so on. But he is not interested in you as you. It cannot be. You are interested . . . in him as this person. This kind of detached presence he cannot have and give (Buber 1966, p. 171).

---

[1]The dialogue between Martin Buber and Carl R. Rogers, moderated by Maurice Friedman, was held at the University of Michigan on April 18, 1957. It is printed as the Appendix to Martin Buber, *The Knowledge of Man* (Buber 1966).

Buber went on to say that in the common situation Rogers was able to observe, know, and help the patient from both his own side and that of the patient. The therapist can experience bodily the patient's side of the situation and feel himself touched by what he does to the patient, whereas the situation itself makes it impossible for the patient to experience the therapist's side of the relationship. "You are not equals and cannot be. You have the . . . great self-imposed task to supplement this need of his and to do rather more than in the normal situation. . . . I see you *mean* being on the same plane, but you cannot." These are the, sometimes tragic, limitations to simple humanity.

Rogers agreed that if the patient really could experience his side of the situation fully, the therapy would be about over, but he also insisted that the patient's "way of looking at his experience, distorted though it might be, is something I can look upon as having equal authority, equal validity with the way I see life and experience. It seems to me *that* really is the basis of helping." What Rogers said here is the essence of what I shall have to say about the "dialogue of touchstones" as an approach to therapy, but it does not, as Buber pointed out, change the fact that the situation is not equal, however much Rogers *feels* the equality. "Neither you nor he look on *your* experience. The subject is exclusively him and his experience." Rogers suggested, in response, that what Buber said applied to the situation looked at from the outside. This has nothing to do with the relationship that produces therapy, which is "something immediate, equal, a meeting of two persons on an equal basis—even though, in the world, of I–It, it could be seen as a very unequal relationship." Buber replied that effective human dialogue must be concerned with limits and that these limits transcend Rogers' method, especially in the case of the schizophrenic and the paranoid.

> I can talk to a schizophrenic as far as he is willing to let me into his particular world that is his own. . . . But in the moment when he shuts himself, I cannot go on. And the same, only in a terrible, terrifyingly strong manner, is the case with a paranoiac. He does not open himself and does not shut himself. He *is* shut. . . . And I feel this terrible fate very strongly because in the world of normal men, there are just analogous cases, when a sane man behaves, not to everyone, but behaves to some people *just so*, being shut, and the problem is if he can be opened, if he can open himself. . . . This is a problem for the human in general (Buber 1965b, p. 175f.).

In my own role as moderator of this dialogue between Buber and Rogers I suggested that the real difference was that Buber stressed the patient's inability to experience Rogers' side of the relationship, whereas Rogers stressed the meeting, the change that takes place in the meeting, and his own *feeling* that the patient is an equal person he respects. Rogers replied that in the most real moments of therapy the intention to help is only a substratum. Although he would not say that the relationship was reciprocal in the sense that the patient wants to understand him and help him, he did assert that when real change takes place it is reciprocal in the sense that the therapist sees this individual as he is in that moment and the patient really senses his understanding and acceptance of him. To this Buber replied that Rogers gives the patient something in order to make him equal for that moment, but that this is a situation of minutes, not of an hour, and these minutes are made possible by Rogers who "out of a certain fullness" gives the patient what he wants in order to be *able* to be, just for this moment, on the same plane with him.

We can get further insight into the problematic of mutuality from the findings of Elaine Archambeau's perceptive study, "Beyond Countertransference." Archambeau interviewed Carl Rogers, John Weir Perry, a Jungian analyst, and Sidney Smith, a Freudian analyst, to discover concrete instances in which the therapist felt that he was being healed by the patient. On the basis of these interviews, she describes a process that begins when the patient elicits feelings in the therapist, and the therapist struggles with the "rightness" or accuracy of his feelings. The therapist then becomes aware of unexpressed feelings or parts of himself that have been pulled into the therapeutic relationship. This leads to an understanding of mutuality that goes counter to psychoanalytic theory: "Mutuality for all three therapists is not only the act of seeing and experiencing the other or the patient, but themselves as well in the therapeutic relationship." The recognition of such mutuality leads to a turning point in the therapeutic relationship, one in which the therapist feels confirmed and experiences the validation of feelings or actions previously perceived as "questionable." What is confirmed most of all is the personal "realness" of the therapist that has arisen from and been brought into the therapeutic relationship (Archambeau 1979, pp. 141–158).

Archambeau places this process squarely within the ontology of the between—"a mutual process of begetting between therapist and client" rather than the therapist's healing being experienced by an isolated entity due to some internal revelation. She makes this betweenness most explicit in her interpretation of Carl Jung's *Psychotherapy of Transference* (1966):

> The therapist and the client find themselves in a relationship built on mutual unconsciousness. The therapist is led to a direct confrontation of the unreconciled part of himself. The activated unconsciousness of both the client and the therapist causes both to become involved in a transformation of the "third." Hence, the relationship itself becomes transformed in the process (Archambeau 1979, p. 162).

Both Freud and Jung, as we have seen, recognize that there may be a direct meeting of one unconscious and another between therapist and patient, and Jung explicitly states that when projections are recognized by both patient and therapist, the form of rapport known as transference is at an end and the problem of individual relationship begun.[2] To confine the interaction to the unconscious, however, is to limit it to less than the whole person and to exclude that type of personal response for which Jourard and others have called.

Archambeau joins Richard Stanton in attacking what Stanton describes as "an operational myth" within psychoanalysis "that allows the therapist to reflect upon the session as if there was only one person there: the client" (Stanton 1978, p. 105). Mutuality is usually present, but it is also not usually attended to. The ultimate touchstone for the therapist of the rightness of including himself consciously in the therapeutic relationship is the outcome for the patient. Thus in the end, Archambeau, too, is advocating a one-sided mutuality that is normatively limited by the goal of therapy itself:

> It is imperative that the therapist be encouraged to view his/her own woundedness and to enter the therapeutic relationship with that in mind. To believe that the therapist enters the relationship without the client viewing his person on some level is unrealistic (Stanton 1978). . . . The therapist falls in to the danger, not so much of losing the therapeutic focus on the other, but of not including himself, his "realness" in the therapeutic relationship, that in turn, may stand in the way of healing for the other (Archambeau 1979, p. 167f.).

One-sided inclusion does not mean, says Lynne Jacobs, that the person the therapist differs in worth from that of the patient: "The difference comes from the fact that the task sets the two people in different relations to each other and to the task. . . . The patient is invested in his/her learning, not that of the therapist." Erich Fromm once said to me, as we have seen, that he liked very much the phrase "healing through meeting" and added, "I am healed by my patients." Undoubtedly any good teacher learns from his or her students and any good therapist from his or her patients. But the *goal* of the therapy cannot be the healing of the therapist, nor can the therapist impose his hope of being healed upon the patient as a demand or even as an expectation. "To engage at the level of I–Thou without the demand that the other confirm one is the essence of the therapist's dialogical attitude," writes Jacobs.

---

[2] C. G. Jung, *Psychotherapy of Transference* (1966), p. 136f., quoted in Archambeau, 1979, p. 162f.

It is the dilemma of the therapist that he/she encounters the patient with the attitude and involvement of I–Thou, yet he/she does not seek to be confirmed through the direct human encounter. The therapist's confirmation comes through the expression of him/herself in the service of the task. The therapist's own self-acceptance, self-esteem, and faith in the "truth" of the task, in the liberation of both people that the task will allow, enables him/her to hold aside the wish to be confirmed by the other, and instead to be confirmed through knowing that the task is most creatively served in this way (Jacobs 1978, p. 113).

What must be emphasized here is that the therapist cannot *demand* that the patient confirm her/him. I would not agree that the confirmation of the therapist comes only through the service of the task and not through the patient. For another person to *allow* me to help her or him means that the person *is* confirming me. He is giving me one of the rarest gifts I may receive, even if it cannot be fully mutual by the very structure of the therapy situation.

Essentially Archambeau documents what Erich Fromm stated of himself—that the good therapist is also healed by his patients—and what Jourard asserts—that change in the therapeutic relationship works both ways. No one, including Rogers, claims that the *goal* of the therapeutic relationship is the healing of the therapist or that any demand or expectation can be placed upon the patient with such healing in mind. A more radical understanding of the reversal of roles that may take place within the therapeutic relationship and of the extension of the possibilities of mutuality within that relationship is to be found in the work with schizophrenics of two Sullivanian analysts both of whom were connected with Chestnut Lodge: Frieda Fromm-Reichmann and Harold Searles.

The psychiatrist must avoid an attitude of "personal irrational authority," testifies Fromm-Reichmann, in favor of real listening and conducting therapy in the spirit of collaborative guidance. The therapist is only superior to the patient by virtue of his special training and experience and not necessarily in any other way. The emotional difficulties that lead the patient to the therapist or even to the mental hospital do not imply any basic inferiority on the part of the patient. "The mental patient, who is supposed to be out of his mind, may say meaningful things which the psychiatrist, who is supposedly in his right mind, cannot understand."

A part of this collaborative guidance entails offering interpretations as open-ended invitations for the patient to corroborate or reject them and to take them further. In Buber's language, these interpretations should be in the nature of a mutual dialogue rather than a one-sided monologue. The therapist "addresses himself to a psychotherapeutic co-worker" and "invites further interpretive collaboration on the patient's part." The schizophrenic patient, as a rule, is aware of the content meaning of what he communicates about his inner experience in his private world. The help he needs from the therapist is not immediate content meaning, but rather becoming aware of and learning to understand the genetic and dynamic background of the unknown implications of his conflicts and his symptomatology. In this sense, Fromm-Reichmann engages even her schizophrenic patients in what I shall discuss below as a "dialogue of touchstones."

One of the most remarkable examples of healing through meeting that Fromm-Reichmann gives is the occasion in which she had deliberately imitated a patient's physical presence or stance in order to gain insight into where the patient is coming from. By holding her breath and trying to think away a part of herself, as her patient did, she came to understand that he was identifying himself with a pregnant woman (his wife). In another case, by trying to sit lotus fashion, like her patient, she came to understand his self-involvement and, through it, the overt homosexuality that until then he had never confided in her. These are acts of "inclusion" in the precise sense in which Martin Buber uses the term—the quite concrete imagining, through the most intense action of one's being and bold swinging to the other, of what the other person is feeling, thinking, and willing (Fromm-Reichmann 1950).

Although such inclusion from the patient's side is not a demand the therapist can or should place upon the patient, it does take place, especially on the part of schizophrenics:

> Because of their marked anxiety, these people have developed a consistent watchfulness of their environment and great alertness regarding interpersonal experiences. Therefore, they are frequently capable of emotional eavesdropping, as it were, on other persons, including their psychiatrists. From the gestures, attitudes, inadvertent words, and actions of the therapist, the psychotic may, at times, gain an empathic awareness of certain personality aspects of which the therapist himself may not be aware. Well-developed security is necessary for the therapist to be able to listen without resentment to his patients' comments on these more-often-than-not undesirable personality trends of which he may have been previously unaware (Fromm-Reichmann 1950, p. 24).

Such "inclusion" is not, of course, for the sake of the healing of the therapist, and it is, as often as not, accompanied by distorted (parataxic) interpretations on the patient's part. If the therapist is afraid of the patient's impulses to kill or otherwise made anxious by the patient, the sensitive patient will pick this up, and it will, in turn, increase the patient's own fear and anxiety:

> To the patient the psychiatrist's anxiety represents a measuring rod for his own anxiety-provoking qualities. If the therapist is very anxious, the patient may take that as a confirmation of his own fear of being

threatening, that is, "bad." In other words, the therapist's anxiety decreases the patient's self-esteem (Fromm-Reichmann 1950, p. 25).

Harold Searles also offers us insight into the possibility and limitations of inclusion from the side of the patient in his remarkable essay, "The Patient as Therapist to His Analyst." Searles claims that all human beings have a desire to heal that arises in infancy in the relation of the infant to the mother. When such therapeutic strivings are not fulfilled or even acknowledged, they become inordinately intense and, with unduly intense components of hate, envy, and competitiveness, they are necessarily repressed. Because and to the degree that this happens, claims Searles, the person becomes ill. Yet when such patients enter therapy, they are likely to have, over time, a genuine caring as to whether the analyst has been growing and thriving through the patient's ministrations to him or her.

Searles sees this process as largely unconscious, since the analyst's psychopathology tends to remain masked—by introjective processes within the patient and projective processes within the analyst. But what Searles is talking about definitely transcends transference, since it has a reality core. Of a schizophrenic woman with whom Searles worked for 13 years and whom he characterized as "the most deeply ill patient I have ever treated," Searles wrote:

> It was clear that her own needs included a need for me to become a stronger, more firmly limit-setting father toward her; but it was quite clear that she was trying persistently to help me resolve the genuine flaw in myself which formed the nucleus of reality upon which her transference was based. Through outrageously and persistently obstreperous behavior, which involved both blatant sexual provocativeness as well as physical onslaughts of various kinds, she eventually succeeded in fostering in me a degree of decisiveness and firmness, expressed in masterful limit-setting, which I had not achieved before with anyone, either patients or other persons in my life (Searles 1975, p. 100).

Searles, like Archambeau, holds that the healing of the patient is promoted by the analyst's awareness of his own feelings: "The more readily accessible to himself are the therapist's own symbiotic-dependent feelings, the better he is equipped to help the patient to become conscious of similar feelings, so that the patient need no longer act out symbiotic yearnings through the schizophrenic postponement of individuation" (original italicized). But he goes beyond Archambeau and, by implication, Rogers, Perry, and Smith, in claiming that one of the patient's strivings is to help the analyst fulfill his human potentialities:

> The patient strives to help the analyst to share those modes of interpersonal relatedness which are relatively anxiety-free for the patient and

anxiety-laden for the analyst. . . . Another way of putting it is that the patient endeavors to help the analyst to share in the patient's relatively nonneurotic areas of ego functioning. He is endeavoring to contribute to the analyst's emotional growth, integration, and maturation (Searles 1975, p. 126).

Searles acknowledges that in more severely ill schizoid or schizophrenic patients, these therapeutic "goals are relatively undifferentiated from the goal of the patient's endeavoring to provide himself with an increasingly constructive model for identification, in the person of the analyst, that can be used for the patient's further maturation." Nonetheless, he sees the patient as using actual psychotherapeutic techniques—catharsis, verbal and nonverbal reassurance, introjection of the analyst's more ill components, and projection upon the analyst of his own areas of relative strength. Searles suggests that the analyst share the fact that these efforts are personally helpful to him in a relatively nonanxious, nonguilty, and therefore nonconfessional way as data to be talked over with a collaborator. But Searles warns both against the hazard of failing to recognize and interpret the patient's therapeutic strivings and the hazard of prematurely interpreting them. "As long as the patient remains oppressed by feelings of guilty responsibility, he will react with intensified guilt to any intimation from the analyst that he is finding the sessions personally helpful" (Searles 1975, p. 127). This is another way of saying that, though the patient has therapeutic strivings, these must be related to by the therapist in such a way as to help the patient. Thus the patient still remains the patient and the therapist still remains the therapist.

Searles also sees the analyst as regressing to relatively raw aggressive and sexual urges as a result of his own frustrated therapeutic strivings. This frustration can result in a tragic perversion of therapy, in which the therapist's incestuous urges become acceptable in the guise of healing:

> In many instances the primitive healing strivings are no less powerful than are the sexual strivings, and the therapeutic strivings can be the most powerful of all in bringing about a tragic deforming of the therapeutic endeavor, predatory sexual behavior by the therapist under the guise of the emancipated healer. A need for therapeutic omnipotence can lead the therapist to seize upon any available, intentionally therapeutic measures, including actual sexual involvement with the patient (Searles 1975, p. 130).

This danger arises when the therapist loses sight of his usual working knowledge and awareness of the dimension of transference and countertransference.

On the positive side, Searles tells of a teaching interview with a borderline schizophrenic young woman at a hospital, which was not only helpful to her, but also "deeply fulfilling and confirming for me in my identity as someone wanting to be a useful psychoanalyst." This is exactly what I said above about the confirmation that the therapist receives when the patient allows himself to he helped:

> It struck me how illusory is an assumption that the therapist experiences such professional gratification as an expectable, everyday, mundane part of his work. I am trying here to suggest that the therapist has reason to feel as rare and memorable and intense a form of gratitude as has the patient whose therapist has effected, as we conventionally say, a remarkable cure (Searles 1975, p. 134).

In both cases, the gratitude is for the grace of the "between," the healing through meeting that cannot be willed and is never simply the effect of which one or another partner in the therapeutic relationship is the cause.

In his discussion of pertinent literature, Searles reinterprets the "therapeutic alliance" not as being an alliance for therapy for the *patient*, as is usually held, but rather "an alliance for therapy for *both* participants in the treatment situation." At the same time, he explicitly rejects any idea of sharing with the patient information about the therapist's own personal life. "For in my own work I probably do little more of this than does any classical psychoanalyst." Searles quotes at length from Erwin Singer's closely similar paper, "The Patient Aids the Analyst," in which Singer too claims "that the capacity to rise to the occasion when compassion and helpfulness are called for is part and parcel of the makeup of all human beings." Singer sees his own disclosures as accelerating the therapeutic process through remarkable insights, memories, and heightened awareness in his patients: "Strict psychoanalytic anonymity would have reduced my patients' opportunities to see their own strengths; and certainly it would have limited my knowledge of their caring and compassionate capacities."

Searles takes exception to Singer's conclusion that "a marked reduction of the analyst's anonymity is essential to therapeutic progress," in connection with which Searles makes a distinction very close to that made by Jourard: "In my own work, while I am relatively free about revealing feelings and fantasies which I experience during the analytic session itself, I tell patients very little of my life outside the office." Nonetheless, he concludes on a note totally akin to the observation cited above from Richard Stanton: "The classical analytic position contains an element of delusion to the effect that the analyst is not at all a real person to the patient, and therefore simply will not do" (Searles 1975, p. 134).

Searle's paper is clearly the exception that proves the rule as far as the problematic of mutuality is concerned. It goes as far as can be imagined in the direction of seeing the healing as a two-way process in which both therapist and patient may be helped and healed. Yet this two-way process takes place within the structure of the therapist–patient relationship, and the nature and goal of this structure, for Searles, Jourard, Rogers, John Weir Perry, and Fromm-Reichmann, remains one in which the healing of the therapist is never aimed at nor is the expectation or demand for such healing ever placed upon the patient.

A number of contributors to Kenneth Frank's collection *The Human Dimension in Psychoanalytic Practice* give us further valuable insight into the problematic of mutuality in psychoanalytic psychotherapy. Frank himself concludes his Introduction with the statement:

> The viability of psychoanalytic psychotherapy depends upon the recognition, minimized in the past, that even the most perceptive possible grasp of the patient's psychodynamics, combined with optimally timed and focused interpretation, is of limited value unless implemented within a relationship characterized by an affectional bond of mutual trust and respect, and where the analyst is willing to fully experience and to be experienced, on an authentically human level. Consequently, the ultimate developmental task of the psychoanalyst is the integration of theory and technique with his unique person. This is necessarily a challenging and lifelong task. But it need not be a secret struggle (Frank 1977, p. 6).

Closely similar to Frank, Harry Guntrip, the British "object-relations" analyst, defines psychoanalytic therapy as "the personalities of two people working together towards free spontaneous growth." At the same time that it implies that the analyst grows as well as the analysand, it is one-sided in its focus on the healing of the patient. Psychoanalytic psychotherapy, says Guntrip, is

> the provision of a reliable and understanding human relationship of a kind that makes contact with the deeply repressed traumatized child in a way that enables one to become steadily more able to live, in the security of a new relationship, with the traumatic legacy of the earliest formative years, as it seeps through or erupts into consciousness (Guntrip 1977, p. 65).

The American psychoanalyst David Shainberg describes the analytic process as one in which the analyst and the patient work together to create and enlarge a mutual vision that grows between them:

> It is like a team coming to the edge of a forest and working its way through each thicket to a clearing and then on to another thicket. The spirit is one of teasing out the brambles and the vines together until there is a clearing through which first one and then the other can walk (Shainberg 1977, p. 125).

Shainberg sees most relationships, including analytic ones, as inauthentic processes based on communal deception and an unspoken agreement that neither person will really disturb the archaic structures of the other.

In contrast, a moment of transformation in psychoanalysis takes place when my patient and I give up the protectiveness of our isolation and begin willingly to move toward helping each other toward greater self-articulation and acceptance of human suffering. We stop decorating the rooms of our minds with fantasies of hoped-for pleasure from one another. We face up to the realities of our existence, albeit the simple one here of the unclearness of our discussion. At these moments, I feel myself in the presence of the mystery of human relating; it is often a monumental experience (Shainberg 1977, p. 126).

In his essay, "The Fiction of Analytic Anonymity," the American psychologist, Erwin Singer, insists that both the hearing and the response of the analyst already entail self-exposure on the part of the analyst quite apart from any explicit sharing. In any genuine meeting, one participant stands equally bared before the other. "He who chances to expose himself by hearing truly his fellow's anguish and ecstasy can hope to be met equally exposed by him." No matter what the analyst may pretend to himself and others, his response to the patient reveals his "private religion." Although patients have quantitatively less data to draw upon, there is a wealth of qualitatively significant and poignant information about their analysis at their disposal *if* they are only courageous enough to avail themselves of it. Ultimately, in fact, the patient becomes "as conversant with the analyst's personal visions, his psychological operations, and his hierarchy of values—including the discrepancies between what he professes and what he truly lives—as the analyst, hopefully, has become conversant with these central aspects of his patients' lives." The analyst may even experience the anxiety of wondering if the patient will accept him if he truly knows him when he recognizes that relevant comments about the patient inevitably reveal himself. As a result, his courage to bare himself via pointed reflections and the posing of pertinent questions is constantly tested. At the same time, Singer warns against construing what he has said about the inevitability of the analyst's self-revealing behavior "as license for his engaging in self-important chatter, self-indulgent ruminations, or intrusive diversions."

Disciplined opposition to such temptation and careful examination of its meaning is part and parcel of the daily struggle the analyst must suffer, but in his self-discipline and self-examination, he reveals to the patient that he, too, must struggle, that the struggle against primitive narcissistic indulgences is always with us, and that it can be carried on, at least at times, successfully (Singer 1977, p. 188f.).

One of the most radical claims of full mutuality between therapist and client is that put forward by the American Jungian analyst J. Marvin Spiegelman. In his 1965 paper on the implications of transference, Spiegelman stated the basic postulates of this position, namely, the therapist and the patient create between them an unconscious betweenness that constitutes an archetype that stands as much in need of clarification as that of individuation. If the analyst resists the realization of his own part in the therapeutic process, "he will either *never constellate the unconscious in its deeper forms or will require that the patient carry the whole burden of the contents activated.*" Spiegelman holds that the analyst must acknowledge to the patient the child in himself that needs the patient's fathering or mothering, as well as acknowledging to the patient his fatigue, boredom, or anger when it occurs, and analyzing it jointly. The unconscious affects both partners simultaneously, which means that the committed and open analyst is as much "in" the analysis as the patient. Although Spiegelman characterizes this as "a genuine 'I and Thou' relation, in which there is real equality," and says that it is just here that "a clearly Jungian analysis, in the sense of the individuation process, begins," he stops short of betweenness in Buber's sense of the term by characterizing the equality between therapist and client as consisting in "the mutual fulfillment of needs, primarily that of the individuation process, as it effects [sic] both partners." What Spiegelman is implying, however, is "an *attitude* of openness in which the analyst can be much freer with his patient than has heretofore been suggested." The acceptance of analysis as a mutual unveiling implies, for Spiegelman, that the dreams that the patient has of the therapist be taken as true, and that the therapist should find out where it is true and acknowledge that to the patient *before* dealing with the patient's projection (Spiegelman 1965, pp. 164–167, 169f., 174f.).

In 1972, Spiegelman updated these reflections in a paper, "Transference, Individuation, Mutual Process" (unpublished). Recognizing that many analysts shied away from the implications of his earlier paper because of the injuries to the healer that were sometimes entailed, Spiegelman confesses that to him such injuries were a common occurrence, a necessary part of the experience of the archetype of the "wounded physician," and, surprisingly, an event that happened more often than the wounding of the patient. At the same time he claimed that he was much helped in his own development by just this wounding. "Indeed, my individuation both demanded this direction and was deeply nourished by it." In this paper Spiegelman defines mutual process as

a *psychological relationship* in which the partners recognize and work with the unconscious as it manifests itself within them and among them. It requires an increasing degree of mutual *openness*, of *intersubjectivity* and a recognition of their *equality* before the gods, the archetypes. It normally enhances both relationship and consciousness, by promoting both differentiation and union. It results in a *creative work*, often one of joint concrete products such as in art or science, or in aspects of relationship itself, such as mutual healing, mutual deepening (Spiegelman 1972, p. 9).

Spiegelman sees this mutual process as an extension of Jung's work to "the union of opposites, both within one's self and *in the relationship*." Because it changes from moment to moment and from relationship to relationship, this mutual process is as difficult to pinpoint and nail down as the individuation process itself. What is more, Spiegelman insists that the analytic relationship should move toward the relationship of equality if its aim of fostering individuation is to occur. The aim of analysis, in fact, can be defined as "helping the analysand toward a true independence of spirit and, at the same time, of enhancing the capacity for relating equally." Spiegelman sees his emphasis on mutual process as going beyond that of Rogers, Bion, the Tavistock group, and Gestalt in its contract to work together consciously on the interaction of unconscious transference and countertransference (Spiegelman 1972, pp. 12, 15, 21 *n*, 31).

In his most recent paper on this subject, Spiegelman makes an interesting practical application of mutual process in his insistence that he has a moral responsibility in the name of honesty to tell his fantasies, as well as to hear the patient's.

> From such sharing . . . both patient and therapist gain insight as to what is transpiring in *the* unconscious (as opposed to "my" and "your" unconscious) and we are now mutually connected to the "third" or the relationship itself. I have called this third the "God among" (as opposed to the "God within"). Objectivity and authority is hence transferred to the unconscious itself, as revealed in the fantasies and dreams of the participants, as partners, who can now attend to themselves and the other as well as to this third, thus performing the work of alchemical transformation Jung was writing about (Spiegelman 1980, p. 104f.).

Perhaps the most famous and radical departure from Freud's counsel of mirrorlike impassivity and the other traditional structures that hedge round the analytic hour is the Swiss psychotherapist Margaret Sechehaye's work with a schizophrenic girl whom she calls Renée. In Renée's autobiographical account, the absolutely central importance of contact with her therapist is stressed repeatedly, and the remarkable lengths to which Sechehaye went to help her are equally evident. In Sechehaye's own commentary at the end of the autobiography, ironically, the sole concern is with Renée's individual developmental phases, and the centrality of healing through meeting is never touched on. When Sechehaye has to refer to herself, she does so in the third person as "the analyst."

"Mama," as Renée called Margaret Sechehaye, quickly became for the tormented Renée "the precious little oasis of reality in the desert world" of her soul. "Mama" dared declare herself stronger than the System (the "Enlightenment," as Renée called it) that imprisoned her in guilt and lifelessness and robbed her of all sense of contact and reality in her relation to other people and even to the objects of the natural and man-made world. By speaking of herself and Renée in the third person, Mama was able again and again to break through the unreal wall that hemmed her in and bring her into some contact with life. In order to do this, Sechehaye not only took her on holiday to the seashore, as Ferenczi had done with one of his patients, but also took her into her home for extended periods. She allowed her to regress to the point where she felt she was re-entering her mother's body, thus becoming one of the first of those therapists who have literally undertaken to "reparent" schizophrenic clients. She let her lean on her bosom and pretended to give milk from her breasts to the doll with whom Renée identified (Sechehaye 1951a). Renée describes the healing effect of these actions with utmost vividness:

> My perceptions of things had completely changed. Instead of infinite space, unreal, where everything was cut off, naked and isolated, I saw Reality, marvelous Reality, for the first time. The people whom we encountered were no longer automatons, phantoms revolving around, gesticulating without meaning; they were men and women with their own individual characteristics, their own individuality. It was the same with things. . . .
>     As I entered my room after arriving at the hospital, it was no longer my room, but living, sympathetic, real, warm. And to the stupefaction of the nurse, for the first time I dared to handle the chairs, to change the arrangement of the furniture. . . . Until now I had tolerated no change, even the slightest (Sechehaye 1951a, pp. 79–81).

Renée's voices no longer assailed her; she no longer risked being changed into a cat; she enjoyed everything she saw and touched; and Mama, too, changed in her eyes from a statue that she liked to look at into an alive, warm, animated person whom she cherished deeply and wanted to remain near. At first Renée could maintain contact with Mama only if Mama met her on the level at which she was. But by degrees she became independent of Mama, first through feeding, then through cleanliness and personal care until finally she could think differently from her and even oppose her without endangering her perception of reality. "Now I can accept Mrs. Sechehaye in her own right," Renée concludes. "I love her for herself and I am eternally grateful to her for the priceless treasure she has granted me in restoring reality and contact with Life" (Sechehaye 1951a).

The only explicit recognition Sechehaye gives of the centrality of her meeting with Renée in her recovery is the statement early in her interpretation:

> At this period she seemed not even to recognize the analyst; nonetheless an effort was made to create some bond, tenuous though it might be, capable of establishing contact. This could be accomplished only by

satisfying the need inherent in the current phase of regression (Sechehaye 1951a, p. 125).

That Sechehaye was far more involved personally than even the most
humanistic of therapists usually are we can infer from the accounts of how
she gave instructions for her meals, saw to her baths, and in general played
for Renée the nourishing mother that she had been denied as an infant.
That this took an emotional toll far beyond the ordinary is evident from
Renée's own account that "'Mama was extremely upset" or that she
regained consciousness and found Mama weeping over her (Sechehaye
1951a).

It is a pity that Sechehaye did not tell us more directly of her own
personal involvement in this remarkable healing partnership that lasted
over many years. In *Symbolic Realization*, the companion volume to
Renée's autobiography, Sechehaye does detail her role and spells out her
thoughts on Renée's unprecedented near total recovery from her schizophrenia. Sechehaye quickly discovered that the traditional analyst's position behind the couch left Renée feeling completely abandoned. By sitting
next to her on the couch she assured her that she was being listened to and
had a partner. Later, during the acute period of Renée's illness, Sechehaye
realized that since the apples represented maternal milk, she had to give
them to her directly, without intermediary: "Renée then leans up against
my shoulder, presses the apple upon my breast, and very solemnly, with
intense happiness, eats it." Sechehaye thus substituted the "bountiful
mother" for the "depriving mother" Renée had known, thereby permitting
Renée to live and to love herself and to abandon self-punishment (Sechehaye 1951b, pp. 41f., 51, 53).

Sechehaye saw the re-education of Renée as made possible by a
number of attitudes and actions on her part. Sechehaye gained Renée's
confidence through an understanding attitude coupled with absolute
sincerity in the interest and devotion shown her, simplicity that was ready
to acknowledge mistakes, an accommodating and flexible attitude, and
helping her beyond what seemed necessary. She reassured her constantly
about the possibility of her recovery and guessed the legitimate needs of
her libido and her real ego, including giving attention to her nourishment,
her bodily care, and her clothing. Whenever possible, she gave Renée
whatever she desired, devising pleasurable projects for her at each stage,
giving her small gifts, and walking with her in the country—"an intermediary stage between the narcissistic needs and the social needs." She fixed
time carefully for all her work, making out a daily program including the
duration of all activities. She also avoided don'ts, protests, and blame that
would have pushed Renée to want to die, overwork that might lead her to
depression and setback, and going too fast or skipping stages (Sechehaye
1951b, pp. 109–117).

So far from recognizing the role of healing through meeting, Sechehaye explicitly rejects the notion that it was the maternal love that she gave Renée that saved her. She recognizes the importance of her affection in stimulating a positive transference from her unconscious mother image to a new, loving mother. She recognizes, too, that her profound interest in the patient and her affection for her gave her the determination to see it through to the end, preventing the therapy from leaving off halfway, which would have abandoned Renée to mental lapse or suicide.

> But I insist that this is not the primary element of the cure. The proof is that I acted as "loving mother" from about the second year of the treatment, and that I have remained the same until this day. During this time, the patient became worse and then improved, then worsened again, then was cured. Therefore, if the affection had sufficed, the progress of the cure would have been regular up to the success. But, on the contrary, we see that the positive transference lost itself at certain times, even to the quasi-complete withdrawal into autism (Sechehaye 1951b, p. 130f.).

Sechehaye attributes some part of the cure in its beginning stages to orthodox psychoanalytic procedure:

> the objective attitude of the analyst, who simply wanted to look clearly into her and with her, and who did not demand gratitude, or affection, or religious consecration in exchange for her help (as had some of her friends), delivered her from the heavy obligation which her guilt feelings made even more oppressing and binding. At last she felt free toward a human being, and this made the establishment of a positive transference possible and constituted a support for her (Sechehaye 1951, p. 132).

In her conclusion, however, Sechehaye recognizes that it was the maternal love that she gave Renée that enabled Renée to get rid of her aggressiveness toward the material world and other people and to love and accept herself (Sechehaye 1951b, pp. 140, 142). These are, to be sure, "symbolic realizations." Yet they were made possible by the fact that Sechehaye's love was not "symbolic," but rather was quite real and remarkably sustained, beyond what most actual mothers could conceivably have given. Because this was a conflict that occurred prior to the formation of the ego, Renée had to be allowed to go again through the entire evolution. Only the grace of Sechehaye's remarkable gift of informed and discriminating love enabled her to do this. Sympathy and maternal love were not all the cure, to be sure, but they were clearly as primary as the symbolic realizations with which they went hand in hand. Although Sechehaye points out that a traditional analysis would take almost as much time as she gave Renée, what she did for her *in* that time went far, far beyond what any traditional analyst is willing or able to do.

In his essay, "Education," in *Between Man and Man*, Martin Buber wrote: "In the moment when the pupil is able to throw himself across and experience from over there, the educative relation would be burst asunder, or change into friendship." Friendship is that "form of the dialogical relation which is based on a concrete and mutual experience of inclusion. It is the true inclusion of one another by human souls (Buber 1965, p. 101). One therapist who carried the therapist–patient relationship so far that it almost became friendship is Hanna Colm. A psychiatrist working with the Washington School of Psychiatry, but strongly influenced by Tillich and by Buber, Colm wrote just before her death a moving testimony on "the therapeutic encounter" as she had experienced it:

> Healing does not result merely from greater *knowledge* of oneself but from *experiencing* oneself (as one *is*) in relation to another person and in the struggle towards mutual acceptance in spite of the humanness one finds in oneself and in one's partner. I am not afraid of letting counter-transferences enter into my reactions. . . .
>
> Once a certain rapport has been established the therapist can go ahead of his patient in daring to be himself. He should be open for a genuine encounter in feeling, be it affection, or irritation, or even temporary hate, or the thousands of feelings that each patient will provoke in his therapist and the therapist in the patient.
>
> At the right time the therapist will dare to show the patient that he too is only a human being who has reactions, positive and negative, which the patient must learn to accept or refuse. Thus the patient, in the encounter with the therapist, must again become a full person and will gradually gain trust in his own judgment not only in his dealings with his therapist, but also in dealing with his own life situations (Colm 1965, p. 139f.).

The therapist can help the patient recognize that the negative reactions he provokes in the therapist are similar to those he provokes in daily living and perhaps, too, the way in which he tries to destroy genuine basic affection out of fear of closeness. This is only possible if the therapist approaches the patient not as an authoritative expert, but rather as a partner in a joint undertaking who may be mistaken. If the therapist feels guilt about his responses to the patient, working through such guilt feelings is part of the encounter. The ideal world is dissolved in favor of the actual, and the hostility engendered by disappointment is dissipated as one accepts present reality as worthwhile. The self-inflicted isolation of the patient will cease and he will become a part of the human community, while the therapist will emerge from each successful encounter a wiser therapist and person. Both will be able to move back to their own lives ready to transcend temporary estrangement in a never-ending struggle for communion. This mutually developing openness and sharing of each other's humanness in living and being is the core of the healing process, according to Colm. "When this stage is reached fully, therapy has reached its end and in some cases an enduring friendship will be born of a depth that is rare in our culture." Colm recognizes that what she has described is the "ideal type" of therapy, an ideal that cannot even be approximated when the anxiety of the patient or his fear of closeness is too great.

Colm tells of sharing a negative dream with a patient, but adds that she would only share a dream with strong feeling, positive or negative, if a relationship of some depth had already developed so there might be hope of a mutual acceptance of the possibility of the presence of both positive *and* negative feelings. As the relationship grows, the patient becomes alerted to the therapist's integrity and both help each other in moving toward genuine living. Through the therapist sharing his feelings, the patient is able to experience how seriously the therapist takes his partnership. "The therapist's expression of his reactions and even of his irrational counter-transference makes for far shorter periods of regression in the patient," Colm claims. Loneliness decreases and closeness is less frightening. "Encounter reveals itself as a slowly developing process on both sides, which centers around the patient's needs especially in the beginning, but then slowly develops into a genuine relationship, with growth on both sides."

Colm concludes by reasserting that the closeness between patient and therapist will eventually be that of two friends, who see each other when they both feel like it and conditions permit:

> Sometimes they can meet occasionally and then it feels like a gift of grace if the center-contact has stayed alive and can be immediately re-established without one-sided dependency but in a dependency on each other and in mutual openness towards each other, which leaves the friend, whom one helped to grow and through whom one grew oneself, free in communion and trust (Colm 1965, p. 159).

The amount of mutuality possible and desirable in therapy depends not only upon the stage of the relationship, but also upon the unique relationship between this particular therapist and client and upon the style and strength of the therapist. Colm's testimony is impressive because it shows how far one can go in the direction of mutuality without turning healing through meeting into injury through mismeeting. Other therapists also testify to bringing their feelings into the therapeutic encounter to a greater or less degree, and many testify to themselves being healed through that encounter or at the very least growing in creativity and wisdom. None of this changes the basic fact that the therapist's expression of emotion, Colm included, is always made in the service of the therapy and never in the service of the healing of the therapist or of mere self-indulgence on the part of the therapist. If the eventual result of an "ideal type" of therapy, such as Colm describes, is mutual friendship, that friendship is definitely not any longer a healing and helping relationship, but rather just what both Colm and Buber describe it as—one of concrete and mutual inclusion, mutual dependency, and mutual concern.

The healing relationship must always be understood in terms of the quite concrete situation and life-reality of those participating in it. It is not always necessary or even helpful to label the client by such terms as "schizophrenic," "neurotic," "obsessive-compulsive," "borderline psychotic," or any of the other categories of the DSM Manual. But it is necessary to recognize that in the healing partnership one person feels a need or lack that leads him or her to come to the other for help and that the other is a therapist or counselor who is ready to enter a relationship in order to help.

This excludes neither Erich Fromm's conviction that the therapist at the same time heals himself in some measure through his own response to the patient nor Carl Rogers' feeling of the equal worth and value of the patient (which leads Rogers, mistakenly in my opinion, to stress the *full* mutuality of the patient–therapist relationship). But it does preclude accepting the therapist's *feeling* of mutuality as equivalent to the actual existence of full mutuality in the situation *between* therapist and patient. The "scientific" impersonalism that characterized orthodox psychoanalysts (though not so much even by them, particularly Freud, as some imagine) is rightly rejected by many present-day therapists. But this should not lead us to a sentimental blurring of the essential distinction between therapy and other, less structured types of I–Thou relationships. In the latter, as Buber puts it, there are "no normative limitations of mutuality," but in the former, the very nature of the relationship makes full mutuality impossible.

Having stressed this limitation, we must also stress the fact that healing through meeting *does* imply mutuality between therapist and patient, that the therapist is called on to be present as a person as well as a smoothly functioning professional, that he is vulnerable and must take risks, that he is not only professionally *accountable*, but also personally *responsible*. The professionally oriented therapist tends to regard those of his patients who commit suicide as his personal failures and those who get better as his personal successes, as if the patient's actions were simply the effect of which the therapist is the cause. Healing through meeting suggests a very different approach.

This approach, to begin with, accepts the uniqueness of each relationship and does not imagine that what worked in one case will necessarily work in another. In the second place, it accepts the limitations that are discovered in that unique relationship—not theoretical limitations, but actual ones, though it is also willing on another occasion to try to test those limits and see how they can be pushed back. Above all, it accepts the reality of the *between* and recognizes that it is not entirely to the therapist's credit if the therapy goes well, or to his discredit if it does not.

Harry Stack Sullivan was deeply affected by a patient who almost committed suicide, and Martin Buber by a man who was in despair and did not oppose his own death. Sullivan concludes his narration of this event with the statement of how it affected his subsequent approach to the therapeutic relationship:

> The subsequent course of his mental disorder was uninterruptedly unfortunate and he has resided for years in a State hospital. I have not since then permitted a patient to enter upon the communication of a gravely disturbing experience unless I have plenty of time in which to validate his reassurance as to the effect of the communication on our further relations (Sullivan 1940, p. 90).

Leslie Farber in his essay, "Martin Buber and Psychotherapy," compares these two events and what Buber and Sullivan concluded from them. In his lengthy comment, Farber delineates the very contrast we have made above between the prideful "responsibility" of the "professional scientist" and the more modest and truly responsible acceptance of the reality of the "between":

> Each instance, touching in its confession of failure, speaks of "conversion": Buber is converted from the private, the rhapsodic, the mystical, into the world; Sullivan, on the other hand, shakes the claims and interruptions of the hospital world to move into a more private attention to his patient's existence which would allow for relation. While Buber convicts himself for his fragmentary response to his friend's despair, he resists arrogating to himself prideful responsibility for the other's fate: he could not necessarily save this young man; he could only have been "present in spirit" when his visitor sought confirmation and meaning from him.
>
> If we turn now to the instruction Sullivan derived from his tragedy, we find him perhaps more faithful to his science than to his humanity. On the one hand, psychiatry is indebted to him for his ideal, still unachieved, that the psychiatric hospital should exist primarily for the psychiatric patient. On the other hand, unlike Buber, Sullivan's devotion to the techniques of his science leads him to the immoderate claim that such desperate moments may be postponed until there is time to "validate" the "reassurance." Leaving aside the question whether "reassurance" can or should be "validated," I believe that with more modesty or less devotion, he might not have taken on the sole responsibility for his patient's fate (Farber 1967, p. 581).

A few years after Farber wrote the above essay, one of his patients, who was also a good friend and a person of stature in the community, committed suicide. When I asked Farber how he felt about this tragic event, he replied: "I knew when he said he wanted to enter Chestnut Lodge as a patient that that would be the result." "If you insist on putting yourself into Chestnut Lodge," Farber said to him, "I shall still be your friend, but I shall no longer be your therapist." Farber's patient did enter Chestnut Lodge; Farber ceased to be his therapist; and on a weekend leave this person committed suicide. I do not think that any therapist could accept the suicide of a patient with equanimity and without searching for his own responsibility in the situation. Yet part of the realism and seriousness of what we are talking about is to recognize that the responsibility of whether the therapy works or not does not lie entirely on the therapist, any more than it rests entirely with the patient. In the final analysis, it is a matter of the "between."

# Chapter 17

# Empathy, Identification, Inclusion, and Intuition

Before we bring our thoughts on confirmation and healing through meeting into sharper focus through our discussion of the "dialogue of touchstones," we should look at one more contour of dialogical psychotherapy, that whole range of relations between therapist and client that is popularly called "empathy." The chief problem with empathy is not that it is neglected, as Kenneth B. Clark (1980) and Carl R. Rogers have suggested, but that it is overwidely and much too loosely used. Those psychologists who employ the term do so in such general, vague, and varying ways that it is impossible to deal with as a really concrete phenomenon. For example, Freud in 1921 wrote: "A path leads from identification by way of imitation to empathy, that is, to the comprehension of the means by which we are enabled to take up any attitude at all towards another mental life."[1] Heinz Kohut, following Freud, defined empathy as "our ability to know via vicarious introspection what the inner life of man is, what we ourselves and what others think and feel" (Kohut 1977, p. 306).[2]

In his essay, "That Impossible Profession," the psychotherapist Ralph R. Greenson emphasizes the place of empathy in psychoanalysis far more than either Freud or Kohut:

---

[1] Sigmund Freud, *Group Psychology and the Analysis of the Ego, Standard Edition*, Vol. XIX (London: Hogarth Press, 1955), p. 110, quoted in Kohut 1977, p. 306.

[2] See also Heinz Kohut, *The Search for the Self: Selected Writings of Heinz Kohut*, 1950–1958, ed. by Paul Ornstein (New York: International Universities Press, 1978), 2 vols., "Introspection, Empathy, and Psychoanalysis."

The ability to empathize with the patient is an absolute prerequisite for psychoanalytic practice. It is our best method for comprehending the complex, subtle, and hidden emotions in another human being. Empathy means to share, to experience partially and temporarily the emotions of another person. It is essentially a preconscious phenomenon. It can be consciously instigated or interrupted, and it can occur silently and automatically, alternating with other forms of relating to people. The essential mechanism in empathy is a partial and temporary identification with the patient. In order to accomplish this it is necessary to regress from the position of detached, intellectual observer to a more primitive kind of relationship in which the analyst becomes one with the person he is listening to. It requires the capacity for controlled and reversible regressions.

Empathy is a special variety of intimacy with another human being. In order to empathize the analyst must be willing to become emotionally involved with his patient. He cannot empathize coldly; he can only empathize out of some wish or willingness to become close. Then he must be able to give this up and become the observer, the thinker, and the analyzer again. Empathy is most likely to come into play when the analyst feels lost or out of touch. Empathy becomes a means of regaining contact with the un-understood patient. It resembles other identificatory processes which occur when one is attempting to reestablish contact with a lost love object. One must be able to do this again and again and yet retain the ability to return to the detached and uninvolved position of analyzer. This is one of the important antithetical, bipolar demands of psychoanalytic practise.

. . . . . . . . . . . . . . . . . . . . . . . . . . . . . . . . . . . . . . . . . . . . . . . . . . . . . . . . . .

I believe that the capacity to empathize requires a willingness temporarily and partially to give up one's own identity. People with a rather narrow sense of identity, rigid and fixed, are unwilling or unable to empathize; the analyst's self-image has to be flexible and loose. Yet he may not lose his identity. At the end of the hour, he has to end up being the analyst. Furthermore, I am not referring to consciously playing a role, which implies conscious deception. . . . Empathy—and I dwell on it because it is so crucial—is a special kind of nonverbal, preverbal closeness which has a feminine cast; it comes from one's motherliness, and men (and women too) must have made peace with their motherliness in order to be willing to empathize. . . . People who are empathizers are always trying to re-establish contact, like people who are depressed. I believe that analysts who have been depressed and have overcome their depression make the best empathizers. One must be able to regress to empathic contact with the patient and then be able to rebound from it in order to check on the validity of the data so gathered (Greenson 1977, pp. 101, 105).

As we are not likely to be able to overcome the negative connotations of "guilt" that prevent people from using it in a fully meaningful sense, we are also unlikely to be able to get psychologists and psychiatrists and philosophers, not to mention the rest of us, to use empathy in a more exact sense. Nevertheless, it may be helpful here to distinguish three quite different uses of the term that ought, because of their different meanings, to have three quite different names. These are empathy proper, identification, and "inclusion," or "imagining the real."

The root meaning of empathy is *em pathos*, to feel in or into. One of the reasons that philosophers and psychologists have been reluctant to accept the term in the past is that they have assumed, like Clark, that human existence is basically and concretely a matter of satisfying individual needs of gratification and power, which makes any sort of understanding of another inexplicable if taken at face value. To explain empathy it has been reduced to something else—a cathected love-object, an ego-ideal, a "selfobject." If we do take empathy at face value, we must still distinguish between empathy and sympathy, feeling *in* and feeling *with*. Feeling in suggests a transposing oneself into the other, feeling with suggests a bipolar process wherein one is with the other and with oneself at the same time.

Empathy in the strict sense of the term then (and not the loose way in which so many use it) means to feel oneself *in* the client through giving up the ground of one's concreteness. One experiences the other's side of the relationship through an imaginative, aesthetic leap. In making this leap one ceases, for the time being, to experience one's own side. One brackets or suspends one's awareness of oneself, as it were, in order better to understand the other. Carl Rogers' earlier use of empathic understanding often suggests this with its emphases upon patient- or person-centered therapy, upon the becoming of the patient, upon acceptance of the patient by the therapist, and upon "unconditional positive regard." Empathy was never, to be sure, an aesthetic category for Rogers, but it seemed to be a category in which one tended to lose sight of oneself and one's own side of the relationship.

Identification, in contrast, means that the therapist resonates with the experiences related by the client only to the extent that they resemble his or her own. It says, in effect, "I am Thou," but it misses the Thou precisely at the point where its otherness and uniqueness takes it out of the purview of one's own life stance and life experience. Once at a Sharman discussion of the passage from the Gospels where Jesus speaks of old wine in new skins and new wine in old skins, I heard a young woman declare: "I believe that Jesus was the wisest man who ever lived. If he was the wisest man who ever lived, he certainly knew this," at which point she proceeded to give the group her own opinion based on her own experience. It struck me that by this method one could never learn anything new, never glimpse how another person saw and related to the world or even to oneself! Above all one could never glimpse the uniqueness of a person like Jesus if one simply made him the mouthpiece of one's own experience.

I suspect that identification is the most common way in which empathy is used in psychology and elsewhere. A particularly clear example of this is the psychologist Sidney Jourard's definition of empathy as "experiencing whatever you have experienced as fully as is possible":

> One means whereby you understand somebody is when you find you have experienced something similar to what he is struggling with. . . . If I can acknowledge the breadth and depth of my own experiencing, I think my empathy has been enhanced and my chances of understanding and communicating my understanding are increased. This is why I say it is good to have been a phony and suffered from it, then rehabilitated from it. It helps you to better understand the agonies of trying to become authentic that a patient is going through (Jourard 1968, p. 79).

The inadequacy of identification as a way of understanding others is made particularly clear through the illustration that Jourard uses of a woman menstruating, which he assumes a male therapist might understand through having had a pain in his gut or lower down. Like Jourard, I, too, have never had a menstrual period; yet I am convinced that the full context and meaning of that experience and all it implies about being a woman is in no way captured by pains that I have had in any parts of my anatomy! A Hasidic tale that Martin Buber has entitled "The Standard" illustrates vividly the difference between "identification" such as this and real "inclusion," or experiencing the other side of the relationship:

> Rabbi Mordecai of Neskhizh said to his son, the rabbi of Kovel: "My son, my son! He who does not feel the pains of a woman giving birth within a circuit of fifty miles, who does not suffer with her, and pray that her suffering may be assuaged, is not worthy to be called a zaddik."
> His younger son Yitzhak, who later succeeded him in his work, was ten years old at the time. He was present when this was said. When he was old he told the story and added: "I listened well. But it was very long before I understood why he had said it in my presence." (Buber 1961, p. 164).

In contrast to both empathy and identification, inclusion means a bold imaginative swinging "with the intensest stirring of one's being" into the life of the other so that one can, to some extent, concretely imagine what the other person is thinking, willing, and feeling and so that one adds something of one's own will to what is thus apprehended. As such, it is the very opposite of the abstraction to which Kenneth Clark relegates empathic concern for others. It means, on the contrary, grasping them in their uniqueness and concreteness. As such, too, it presupposes a philosophical anthropology in which we become human in our interaction with other persons, not secondarily, but primarily and ontologically.

A person finds himself as person through going out to meet the other, through responding to the address of the other. He does not lose his center, his personal core, in an amorphous meeting with the other. If he sees through the eyes of the other and experiences the other's side, he does not cease to experience the relationship from his own side. We do not experience the other through empathy or analogy. We do not know his anger because of our anger; for he may be angry in an entirely different way from us. But we *can* glimpse something of his side of the relationship. That is because a real person does not remain shut in himself or use his relations with others merely as a means to his own self-realization.

Inclusion, or "imagining the real," does not mean at any point that one gives up the ground of one's own concreteness, ceases to see through one's own eyes, or loses one's own "touchstone of reality." In this respect, it is the complete opposite of empathy in the narrower and stricter sense of the term in which we discussed it above. It is striking that in his later formulations of "empathic understanding" Rogers has stressed this very point. Rogers, we will recall, said to Buber in describing his own therapy: "I am able to sense with a good deal of clarity the way his experience seems to him, really viewing it from within him, and yet without losing my own personhood or separateness in that." We have also seen in Rogers' discussion of empathic understanding in his later essays that he stresses accurately seeing into the client's private world *as if* it were his own without ever losing that *as if* quality. This, too, is very close to Buber's definition of "inclusion" as the bipolar experiencing of the other side of the relationship without leaving one's own ground. The therapist runs the risk of being changed by the client, but never loses his or her own separateness or identity in the process. Rogers' placing of congruence before both empathic understanding and unconditional positive regard in these later essays also represents a swing in this direction.

Carl Rogers' latest statements on empathy belie our attempts to point to a clear chronological progression. In his essay, "Empathic: An Unappreciated Way of Being," Rogers quotes his own 1959 definition of empathy as sensing the other's inner feelings as if they were one's own without losing sight of the "as if" and falling into identification. In this same essay, however, he updates his views on empathy in a way that sometimes resembles "inclusion" and sometimes empathy in the narrower sense:

> An empathic way of being with another person . . . means *entering the private perceptual world of the other* and becoming thoroughly at home in it. It involves being sensitive, moment by moment, to the changing felt meanings which flow in this other person, to the fear or rage or tenderness or confusion or whatever that he or she is experiencing. It means

*temporarily living in the other's life*, moving about in it delicately without making judgments; it means sensing meaning of which he or she is scarcely aware, but not trying to uncover totally unconscious feelings, since this would be too threatening. It includes communicating your sensings of the person's world as you look with fresh and unfrightened eyes at elements of which he or she is fearful. It means frequently checking with the person as to the accuracy of your sensings, and being guided by the responses you receive.

Entering the private perceptual world of the other and temporarily living in the other's life suggest empathy in the narrower sense of losing one's own ground, whereas communicating one's sensings of the person's world with fresh and unfrightened eyes and checking as to the accuracy of one's sensing suggest inclusion, which remains on its own side of the dialogue even while swinging over to the other. Rogers' frequent checking with the other is close to my own experience as a counselor. I like to say, "If this rings a bell, fine. If it does not, fine," and to discover whether it does, in fact, ring a bell.

Rogers continues with a statement that once again suggests empathy in the narrower sense: "To be with another in this way means that for the time being, *you lay aside your own views and values in order to enter another's world* without prejudice. In some sense it means that *you lay aside your self*." Yet it presupposes that you are, in fact, holding your own ground as inclusion does and empathy in the narrower sense does not:

> This can only be done by persons who are secure enough in themselves that they know they will not get lost in what may turn out to be the strange or bizarre world of the other, and that they can comfortably return to their own world when they wish (Rogers 1980, p. 142f., italics added).

Sidney Jourard seems to have had something close to inclusion in mind when he uses Buber's term "imagining the real" in connection with empathy in *The Transparent Self* and claims that effective psychotherapy creates a greater flow of mutual understanding within the relationship of the patient and the therapist as well as the patient's relationship to other persons:

> Now, one outcome of effective psychotherapy is that the patient becomes increasingly sensitized to the nuances of his own feelings (and those of the therapist) as they ebb and flow in the relationship. The patient becomes more transparent to himself! Coincident with this increase in insight is an increase in empathy with others, an increase in his ability to "imagine the real" (Jourard 1971, p. 37).

Imagining the real, or inclusion, is even more clearly present in Jourard's discussion of loneliness in *Disclosing Man to Himself*:

The healthier personality, because he is less self-concealing and has readier access to his own fantasy, feelings, and memories, is less afraid of solitude when that is his lot; and when he is with others he can feel secure enough in his own worth that he can let encounter and dialogue happen. During the process of such dialogue, the shell which encapsulates him as a separate, isolated being ruptures; and his inner world expands to include the received world of experience of the other. When the dialogue ends, he has experienced himself in the new dimensions evoked by the other person, and he has learned of the personal world of another—thus he is enlarged and changed (Jourard 1968, p. 50).

Those who are used to using "empathy" in the customary larger, looser way may well ask what practical difference is made by the fine distinctions between empathy in the stricter sense, identification, and inclusion. A first answer would be that empathy (in the narrower sense) and identification are both very limited means of understanding, within therapy and without, and for the same reason: both rely on only one side of the relationship. Empathy attempts to get over to the other while leaving oneself; identification tries to tune in to the other through focusing on oneself. Neither can grasp the uniqueness of the other person, the uniqueness of oneself, and the uniqueness of the relationship.

A second, deeper answer is that neither empathy, in the strict sense, nor identification can really confirm another person, since true confirmation means precisely that *I* confirm *you* in your uniqueness and that I do it from the ground of my uniqueness as a really other person. Only inclusion, or imagining the real, can confirm another; for only it really grasps the other in his or her otherness and brings that other into relationship to oneself.

Leslie Farber provides us with an excellent example of this relationship between inclusion and confirmation—not from the realm of therapy, but rather from that of the relationship between man and woman:

Equally important, perhaps more important [than the attraction of sexuality] in real man/woman talk, is the exciting possibility of receiving and offering a range of perception and sensibility whose otherness can be uniquely and surprisingly illuminating. . . . So long as equality and honesty prevail, and so long as each person tries to imagine the other's reality without dishonoring his own, the manner or mood of such talk can be various: humorous, serious, philosophical, concrete, abstract, gossipy, and so on. Employing Martin Buber's terminology, and at the same time shifting its focus from friendship between people of the same sex, I would maintain that such talk contains the supreme potentiality of confirming the other, not only as a particular human being, but as a particular man or woman, and, of course, of being confirmed in the same way (Farber 1976, p. 165).

Our distinction among inclusion, identification, and empathy may also illuminate another very loosely used term—"intuition." Often the word intuition is used in a way very similar to empathy in the narrow sense of the term, or identification. The French philosopher, Henri Bergson, goes even further and suggests that there is an absolute intuition through which one can make oneself identical with the *élan vital*, or *durée*, of other persons and brings in their particularity. In his Introduction to the Hebrew edition of Bergson's works, Martin Buber offers a definition of intuition that does not make this claim of absoluteness and that, by the same token, distinguishes intuition from both empathy and identification and links it to imagining the real:

> Intuition, through vision, binds us as persons with the world which is over against us, binds us to it without being able to make us one with it, through a vision that cannot be absolute. This vision is a limited one, like all our perceptions, our universal–human ones and our personal ones. Yet it affords us a glimpse in unspeakable intimacy into hidden depths (Buber 1957b, p. 86).

Intuition as imagining the real is the very stuff of "betweenness" because it is, in the first instance, the stuff of immediacy that only later becomes something we may ruminate over and think about. The therapist with years of experience and with the knowledge of the many case histories that are reported in the literature will naturally think of resemblances when a client tells him something. But if he is a good therapist, he must discover the right movement back and forth between his patient as the unique person he is and the categories and cases that come to his, the therapist's, mind. He cannot know by scientific method *when* a particular example from case histories, his earlier clients, or even his own experience applies. This is where true intuition—imagining the real or inclusion—comes in. That is what some people mean when they describe psychotherapy as an art, or what I would call a grace of allowing oneself to be led.

Some people seem to possess this grace more than others. There are people who are gifted with an unusual degree of inclusive intuition who do not have any degrees in psychiatry or psychology. And there are other people who somehow seem obtuse. These latter either do not pick up cues or do not allow themselves to be aware of what they do pick up. That may be because they come to therapy with a certain mind-set, perhaps that of their school of therapy or just their own ways of thinking. But it may also be because it makes them anxious. We communicate to each other all the time far beyond our words—by our gestures, our actions, our silences, the set of our head. And we pick up far more than we know from others. Often, however, we do not allow ourselves to be aware of what we are picking up because it carries a double meaning or because the nonverbal communication contradicts the verbal, which we want to believe!

Buber's statement about the interpretation of dreams at the seminars of the Washington School of Psychiatry in 1957 is a good example of the contrast. There are two sorts of relation to dreams, he suggested. One is the scientific one that wants to interpret the dream according to the tenets of a particular school of psychoanalysis or psychotherapy. The other is a musical, free-floating relationship that relates to each dream as one might interpret a poem—in its own terms and not in the way in which one would interpret the dreams (or novels, plays, and poems) of another.

There is no system for being intuitive in this broader and more concrete sense of imagining the real, other than what I have called the courage to address and the courage to respond—existential trust. On the other hand, there is one sort of intuition I profoundly distrust. This is the "intuition" that can reach right into the heart of the person and say, "This is what makes that person tick." This intuition sets itself up even against the other's own responses. It does not see the relationship through the eyes of the other or imagine the real. Rather it reaches into the person and discovers a brilliant, but partial truth that imprisons that person in a still more sophisticated category or label than the ones that are already besieging him or her. This intuition is dangerous and destructive to human relationships, and it is one that is all too often used by therapists, gurus, teachers, ministers, and friends.

Once a group of Hasidim came to see a Hasidic rabbi who was known for being able to look through the forehead of a person and tell what was in the person's mind. When the Hasidim entered the rabbi's study, they all pulled their hats over their foreheads. "Do you think that if I can see through your forehead, I won't be able to see through your hat too!" asked the rabbi. Some people think of such gifts of seeing as magic powers. I, rather, think of it as being in touch—as touching, contact, a "dialogue of touchstones." If we keep in view the concrete reality of the between that underlies such intuition, we shall not be tempted to think of ourselves as *possessing* unusual powers. Those who feel they possess intuition sometimes try to use it for the spiritual or psychological domination of others. If we take seriously the "partnership of existence," the between, we shall not imagine that it is *our* power. What we contribute to the event is that we allow the intuition to happen between us and the other rather than preventing it from happening by blocking it from our awareness, as is usually the case. But we cannot take credit for it. If the other person does not want to reveal him- or herself to us at all, then this inclusive intuition will not take place. We cannot force the other to reveal himself. So when such revelation does happen, it is part of an event happening *between* us and the other. Such a knowing through mutual contact I *would* trust as opposed to the "intuition" that turns the other into an object.

There was a time, which I describe in my book *Touchstones of Reality* (Friedman 1972), when all my touchstones had been shattered, and I was going through a very difficult period. My mother had come up to Philadelphia to be with me, and I was reading aloud to her Martin Buber's novel *For the Sake of Heaven.* I came to a part in the novel where I broke down and wept and could not continue reading. The only thing my mother could suggest was that I take a hot bath. But there was a person in the Brudercoop in Philadelphia where I was staying who had just recently got out of prison as a conscientious objector. He was a very tall man with very large hands, blond hair, and high forehead. I remember distinctly how this man came down to the front room from the second floor and looked at me with an open yet penetrating glance. I had not talked with him at all; yet he said to me, "Would you like to go with me to meditate?" I said yes, and we went upstairs. Quiet meditation was at that moment the one thing I really needed, the one thing that could really help me. That is what I would call an active, inclusive intuition arising through mutual contact in the "between."

# Chapter 18

# The "Dialogue of Touchstones"

Our understanding of confirmation and of healing through meeting may be deepened if we look at them through one final perspective—that of the "dialogue of touchstones." The dialogue of touchstones is a phrase from my book *Touchstones of Reality* (Friedman 1972), an autobiographical book largely concerned with the world religions with which I have been in dialogue, but also centrally concerned with existential trust, the partnership of existence, and the courage to address and to respond.

In speaking of "touchstones of reality" I imply no separate and prior definition of "reality." I know of no "reality" independent of "touchstones," but also of no "touch" independent of contact with an otherness that transcends my own subjectivity even when I respond to it from that ground and know it only in my contact with it. A coloration that we take on from the culture or *Zeitgeist* but have not made our own is not a touchstone: it is only fool's gold. A touchstone cannot be passively received. It must be won by contending, by wrestling until dawn and not letting the nameless messenger go until he has blessed us by giving us a new name. Walking on our path, we encounter something that lights up for us—an event, a teaching, a breathless view of nature, an hour of unusual calm.

Touchstones of reality are like insights, except that they are closer to events. An insight arises from a concrete encounter, but we tend to remove it too quickly and completely to a plane of abstractions. To walk on the road from touchstone to touchstone means holding in tension the question of when it is right to move in the direction of insight and philosophical abstraction and when to move back into the stream of living. Every form of intellectual, philosophical, theological, psychological, sociological, economic, or political "party line" that tells us in advance how we ought to regard a situation comes between us and the possibility of a fresh, unique response.

I claim for touchstones what I claim for touching. In touching you do make contact. Even if it is only a partial contact, like that of "The Blind Men and the Elephant," that contact itself is a reality and a form of direct knowing, however illusory the inferences from the contact may be. It is not just that we have the *experience* of touching. On the contrary, to touch is to go through *and beyond* subjective experiencing: if I touch, if we touch, then there is a communication that is neither merely objective nor merely subjective, nor both together. The very act of touching is already a transcending of the self in openness to the impact of something other than the self. When two people really touch each other as persons—whether physically or not—the touching is not merely a one-sided impact: it is a mutual revelation of life stances.

In their chapters on "contact" in *Gestalt Therapy Integrated*, Erving and Miriam Polster include some illuminating pages on touching in the literal sense of the term. They recognize that the current trend toward overcoming the taboo of touching has resulted in much self-conscious exhibitionism or the staging of touching under conditions where it emerges as artifice instead of ripe culmination. "People may feel constrained to touch someone whom they are either not yet ready to touch or whom they would rather not touch at all." At the same time they recognize that in groups, especially, the restoration of touching may be a means of completing important unfinished business. "The immediacy of touch breaks through the intellectual layers into palpable personal recognitions." Most important of all for our purposes, they see in touching a means of facilitating the "dialogue of touchstones":

> Once some of the taboos against touching are relaxed, we may not only touch but we may also engage in a whole range of experiences which must be prohibited lest they *result* in the tabooed action—touch. . . . Thus, the avoidance of touch would not be nearly such a sweat if it didn't also prevent us from getting out from behind our desks, telling intimate stories about ourselves, standing close to other people, speaking warmly or colorfully, and many of the other actions where we might come to touch another person (Polster and Polster 1974, p. 144f.).

Once Martin Buber asked me why I had undertaken to edit a book on problems of the Mideast. When I explained my reasons, he sprang up from his chair, touched my shoulder, and said, "That was a mistake!" I felt that he could not have said it as he wanted to if he had not touched me at the same time.

Equally as important as the question of how we continue to remain faithful to our touchstones without objectifying them into abstractions is the question of how we communicate them to others. Indeed, many of our touchstones come to us precisely through such communication. Real communication means that each of us has some real contact with the otherness of the other. But this is only possible if each of us has related to the other's touchstones in his or her unique way. If instead I take on the role of the "objective observer," or even of the sympathetic "receptive listener," and fail to respond from the ground of my own uniqueness, then I have not even heard you, much less learned anything myself. We can only really listen if we are willing both to be open and to respond personally. The product of such communication will be something different from what either you or I intend. But it will be real communication, in contrast to that habitual misunderstanding in which we are all too often imprisoned—closed circuits in which we make a little voyage toward the other and then come back.

The real "dialogue of touchstones" means that we respond from where we are, that we bring ourselves into the dialogue. The other person needs to know that he is really coming up against us as persons with touchstones and witnesses of our own. Sometimes the strongest opposition is more confirming by far than someone who defends your right to your opinion, but does not take it seriously. To communicate a touchstone is to witness. When we really witness, we hold the tension of the event out of which it took root, nor do we imagine that we can hand the event over as an objective fact minus the interpretation that we have made of it. For this same reason we have the right to ask that those to whom we witness do not limit themselves to the words that we use minus ourselves, the persons using them, and what we are witnessing to in our own life. If we are making a witness, we are sharing something really unique with a unique person in a unique situation. Because this sharing is real, it often happens that more than one touchstone is real to us at the same time. When this is so, we cannot exclude either voice, even when they seem to contradict each other.

Although each of us has his or her own viewpoint, we are not completely alone. We are able to share what is uniquely our own and, each of us in his or her own way, bring it into a common reality. The sad thing is that so much of our sharing is pseudosharing because we lift it to a plane of objective discourse. In order to have real contact with one another, we must overcome our "education"; for we are programmed to "hear" in such a way that we rarely really hear. Most of our education is an education in the methods of abstracting. Consequently, we do not hear the person who speaks but only his "opinion" or "point of view." We put him into this or that category—Freudian, behaviorist, Jungian, or Rogerian; neurotic, borderline, schizophrenic; existentialist or logical analyst—and this putting into categories we call being educated.

True education is an education in the communication of touchstones. Touchstones of reality always include the component of our unique response to them. We think we communicate when we set ourselves aside as persons, agree on definitions, and meet on the high plane of abstractions. But this is really another form of subjectivism, since only a few people, if any, will agree with our terms and what we propose that they should mean, and even those who "agree" will do so from the ground of a different life stance. For the rest, most of what we call communication is simply misunderstanding and mismeeting—people using words in different ways and not even caring enough to ask the other person what he means by what he says.

We help one another along the road when we share our touchstones *and* the confusion that sometimes accompanies them. We evolve our touchstones in relation with one another; we witness to one another. We have an impact on one another through which we grow in our own touchstones. Growing in this way, we come to recognize that the "dialogue of touchstones" is itself a touchstone of reality.

When I wrote *Touchstones of Reality* I thought of the "dialogue of touchstones" as fully mutual. Shortly after its publication, while I was a visiting fellow at Carl Rogers' Center for the Study of the Person in La Jolla, I came to understand the possibility of the dialogue of touchstones as an approach to psychotherapy in which there would be both mutuality and a "normative limitation of mutuality."

I came to this insight through a simple incident, one which at first glance seems to have nothing to do with therapy, but in fact, represents the meeting of therapy and teaching. During the spring semester of 1972, when I was Visiting Distinguished Professor at San Diego State University, I taught a course in religion and literature. In the class of 30 students was a young man of 25 who described himself as always having been a loner and who demonstrated an astonishing capacity for alienating the other members of the class. After a moving discussion in which several persons shared the suffering over the death of a daughter by cancer, the sickness of a friend, or their own personal hurt, this young man said, "None of you has ever really suffered." Later he told me that he had been sent to a writing clinic where a philosopher had criticized a paper he wrote because it began with the sentence, "We exist in order to survive." "Which should I accept," this student asked me, "this philosopher's view or my own?" It struck me that this was an impossible question, which admitted of no answer. If he gave up his sentence, he was submitting to authority and suppressing his own unique touchstones of reality. On the other hand, if he tried to speak as he was, he would not communicate at all. Either way he was condemned to isolation.

It struck me shortly afterward that this must be overwhelmingly and terrifyingly the case for the so-called psychotic, the schizophrenic, or the paranoid who also live facing the impossible choice of retreating within and pretending to go along with socially approved ways of speaking and acting or of "expressing" themselves and alienating everyone else in so doing. If, as I felt, they too have their "touchstones of reality," such an impossible choice represents a sort of death for them. Carl Rogers shows a clear understanding of this impossible choice in his discussion of loneliness in his commentary on Ellen West:

> The other element in our loneliness is the lack of any relationship in which we communicate our real experiencing—and hence our real self—to another. When there is no relationship in which we are able to communicate both aspects of our divided self—our conscious façade and our deeper level of experiencing—then we feel the loneliness of not being in real touch with any other human being (Rogers 1980, p. 166).

In his discussion of the injection and concealment of meaning, Lyman Wynne speaks of a wife who surrendered her belief in her own ideas and took on those of her husband with the result that her own experience was invalidated. "Her consensual validation of his viewpoint was at the cost of her own belief system and her own integrity." In *The Politics of Experience*, Ronald Laing extends this consensual *in*validation to the relationship between psychiatrist and patient in which the psychiatrist acts as if there were only *one* valid point of view, his own:

> The psychiatrist's part . . . is taken as the very touchstone for our common-sense view of normality. The psychiatrist, as *ipso facto* sane, shows that the patient is out of contact with him. The fact that he is out of contact with the patient shows that there is something wrong with the patient, but not with the psychiatrist.
>
> . . . . . . . . . . . . . . . . . . . . . . . . . . . . . . . . . . . . . . . . . . . . . . . . . . . . . . . . .
>
> Psychiatrists have paid very little attention to the *experience* of the patient. Even in psychoanalysis there is an abiding tendency to suppose that the schizophrenic's experiences are somehow unreal or invalid; one can make sense out of them only by interpreting them; without truth-giving interpretations the patient is enmeshed in a world of delusions and self-deception (Laing 1967, p. 108).

Laing quotes Bert Kaplan's introduction to his collection of self-reports on the experience of being psychotic:

> "The process of psychotherapy consists in large part of the patient's abandoning his false subjective perspectives for the therapist's objective

ones. But the essence of this conception is that the psychiatrist understands what is going on, and the patient does not (Kaplan 1964, p. vii).

When a person is put in the role of a patient, Laing concludes, he "tends to become defined as a nonagent, as a nonresponsible object, to be treated accordingly, and even comes to regard himself in this light," as Erving Goffman has shown at length from his look from within at asylums (Goffman 1961).

> The "committed" person labeled as patient, and specifically as "schizophrenic," is degraded from full existential and legal status as human agent and responsible person to someone no longer in possession of his own definition of himself, unable to retain his own possessions, precluded from the exercise of his discretion as to whom he meets, what he does. . . . More completely, more radically than anywhere else in our society, he is invalidated as a human being. . . . Once a "schizophrenic," there is a tendency to be regarded as always a "schizophrenic" (Laing 1967, p. 122).

Psychotic experience goes beyond the horizons of our common, communal sense and may therefore be judged as invalidly mad, Laing points out. But it may also be validly mystical. An exile from the scene of being as we know it, the psychotic "is an alien, a stranger signaling to us from the void in which he is foundering, a void which may be peopled by presences that we do not even dream of." Madness may be breakthrough as well as breakdown, liberation and renewal as well as enslavement and existential death. Laing also suggests that we do not meet true madness in our society any more than we ourselves are truly sane: "The madness of our patients is an artifact of the destruction wreaked on them by us and by them on themselves" (Laing 1967, pp. 132f., 144f.).

Laing proposes that instead of the *degradation* ceremonial of psychiatric examination, diagnosis, and prognostication, we need for those who are about to go into a schizophrenic breakdown, an *initiation* ceremonial, through which the person will be guided with full social encouragement and sanction into inner space and time, by people who have been there and back again (Laing 1967, p. 128f.). Laing has tried to make this a reality in Kingsley Hall and the other centers of the Philadelphia Association in London. The Jungian analyst John Weir Perry has taken a kindred approach in such books as *The Far Side of Madness* (Perry 1974) and in Diabasis House in San Francisco where a small group of acute schizophrenics may go through their journey in dialogue with sympathetic attendants and without the deadening effect of drugs.

In *The Politics of Experience*, Laing sometimes falls into romanticization of the schizophrenic as the pioneer of the Twenty-First Century.

Schizophrenics are often terribly literal, rather than imaginative or creative, as Leslie Farber has pointed out, and *most* of them, in part certainly because of the way our society treats them, do not break through to a higher level of integration. Nonetheless, what Laing says in his soberer moments is entirely consonant with the dialogue of touchstones as an approach to human existence in general and to therapy in particular:

> Existence is a flame which constantly melts and recasts our theories. Existential thinking offers no security, no home for the homeless. It addresses no one except you and me. It finds its validation when, across the gulf of our idioms and styles, our mistakes, errings and perversities, we find in the other's communication an experience of relationship established, lost, destroyed, or regained (Laing 1967, p. 56).

Freud and many of the analysts who have followed him have been concerned with "reality-testing," and Adler, Jung, Reich, Sullivan, Fromm, Glasser, and Mowrer have each, in his way, been concerned with what Glasser has called "reality therapy." Yet few if any of them have gone beyond a monological approach to reality to an understanding of the central place of the dialogue of touchstones of reality. Sullivan, to be sure, used to say to young psychiatrists when they came to work with him, "I want you to remember that in the present stage of our society, the patient is right, and you are wrong" (Laing 1967, p. 109). And Jung, as we have seen, had gone surprisingly far in the direction of taking fully seriously the dialogue between therapist and patient and the extent to which each learns and changes in this dialogue.

Ivan Boszormenyi-Nagy has perhaps come closest to an explicit rejection of the old formula of "reality-testing" in favor of a dialogue of touchstones. Boszormenyi-Nagy concludes an imaginary vignette in which one friend complains that he has been treated unfairly with the statement: "Even though you may not be aware of having violated any mutually shared ethical principle, our parallel subjective reactions have consensually validated the relative objectivity of my suffered injustice." Then Boszormenyi-Nagy comments:

> The importance of the argument illustrated by this vignette lies in its emphasis on the mutuality of an action dialogue which is more than the sum total of two persons' subjective experiences. Thus, while the concept of reality-testing in psychology is a comparatively monothetical notion (one is either reality-bound or subject to distortion), the concept of the just order of the human world is a dialectical [I would say dialogical] one. A man's betrayal of his friend involves more than the vicissitudes of his repressed childhood wishes, depressions, etc. To decide on the extent of distortion would depend on his friend's vantage point too (Boszormenyi-Nagy and Spark, 1973, p. 82).

Hanna Colm has also explicitly portrayed a dialogue of touchstones in her report of her personal experience in the "therapeutic encounter." Instead of looking at the patient's disturbed behavior as "pathology," she asks herself what its meaning is for his whole living. She recognizes that neurotic behavior and neurotic symptoms often express the degree to which a patient can live *with integrity.* "I look not for his pathology but for his integrity." This approach helps her to find the thwarted, yet basically positive angles in the patient's behavior, to overcome her own obstacles to entering into the struggle with the patient, and to observe what genuine reactions his behavior causes in her. She uses these observations "as a starting point towards experiencing him and me in interaction, in a back and forth process of questioning both of us."

> In this process we both must be open to correct our experience of each other where it belongs to our past and is not a genuine reaction to the other person. This is the process which gradually heals, most of all the patient, but also the therapist, from leftover childhood ideals of perfection and the resulting disappointment about oneself, others, and life in general (Colm 1965, p. 139).

Sidney Jourard also offers what amounts to a summing up of confirmation and healing through meeting in terms of dialogue of touchstones. "In true encounter," he says, "there is a collapse of roles and self-concepts." The therapist's willingness to disclose himself to the client and to drop his mask is a factor in the client's trusting him and daring to disclose himself. "As I disclose myself to you, I am your world, and this world discloses new possibilities to you—it evokes new challenges and invitations that may stir you and enliven your imagination." Jourard holds that if he remains in dialogue with his client, he "may actually lead him to the edge of going out of his mind, thus clearing the way for the emergence of a new self." (A rather Laingian note.)

> In dialogue at its best, the participants remain in contact and let their reciprocal disclosures affect one another. If the dialogue occurs in the context of letting be and confirmation, then the weaker of the two may indeed flip into raw experiencing, find it safe and emerge in a more awakened state (Jourard 1968, p. 124f.).

The most impressive confirmation of my insight concerning the dialogue of touchstones as an approach to therapy is the writings of Harold Searles. Like Kaplan and Laing, Searles recognizes that "reality" and, by extension, the ability to be of help has mostly been considered the monopoly of the therapist:

> Psychoanalytic literature is written with the assumption that the analyst is healthy and therefore does not need psychological help from the

patient, who is ill and is therefore in need of psychological help from, and unable to give such help to, the analyst . . . it is a source of lasting pain to me that my analyst [of his training analysis], like each of my parents long before, maintained a high degree of unacknowledgment of my genuine desire to be helpful to him (Searles 1975, p. 96).

From his earliest papers, Searles has consistently stressed that there is an element of reality in all the patient's distorted transference projections of the analyst and that the transference symbiosis can itself become so reality related that it can evolve into a therapeutic symbiosis that is mutually growth enhancing and can lead to a healthier individuation for both therapist and patient (Searles 1975, p. 97f.).

It is in the last part of his discussion of the schizophrenic individual's experience of his world that Searles becomes startlingly explicit and richly concrete in his exposition of the dialogue of touchstones. No matter how unwittingly, the patient has an active part in the development and maintenance of his illness. It is only by making contact with this essentially assertive energy in him that the therapist can help him to become well.

Searles makes six suggestions concerning psychotherapeutic technique that offer us a range of specific approaches to the dialogue of touchstones in therapy that no one else, so far as I know, has articulated. First, the therapist must realize that the patient has arrived at his perceptual world over years of employing the best judgment of which he is capable and that it is a world deserving of our respect. The therapist cannot ask him to relinquish it in favor of the view of "reality" the therapist offers him. "Invariably, the better I come to know him, and his life, and myself in relation to him, the more I am impressed at how much accuracy, often powerfully incisive accuracy, there is in his perception of me."

Second, Searles found it wise early in therapy to endeavor to accept his patient's feelings about the world as he perceives it rather than challenge the accuracy of his perception of the world. By an active imagining the real, Searles made present to himself how terrified he would be to find himself closeted with a therapist whom he perceived as a homicidal maniac bent on killing him. This enables the patient to share his feelings with his therapist, who never intimates that he is crazy for holding the world-view he holds. The therapist candidly acknowledges and confirms the increments of reality in the patient's distorted view of him—no matter how embarrassing or painful these may be. In this process, the patient comes to remember his own past, but he also is able to replace the repressed, fragmentary, and contradictory self-images derived from conflictual family roles with the therapist's growing perception of him as a single, coherent, three-dimensional whole. Thus through identification with the feeling-image the therapist is developing of him, the patient gradually becomes a whole and integrated human being (Searles 1967, pp. 128–130).

The clearest exposition of the dialogue of touchstones is the sixth step in the therapeutic process in which the therapist looks alternatively, and during varying lengths of time, at the patient's world, sharing it with him, and giving him glimpses of his own view of the world. Through this alternation, the therapist helps the patient realize that there is both an inner and an outer world—something that had been lost to him through the confusion of his perceptions because of the binds imposed upon him by his family. This not only gives the patient back his own sense of reality; it also confirms him as a human being:

> By helping him to see, and at times insisting upon the differences between *his* world and *ours*, we help him to realize that he is a human being among fellow human beings, each of whom has his own individual world-view, and that all these collective world-views can coexist and be meaningfully interrelated (Searles 1967, p. 130).

Gradually both the therapist and the patient become unafraid of each one's own and of the other's world, and this leads to a truly mutual individuation. Passing through the fear of suicide and incurable insanity, "both participants develop the trustful realization that their two worlds can be fully looked at and freely changed." Both come out of this "therapeutic symbiosis" and the mutual individuation that follows deeply changed. The patient, it is hoped, will never again be vulnerable to psychosis. But neither will the therapist ever again need to repress so fully his own more primitive processes, including the kind of nonintegration and nondifferentiation of experience that comprise the defenses of his formerly psychotic patient.

In the last paragraphs of his paper, Searles goes beyond the "normative limitation of mutuality" to focus on what we, the so-called sane, can learn from the schizophrenic. As the shadow of the emotional deficiencies of our culture, schizophrenia casts light on the hypocrisies and previously unquestioned, implicit assumptions in our "normal existence." Through our dialogue with the schizophrenic's touchstones of reality, "we are better equipped to achieve a healthier culture and to live more fully, freely, and knowingly." Just because the schizophrenic has been living on the sidelines of humanity, he is in a position to give us a perspective we could not otherwise attain. The schizophrenic individual has not been faced with the question of *how* but of *whether* to relate to his fellow man. Through the act of inclusion, or imagining his touchstones of reality, we can recognize "that in us, too, this has been, all along, a meaningful and alive and continuing conflict, heretofore hidden from ourselves." Not only shall we no longer take anything for granted about human beings and human behavior, but we shall come to realize "that silence between persons is not necessarily a gulf, a void, but may be a tangibly richer communion than any words could constitute" (Searles 1967, p. 131).

When I say that Searles goes beyond the "normative limitations of mutuality," I do not mean, for a moment, that he changes the structure of the therapy situation in which one person is basically there to help and the other to be helped. Rather he shows us in a most concrete and convincing way that the schizophrenic's touchstones of reality are not just "real for him." They represent a genuine dialogue with "reality" that can deeply enrich our own relation to reality. Put in the language of Buber's "What Is Common to All," the schizophrenic, even in his desire to have a world of his own apart from the common world, helps to build up the common world of speech-with-meaning. His voice and his view cannot be excluded without impoverishing us all.

It is in this spirit of respect for the unique reality that has emerged from even the most psychotic patient's dialogue with the world that I have tried to develop my own thinking concerning the dialogue of touchstones as an approach to therapy. To identify and isolate "reality" has been a problem not just for philosophers, but also for every living human being. I have always been deeply moved by the lines that the American poet Vachel Lindsay wrote in his otherwise joyous poem, "The Chinese Nightingale," not too long before his own suicide:

> Years upon years I but half remember,
> May and June and dead December,
> Dead December, then again June.
> Man is a torch, then ashes soon.
> Life is a loom weaving illusion.
> O who will end my dream's confusion?

"Each person is a more or less naive ontologist," writes Ronald Laing. "Each person has views of what is and what is not." But many have been caught in the tension of multiple "realities" and multiple "touchstones." Some have tried to escape this tension through taking refuge in one or another form of absolutism, others in one or another reductionist point of view, still others in that "common sense" that Whitehead called the bad philosophy of two centuries ago, some in occultism, and some in a crude relativism. Touchstones of reality and the dialogue of touchstones offer an alternative to the either/or's of objective versus subjective, absolute versus relative, mind versus body, and rejection of the "schizophrenic" and the romantic glorification of him.

From the standpoint of the dialogue of touchstones much of what we call "mental illness" can be seen as something that has happened to distort, objectify, or make merely cultural our touchstones of reality. Touchstones and the dialogue of touchstones begin in and are renewed by immediacy. Sickness is what prevents the return to immediacy. From this standpoint, "health" is not "adjustment," becoming rational or emotional, but rather coming to a firmer grasp of one's own touchstones of reality in dialogue with the touchstones of others. In this sense, the dialogue of touchstones may be the goal of therapy as well as the means. This goal helps the therapist avoid three equally bad alternatives—adjusting the client to the culture, imposing his own values on the client, or accepting whatever the patient says and does as healthy and romantically celebrating it.

Kohut speaks of the self-injured patient's fear of disintegrating if he reveals his repressed archaic material to the analyst. But there is a more pervasive fear than that: every client fears that in entering into therapy he will have to sacrifice his own touchstones of reality, that he will have to subordinate himself to an external authority and join in invalidating his own touchstones as "sick." What makes this fear all too real is not only the psychiatrist who sets up his own "reality" as the sole standard of health, but also the "responsible" and "helpful" person who tends to handle both sides of the dialogue and thus *disenables* the other person to bring his own touchstones into the dialogue.

The therapist in the dialogue of touchstones cannot be someone who merely analyzes or reflects what the client says. He must also be someone who brings his own touchstones into the dialogue. The therapist has no monopoly on reality. The normative limitation to mutuality in the therapeutic dialogue of touchstones lies not only in the structure—who comes to see whom for help—but also in the fact that the therapist brings something to the dialogue that the severely neurotic and psychotic patient cannot bring. It is not that his experience is more real, deeper, and certainly, not by a long shot, more intense. It is only that he has more experience in inclusion, in imagining the real, in experiencing the other side of the relationship as well as his own, in seeing through the other's eyes as well as through his own.

If we begin by honoring each person's unique relation to reality, then to say of a person that he or she is "sick" does not imply that this person is outside reality, but only that he or she needs help in being brought into the dialogue of touchstones. When and insofar as the patient is so brought in, he is brought in from where he is. Or rather, to use Jourard's language, the patient responds to an invitation and brings himself into the dialogue. Therefore, the uniqueness of the patient's touchstone remains of primal concern. A uniqueness that is not brought into the dialogue atrophies; for it reaches its reality only in being called into existence and in responding to what calls it.

The terrible dilemma of the "sick" person, we have seen, is having to choose between giving up his touchstones in order to communicate or giving up communication. But a touchstone that is not brought into the dialogue ceases to be a touchstone. Instead the person is divided into an outer "social" mask and an inner hidden reality, and both are less than real. It does not matter whether the outer mask is social conformity or the defenses and postures of the schizophrenic who regards others and/or him or herself as unreal; it is still far less than a human reality.

It also does not matter whether the inner "reality" is one that is repressed from consciousness or is eagerly cherished as the most precious "inward" possession. It too is vestigial, atrophied, less than a fully human or even fully personal reality.

But such a person needs the help of someone who can glimpse and share the unique reality that has come from this person's life experience and can help this person find a way of bringing it into the common order of existence so that he or she too may raise what he or she has experienced as "I" into the communal reality of "We." Thinkers and artists like Blake, Kierkegaard, Nietzsche, Van Gogh, and Jung have had the courage to hold the tension between their faithfulness to their touchstones of reality and their need to enter into communication with others, *and* they have had the genius to create bridges—of poetry, art, theology, philosophy, or psychology—by which a dialogue of touchstones could take place between them and the world. For ordinary persons who experience the gap between their unique experience and the common world, this is usually not possible. Such persons need the help of a therapist who can "imagine the real" and practice inclusion in order to help them enter into a dialogue of touchstones. Harold Searles offers us an example of such therapy from his own training analysis:

> Early in our third session, my first training analyst had suddenly stood up and permanently dismissed me. The despair which I brought into the first session with Dr. Hadley [his subsequent training analyst] was despair lest I would prove hopelessly unable to communicate my innermost feelings to any human being. At the end of that first session . . . I asked, "Do you see any reason why we can't work together?" He assured me, briefly but emphatically, "Hell no!" (Langs and Searles 1980, p. 62).

The help of the therapist is not, in the first instance, a matter of finding the right words, still less techniques of communication. It is a matter of the dialogue of touchstones coming into being between one who cannot reach out and one who can. "When one person is singing and cannot lift his voice," said a Hasidic rabbi, "and another comes and sings with him, another who can lift his voice, then the first will be able to lift his voice." "That," said the rabbi, "is the secret of the bond between spirit and spirit." The title that Martin Buber gave this Hasidic story of healing was not "The Helper," but "When Two Sing." In the language of this book, it might be called "Healing through Meeting" or even "A Dialogue of Touchstones." For that *is* the secret of the bond between spirit and spirit.

The helpfulness of the therapist does not lie in the fact that he or she is a better Socratic dialectician or that he or she articulates better, but rather than he or she can help the patient out of the unfruitful either/or of choosing between faithfulness to one's own emergent touchstones and relation with the community. Yet this is only possible in a situation of mutual trust. If the patient fears to expose himself for fear that the therapist or his family or his friends will invalidate what he has to contribute as worthless, then he will not be able to enter into the venture of the dialogue of touchstones. The goal of healing through meeting, of confirmation, and of the dialogue of touchstones is, therefore, the same— to establish a dialogue on the basis of trust. There is something the patient brings that no one else in the world can—his uniqueness.

The "confirmation of otherness" that the dialogue of touchstones assumes and brings into existence means that no voice is without value, no witness without reality. Every voice needs to be heard precisely because it represents a unique relationship to reality. Even though that voice may be distorted, "sick," and miserable, it still contains the nucleus of a unique touchstone that its very negativity both bears and conceals. People in our culture, especially the educated and the cultured, fear being put down because the emphasis in our culture is on the quick and facile response. The "community of affinity" protects itself through the either/or. Either you are one of us or you are not. If you are one of us, we do not need to hear you because we already know and represent your point of view. If you are different and if you disagree, we do not want to hear you because you "make waves"—you disturb the harmony of our likemindedness. Our society itself is sick—polarized into communities of affinity. Because this is so, the individual cannot help being sick, since he or she does not have the ground on which to stand and from which to enter into a genuine dialogue of touchstones.

Confirming the other, in the end, cannot mean just healing in the negative sense of making a single person whole. It must also mean a movement in the direction of a climate of trust, a caring community, a community that confirms otherness. Thus we can say of healing through meeting what we said of the dialogue of touchstones: It is not only the means to the goal; it is itself the goal. The third alternative to the sickness of conformity and the sickness of rebellion is the community that confirms otherness. Such a community gives each person a ground of his own, a ground from which he can touch the other's touching, a ground in which mutual confirming and healing through meeting can take place in spiraling circles that bring more and more of each person's touchstones—whether born of trauma or of ecstasy—into the reality of life together. This is the secret of the bond between person and person.

# References

Archambeau, E. (1979). *Beyond Countertransference: The Psychothera-pist's Experience of Healing in the Therapeutic Relationship.* Doc-toral Dissertation, California School of Professional Psychology—San Diego.

Bakan, D. (1969). *Disease, Pain, and Sacrifice: Toward A Psychology of Suffering.* Chicago: The University of Chicago Press.

Basescu, S. (1977). Anxieties in the analyst: A personal confession. In *The Human Dimension in Psychoanalytic Practice*, ed. K. A. Frank, pp. 153–163. New York: Grune & Stratton.

Binswanger, L. (1958). The Case of Ellen West. In *Existence: A New Dimension in Psychiatry and Psychology*, ed. R. May, E. Angel, and H. F. Ellenberger, pp. 237–264. New York: Basic Books.

Blakar, R. M. (1984). *Communication: A Social Perspective on Clinical Issues.* Oslo: Universitetsforlaget.

Blum, H. P. (1980). The Borderline Childhood of the Wolf Man. In *Freud and His Patients*, ed. M. Kanzer and J. Glenn, pp. 341–358. New York: Jason Aronson.

Boss, M. (1963). *Psychoanalysis and Daseinsanalysis.* Trans. L. B. Lefebre. New York: Basic Books.

——— (1973). [Selections.] In *The Worlds of Existentialism: A Critical Reader*, ed. with Introductions and a Conclusion by M. S. Friedman, pp. 434–438. Chicago: The University of Chicago Press.

Boszormenyi-Nagy, I. (1965). Intensive family therapy as process. In *Intensive Family Therapy: Theoretical and Practical Aspects*, ed. I. Boszormenyi-Nagy and J. L. Framo, pp. 87–142. New York: Harper & Row, Hoeber Medical Division.

——— (1981). Contextual therapy: Therapeutic leverages in mobilizing trust. In *Family Therapy: Major Contributions*, ed. R. F. Green and J. L. Framo, pp. 395–415. New York: International Universities Press.

Boszormenyi-Nagy, I., and Krasner, B. R. (1980). Trust-based therapy: A contextual approach. *American Journal of Psychiatry 137*: 767–775.

Boszormenyi-Nagy, I., and Spark, G. (1973). *Invisible Loyalties: Reciprocity in Intergenerational Family Therapy*. New York: Harper & Row, Hoeber Medical Division.

Boszormenyi-Nagy, I., and Ulrich D. (1981). Contextual Family Therapy. *Handbook of Family Therapy*. Ed. A. S. Gurman and D. P. Kniskern. New York: Brunner/Mazel.

Buber, M. (1975a). *Eclipse of God: Studies in the Relation between Religion and Philosophy*. Trans. M. S. Friedman et al. New York: Harper & Row (Torchbooks).

————— (1957b). *Pointing the Way: Selected Essays*. Trans. and ed. M. S. Friedman. New York: Harper & Row.

————— (1958). *I and Thou*, 2nd rev. ed. with a Postscript by Author Added. Trans. R. G. Smith. New York: Charles Scribner's Sons.

————— (1960). *The Origin and Meaning of Hasidism*. Trans. and ed. with an Introduction by M. S. Friedman. New York: Horizon Books.

————— (1961). *Tales of the Hasidim: The Early Masters*. Trans. O. Marx. New York: Schocken Books.

————— (1965). *Between Man and Man*. Trans. R. G. Smith, with an Introduction by M. S. Friedman. New York: Macmillan.

————— (1966). *The Knowledge of Man: A Philosophy of the Interhuman*. Trans. M. S. Friedman and ed. R. G. Smith, with an Introductory Essay (Ch. 1) by M. S. Friedman. New York: Harper & Row (Torchbooks).

————— (1969). *A Believing Humanism: Gleanings*. Trans. and ed. with Introduction and Explanatory Comments, M. S. Friedman. New York: Simon & Schuster (paperback).

Clark, K. B. (1980). Empathy: A neglected topic in psychological research. *American Psychologist 35*: 187–190.

Colm, H. (1965). The therapeutic encounter. *Review of Existential Psychology and Psychiatry 5*: 137–159.

Ebner, F. (1921). *Das Wort und die geistigen Realitäten: Pneumatologische Fragmente*. Innsbruck: Brenner-Verlag. In *The Worlds of Existentialism: A Critical Reader*, ed. and trans., with Introductions and a Conclusion, M. S. Friedman, pp. 292–298. Chicago: The University of Chicago Press, 1973 (paperback).

Ellenberger, H. F. (1970). *The Discovery of the Unconscious: The History and Evolution of Dynamic Psychiatry*. New York: Basic Books.

Fagan, J., and Shepherd, I. L. eds. (1970). *Gestalt Therapy Now: Theory/Techniques/Applications*. New York: Science and Behavior Books.

Farber, L. H. (1966). *The Ways of the Will. Essays toward a Psychology and Psychopathology of the Will*. New York: Basic Books.

—————— (1967). Martin Buber and psychotherapy. In *The Philosophy of Martin Buber*, ed. P. A. Schilpp and M. S. Friedman, pp. 577–601. *The Library of Living Philosophers Series*. ed P. A. Schilpp. Lasalle, Illinois: Open Court.

—————— (1967). *lying, despair, jealousy, envy, sex, suicide, drugs, and the good life*. New York: Basic Books.

Frank, K. A. (1977). *The Human Dimension in Psychoanalytic Practice*. New York: Grune & Stratton.

Frankl, V. E. (1970). *Man's Search for Meaning: An Introduction to Logotherapy*. Trans. I. Lasch; Preface, W. Allport. New York: Simon & Schuster (Clarion Books).

—————— (1973). The image of man in psychotherapy. Trans. W. Hallo. In *The Worlds of Existentialism: A Critical Reader*, ed. with Introduction and Conclusions, M. S. Friedman, p. 468. Chicago: The University of Chicago Press (paperback).

Freud, S. (1947). The Ego and the Id. Trans. Joan Riviere. In *The International Psycho-Analytical Library*, ed. E. Jones, No. 12, 4th Ed. London: The Hogarth Press and the Institute of Psycho-Analysis.

—————— (1958). *Civilization and Its Discontents*. Trans. Joan Riviere. New York: Doubleday (Anchor Books).

Friedman, M. S. (1965). Introductory essay. Chapter 1 of M. Buber, *The Knowledge of Man: A Philosophy of the Interhuman*, ed. M. S. Friedman. New York: Harper & Row (Torchbooks).

—————— (1972). *Touchstones of Reality: Existential Trust and the Community of Peace*. New York: E. P. Dutton.

—————— (1973). *The Worlds of Existentialism: A Critical Reader*, ed., with Introduction and Conclusions, M. S. Friedman. Chicago: The University of Chicago Press (Phoenix Books).

—————— (1974). *The Hidden Human Image*. New York: Delacorte.

—————— (1978). *To Deny Our Nothingness: Contemporary Images of Man*, 3rd rev. ed. with new Preface and Appendices. Chicago: The University of Chicago Press (Phoenix Books).

—————— (1983). *The Confirmation of Otherness: In Family, Community, and Society*. New York: The Pilgrim Press.

—————— (1984). *Contemporary Psychology: Revealing and Obscuring the Human*. Pittsburgh, PA: Duquesne University Press.

Fromm, E. (1941). *Escape from Freedom*. New York: Rinehart & Co.

—————— (1956). *The Art of Loving*. New York: Harper & Bros.

—————— (1962). *Beyond the Chains of Illusion: My Encounter with Marx and Freud*. New York: Simon & Schuster (Credo Series).

Fromm-Reichmann, F. (1950). *Principles of Intensive Psychotherapy*. Chicago: The University of Chicago Press.

Glenn, J. (1980a). Freud's adolescent patients: Katharina, Dora, and the

"Homosexual Woman." In *Freud and His Patients*, ed. M. Kanzer and J. Glenn, pp. 23–47. New York: Jason Aronson.

———— (1980b). Notes on psychoanalytic concepts and styles in Freud's case histories. In *Freud and His Patients*, ed. M. Kanzer and J. Glenn, pp. 3–19. New York: Jason Aronson.

Goffman, E. (1961). *Asylums. Essays on the Social Situation of Mental Patients and Other Inmates*. New York: Doubleday (Anchor Books).

Greenson, R. R. (1977). That "impossible" profession. In *The Human Dimension of Psychoanalytic Practice*, ed. K. A. Frank, pp. 99–114. New York: Grune & Stratton.

Guntrip, H. (1961). *Personality structure and human interaction: The developing synthesis of psychodynamic theory*. In *The International Psycho-Analytical Library*, ed. J. D. Sutherland, No. 56. London: The Hogarth Press and the Institute of Psycho-Analysis.

———— (1969). *Schizoid Phenomena, Object Relations and the Self*. New York: International Universities Press.

———— (1977). My experience of analysis with Fairbairn and Winnicott (how complete a result does psychoanalytic therapy achieve?). In *The Human Dimension of Psychoanalytic Practice*, ed. K. A. Frank, pp. 49–68. New York: Grune & Stratton.

Herink, R. (1980). *The Psychotherapy Handbook*. New York: New American Library (Meridian Books).

Hillman, J. (1972). *The Myth of Analysis: Three Essays in Archetypal Psychology. Studies in Jungian Thought*, series. gen. ed. J. Hillman Evanston, IL: Northwestern University Press.

Hycner, R. (1985). Dialogical Gestalt Psychotherapy. *Gestalt Therapy Journal*, Spring 1985.

Jacobs, L. M. (1978). *I–Thou Relation in Gestalt Therapy*. Doctoral dissertation for the California School of Professional Psychology-Los Angeles.

Jourard, S. M. (1968). *Disclosing Man to Himself*. New York: D. Van Nostrand.

———— (1971). *The Transparent Self*, 2nd ed. New York: Van Nostrand Reinhold.

Jung, C. G. (1954). *The Practice of Psychotherapy*. Trans. R.F.C. Hull. *The Collected Works*, vol. 16. New York: Pantheon Books.

———— (1958). *The Undiscovered Self*. Trans. R.F.C. Hull. Boston: Little, Brown.

———— (1961). *Memories, Dreams, Reflections*. Recorded and ed. Aniela Jaffe, trans. Richard & Clara Winston. New York: Pantheon Books.

Kanzer, M. (1980a). Dora's imagery: The flight from the burning house. In *Freud and His Patients*, ed. M. Kanzer and J. Glenn, pp. 72–82. New York: Jason Aronson.

———— (1980b). Freud's 'human influence' on the Rat Man. In *Freud and His Patients*, ed. M. Kanzer and J. Glenn, pp. 232–240. New York: Jason Aronson.

Kanzer, M., and Glenn, J. (1980). Conclusion. In *Freud and His Patients*, ed. M. Kanzer and J. Glenn, pp. 429–431. New York: Jason Aronson.

Kaplan, B. (ed.) (1964). *The Inner World of Mental Illness*. New York: Harper & Row.

Kepnes, S. (1982). Telling and retelling: The use of narrative in psychoanalysis and religion. In *The Challenge of Psychology to Faith, Concilium*, vol. 156, ed. Steven Kepnes and David Tracy, pp. 27–32. New York: Seabury Press.

Kohut, H. (1971). *The Analysis of the Self: A Systematic Approach to the Psychoanalytic Treatment of Narcissistic Personality Disorders*. New York: International Universities Press.

———— (1977). *The Restoration of the Self*. New York: International Universities Press.

———— (1978). *The Search for the Self: Selected Writings of Heinz Kohut, 1950–1978*, ed. P. Ornstein, 2 vols. New York: International Universities Press.

———— (1981). *How Does Analysis Cure?* Ed. Arnold Goldberg with collaboration of Paul E. Stepansky. Chicago: University of Chicago Press.

Kohut, H., and Wolf, E. S. (1978). The disorders of the self and their treatment: An outline. *International Journal of Psychoanalysis* 59 (413): 413–425.

Laing, R. D. (1965). *The Divided Self: An Existential Study in Sanity and Madness*. Penguin Books (Pelican Edition).

———— (1967). *The Politics of Experience*. New York: Ballantine Books.

———— (1971). *Self and Others*. Penguin Books (Pelican Edition).

———— (1972). *The Politics of the Family. And Other Essays*. New York: Vintage Books.

Langs, R. J. (1980a). The misalliance dimension in the case of Dora. In *Freud and His Patients*, ed. M. Kanzer and J. Glenn, pp. 58–71. New York: Jason Aronson.

———— (1980b). The misalliance dimension in the case of the Rat Man. In *Freud and His Patients*, ed. M. Kanzer and J. Glenn, pp. 215–231. New York: Jason Aronson.

———— (1980c). The misalliance dimension in the case of the Wolf Man. In *Freud and His Patients*, ed. M. Kanzer and J. Glenn, pp. 372–385. New York: Jason Aronson.

———— (1982). *The Psychotherapeutic Conspiracy*. New York: Jason Aronson.

Langs, R. J., and Searles, H. F. (1980). *Intrapsychic and Interpersonal*

*Dimensions of Treatment:* A Clinical Dialogue. New York: Jason Aronson.

Laplanche, J., and Pontalis, J. B. (1973). *The Language of Psycho-Analysis.* Trans. D. Nicholson-Smith. Introduction by Daniel Lagache. New York: Norton.

Malcolm, J. (1981). *Psychoanalysis: The Impossible Profession.* New York: Knopf.

May, R. (1958). Contributions of existential psychotherapy. In *Existence: A New Dimension in Psychiatry and Psychology*, ed. R. May, E. Angel, and H. F. Ellenberger, pp. 37–91. New York: Basic Books.

——— (1968). Dreams and symbols. In *Dreams and Symbols*: Man's Unconscious Language, ed. R. May and L. Caligor, pp. 3–128. New York: Basic Books.

——— (1969). *Love and Will.* New York: Norton.

——— (1972). *Power and Innocence: A Search for the Sources of Violence.* New York: Norton.

Mead, G. H. (1934). *Mind, Self, and Society, from the Standpoint of a Social Behaviorist*, ed. C. W. Morris. Chicago: The University of Chicago Press.

Moreno, J. L. (1973). [Selections.] In *The Worlds of Existentialism: A Critical Reader*, ed., with Introductions and Conclusion, M. S. Friedman, pp. 468–472. Chicago: The University of Chicago Press (Phoenix Books).

Perry, J. W. (1974). *The Far Side of Madness.* Englewood Cliffs, NJ: Prentice-Hall.

Pfuetze, P. (1954). *The Social Self.* Reprinted 1973 under the title *Self, Society, Existence: Human Nature and Dialogue in the Thought of G. H. Mead and Martin Buber.* Foreword H. R. Niebuhr. Westport, CO: Greenwood Press.

Polster, E., and Polster, M. (1974). *Gestalt Therapy Integrated: Contours of Theory and Practice.* New York: Vintage Books.

Rogers, C. R. (1951). *Client-Centered Therapy, Its Current Practice, Implications, and Theory.* Boston: Houghton Mifflin.

——— (1961). *On Becoming a Person. A Therapist's View of Psychotherapy.* Boston: Houghton Mifflin.

——— (1967a). The interpersonal relationship: The core of guidance. In *Person to Person: The Problem of Being Human. A New Trend in Psychology*, ed. C. R. Rogers and B. Stevens, pp. 89–103. Lafayette, CA: Real People Press.

——— (1967b). Some learnings from a study of psychotherapy with schizophrenics. In *Person to Person*, ed. C. R. Rogers and B. Stevens, pp. 181–192. Lafayette, CA: Real People Press.

——— (1967c, summer). Article in *Voices.*

———— (1980). *A Way of Being*. Boston: Houghton Mifflin.

Sborowitz, A. (1948). Beziehung und Bestimmung, Die Lehren von Martin Buber und C. G. Jung in ihrem Verhältnis zueinander. *Psyche, Eine Zeitschrift für Tiefenpsychologie und Menschenkunde in Forschung und Praxis* 2:9–56.

Scharfman, M. A. (1980). Further reflections on Dora. In *Freud and His Patients*, ed. M. Kanzer and J. Glenn, pp. 48–57. New York: Jason Aronson.

Schulberg, B. (1941). *What Makes Sammy Run*. New York: Random House.

Searles, H. F. (1967). The schizophrenic individual's experience of his world. *Psychiatry* 30:119–131.

———— (1975). The patient as therapist to his analyst. In *Tactics and Techniques in Psychoanalytic Therapy*, ed. P. L. Giovacchini, pp. 95–151. *Countertransference*, vol. 2. New York: Jason Aronson.

Sechehaye, M. (1951a). *Reality Lost and Regained: Autobiography of a Schizophrenic Girl*, with analytic interpretation by M. Sechehaye. Trans. G. Urbin-Rabson. New York: Grune & Stratton.

———— (1951b). *Symbolic Realization: A New Method of Psychotherapy Applied to a Case of Schizophrenia*. New York: International Universities Press.

Shainberg, D. (1977). Transforming transitions in patients and therapists. In *The Human Dimension in Psychoanalytic Practice*, ed. K. A. Frank, pp. 123–140. New York: Grune & Stratton.

Singer, E. (1977). The fiction of analytic anonymity. In *The Human Dimension in Psychoanalytic Practice*, ed. K. A. Frank, pp. 181–192. New York: Grune & Stratton.

Spiegelman, M. J. (1965). Some implications of the transference. In *Speculum Psychologiae. Festschrift für C. A. Meier*. Zurich: Raschon Verlag.

———— (1980). The image of the Jungian analyst and the problem of authority. *Spring*, pp. 101–116.

Stanton, R. D. (1978). *Dialogue in Psychotherapy: Martin Buber, Maurice Friedman and Therapists of Dialogue*. Doctoral dissertation, Union Graduate School/West, San Francisco, CA.

Stierlin, H. (1974). *Separating Parents and Adolescents: A Perspective on Running Away, Schizophrenia, and Waywardness*. New York: Quadrangle/The New York Times Book Co.

Sullivan, H. S. (1940). *Conceptions of Modern Psychiatry*. New York: Norton.

———— (1953). *The Interpersonal Theory of Psychiatry*, ed. H. S. Perry and M. L. Gawel. New York: Norton.

Trüb, H. (1935). Individuation, Schuld und Entscheidung. Über die Grenzen der Psychologie. In *Die kulturelle Bedeutung der Komplexen Psychologie*, ed. Psychologischn Club Zürich, pp. 525–555. Berlin: Julius Springer Verlag.

——— (1947). Vom Selbst zur Welt. *Psyche* 1: 41–67.

——— (1952). *Heilung aus der Begegnung. Eine Auseinandersetzung mit der Psychologie C. G. Jungs*, ed. Ernst Michel and Arie Sborowitz. Preface, M. Buber. Stuttgart: Ernst Klett Verlag.

——— (1973). Individuation, guilt, and decision (selection). In *The Worlds of Existentialism*. Trans. and ed. M. S. Friedman, p. 497. Chicago: The University of Chicago Press (Phoenix Books).

Weiss, S. S. (1980). Reflections and speculations on the psychoanalysis of the Rat Man. In *Freud and His Patients*, ed. M. Kanzer and J. Glenn, pp. 207–214. New York: Jason Aronson.

Weizsäcker, V. von (1973). [Selections.] In *The Worlds of Existentialism*, Trans. K. Englesing von Rhau, M. S. Friedman, and W. Hallo and ed. M. S. Friedman, pp. 404–410. Chicago: The University of Chicago Press (Phoenix Books).

Whitmont, E. C. (1969). *The Symbolic Quest: Basic Concepts of Analytical Psychology*. New York: G. P. Putnam's Sons for the C. G. Jung Foundation for Analytical Psychology.

Wynne, L. C. (1965). Some indications and contraindications for exploratory family therapy. In *Intensive Family Therapy: Theoretical and Practical Aspects*, ed. I. Boszormenyi-Nagy and J. L. Framo, pp. 289–322. New York: Harper & Row, Hoeber Medical Division.

——— (1971). The injection and concealment of meaning in the family relationships and psychotherapy of schizophrenics. In International Congress Series No. 259, *Psychotherapy of Schizophrenia*, ed. D. Rubinstein and Y. O. Alanen, Proceedings of the IVth International Symposium, Turku, Finland, August 4–7, 1971, pp. 180–193. Amsterdam, The Netherlands: Excerpta Medica.

——— (1976). On the anguish and creative passions of not escaping double binds: A reformulation. In *Double Bind: The Foundation of the Communicational Approach to the Family*, ed. C. Sluzki and D. C. Ranson, pp. 243–250. New York: Grune & Stratton.

——— (1984). The epigenesis of relational systems: A model for understanding family development. In *Family Process*, 23: 297–318.

# Index